W9-CJW-229

eBay®

PowerSeller™ Secrets

eBay®

PowerSeller™ Secrets
Insider Tips from eBay's Most Successful Sellers

SECOND EDITION

Debra Schepp
Brad Schepp

New York   Chicago   San Francisco   Lisbon
London   Madrid   Mexico City   Milan   New Delhi
San Juan   Seoul   Singapore   Sydney   Toronto

The **McGraw·Hill** Companies

Copyright © 2008 by McGraw-Hill, Inc. All rights reserved. Printed in the United States of America. Except as permitted under the United States Copyright Act of 1976, no part of this publication may be reproduced or distributed in any form or by any means, or stored in a data base or retrieval system, without prior written permission of the publisher.

1 2 3 4 5 6 7 8 9 0 FGR/FGR 0 9 8 7

ISBN-13: 978-0-07-149816-6
ISBN-10: 0-07-149816-8

This publication is designed to provide accurate and authoritative information in regard to the subject matter covered. It is sold with the understanding that the publisher is not engaged in rendering legal, accounting, or other professional service. If legal advice or other expert assistance is required, the services of a competent professional person should be sought.
—*From a Declaration of Principles Jointly Adopted by a Committee of the American Bar Association and a Committee of Publishers and Associations*

McGraw-Hill books are available at special discounts to use as premiums and sales promotions, or for use in corporate training programs. For more information, please write to the Director of Special Sales, Professional Publishing, McGraw-Hill, Two Penn Plaza, New York, NY 10121-2298. Or contact your local bookstore.

This book is printed on acid-free paper.

Library of Congress Cataloging-in-Publication Data
Schepp, Debra.
EBay powerseller secrets : insider tips from eBay's most successful sellers / by Brad and Debra Schepp. – 2e [ed.].
p. cm.
Includes index.
ISBN-13: 978-0-07-149816-6 (pbk. : alk. paper)
ISBN-10: 0-07-149816-8
1. EBay (Firm) 2. Internet auctions. 3. Selling–Computer network resources.
4. Internet marketing. 5. Internet advertising. I. Schepp, Brad. II. Title.
HF5478.S34 2007
658.8'7–dc22
2007025211

To my big brother, Mel, brilliant in business and beautiful, too.
Deb

For Steph and Ethan, and they know why.
Brad

Contents at a Glance

Contents

Preface to the Second Edition

We started working on this second edition with both enthusiasm and more than a little concern. The enthusiasm was understandable. We still love eBay and always will, but the concern was a new feeling. It seemed things had gotten almost bleak since the first edition of this book, published in 2004. Everyone wanted to talk about fraud. Sellers seemed disenchanted and were searching for new and greener pastures. With competition on the site greater than ever, and fee increases, listings growth had slowed. We wondered: was anyone making money on eBay anymore? Was the newest PowerSeller secret going to be get off eBay? You know we don't sugarcoat the facts about eBay. Our goal has always been to lay it all out, the good, the bad, and the not so pretty. So how could we write a new edition without depressing our readers?

We'd spent a great deal of time moving among the biggest of the PowerSellers, now called the *TopSellers*. These are the Platinum and Titanium PowerSellers, the big dogs with the big bones to pick with eBay. We'd even seen some of our friends, who had been wildly successful on eBay just three years earlier, either bankrupt or off eBay for other reasons. "Greener pastures" was the goal among many of them.

It was only when we started interviewing some of the newly emerging PowerSellers . . . not the superstars who have been around for years, but those who lay just below the radar, that we discovered that remarkable stories are still there to tell. We saw that for many, eBay was still the greatest business incubator the world has ever known. eBay can still change lives for the better and open doors to opportunity like nothing else ever has.

For this new edition, we've checked every fact, every Web address, every screen shot, and well you get the idea. We've also added a checklist to the end of each chapter to help you track your growth and learning. So you can rest assured the book is now current as of this writing. Some of the new subjects covered in this edition include:

- eMail Marketing, an underused but powerful way to stay in touch with your customers
- Feedback 2.0, which eBay rolled out in mid-2007
- eBay Express, where commodity-type items are for sale at fixed prices
- New tools from eBay including eBay Marketplace Research and Blackthorne software

- The scoop on how Amazon compares to eBay for sellers
- How offering warranties can add thousands to your bottom line
- How to use Skype to get closer to your customers
- Making big money through eBay's thriving Affiliate Program
- Using blogs and eBay Guides and Reviews to drive traffic to your listings
- Hot new auction management services, including one that's *free*
- Hot trends in product sourcing

Finally, you'll catch up with some of the PowerSellers we profiled in the last edition to see how life has changed for them in the last three years. Plus, you'll meet a new crop of PowerSellers who are sure to inspire you. For the next edition, we're hoping to include you!

Deb and Brad Schepp
www.bradanddeb.com

Acknowledgments

This book is the result of the countless hours we spent researching the lives of PowerSellers and writing about those lives. Although it sometimes seemed we'd spend the rest of our days here in our offices, the effort we put into the pages you hold would have gone for nothing if not for the generosity, creativity, and intelligence of the hundreds of PowerSellers who spoke with us, wrote to us, and let us into their business lives. It would be too much to ask of our readers if we called out each seller by name. They know who they are, and we've tried to show them throughout the life of this project just how much we appreciated the treasures they shared with us. It is very humbling to try to return the debt owed to people who have answered our endless questions promptly and with grace, good humor, and wisdom. We'd like to offer them a collective thanks and more admiration than they'll ever know for all they've achieved.

Among that group of PowerSellers, there is a core of people who offered us even more. These are the sellers who agreed to be the subjects of our profiles. We'd like to thank them each individually. To Andy and Deb Mowery, you taught us so much and you made us laugh, too. Dan Glasure and Nick Boyd are collectibles dealers on eBay who gave us great insight into that niche of the eBay world. Chris Santos and Ben Thompkins represent the next generation of eBay PowerSellers. They're young, successful, and completely tuned into eBay's evolution. Thanks for sharing your unique perspectives. Frank Tetro brought business savvy and dedication to his eBay business, and affectionately named it for his beloved great-aunt Tessie. Chris Chapman has taken his love of skiing to new heights with a family-based business that's both successful and satisfying. Bob Buchanan and Greg Scheuer took a career setback and turned it into a vibrant, successful business. Steve Grossberg and Art Clem are our new friends from the Internet Merchants Association. They are both eBay veterans, knowledgeable and always willing to share their expertise. We thank them all for everything they've done to help us, and we look forward to watching their businesses grow and thrive. Finally, to our anonymous SquareTrade mediator, a silent thanks.

Other people who contributed valuable pieces of information were not necessarily PowerSellers, but people who were very savvy about the world of eBay and e-commerce. We'd like to thank Matt Ledwith of eBay's TopSeller program for his kind support and interest in our work. Ina Steiner of AuctionBytes was a wonderful resource about all types of eBay matters. Scott Samuel of Auction Ethics taught us a great deal about auction management software. Win Bent of Bent Sound Research allowed us to feature his eBay Negative/Neutral Feedback tool. David Kay, a PowerSeller, shared his packaging expertise with us. Jerry Weinstein taught us a great deal about providing excellent customer service. Terry Lanier shared his expertise in QuickBooks, and Larra Clark of the American Library Association helped us gather a great deal of information. Robin Cowie of Worldwide Brands was responsive and friendly. The public relations staff of Amazon were thoroughly professional and helpful. Mike Effle of Vendio made sure we got the facts straight. Our friends at MarketWorks and ChannelAdvisor helped us accurately describe their companies' services. Jen Cano of HammerTap was always there when we needed her, and Steve Weber, author of several great books about online marketing—what an inspiration.

Of course, it takes a whole group of people to create any book, and we'd like to thank the talented people who helped us create this one. Agent Margot Maley was the first one who thought this book was a great idea. Bill Gladstone and Ming Russell were a big help with this second edition. We'd also like to thank Dianne Wheeler, our editor at McGraw-Hill. Other people at McGraw-Hill who deserve thanks include Phil Ruppel, who made all the details work out. Tara Cibelli and Bettina Faltermeier, senior publicity managers, both deserve our thanks. It's always a great day when Bettina calls! From the Production Department, we'd like to thank Scott Kurtz.

We owe a special thanks to our technical editor, mentor, and friend, David Yaskulka. His deft editing allowed us to exhale, confident that we weren't neglecting or omitting anything. On a personal note, we'd like to thank our family, who endured our long absences and tremendous preoccupation with all things eBay. Thanks for the phone calls that kept us connected when visiting just wasn't possible. Thank you to Stephanie and Ethan, who made do without us more than we wanted them to. To Max and Mollie, thanks for keeping our desks and monitors warm. Thanks to their diligence, not a single mouse ran across either of our desks throughout this entire project!

Introduction

Have you sold a few things on eBay, enjoyed the whole process, and wondered how you could make eBay selling a full-time job? We have too, and that's why we wrote this book. We love eBay. We love the satisfaction that comes with selling things and making good money in the process. We also love providing people with things they may not be able to get anyplace else. In many ways, running your own eBay business is a new version of the American dream that tugs at so many of us: the dream to be your own boss; to no longer be subject to the forever changing corporate winds; to captain your own ship. Thanks to eBay, that dream is more possible now than it ever has been. Never before has starting your own business been so easy and inexpensive. Selling on eBay can begin as a hobby that supplements your income while you work toward building your dream of independence. Once you've achieved a steady cash flow, you will never again be required to dress a certain way for work, be at work at a certain time every day, or sit in that rush hour traffic.

You may be one of the millions of people who have sold items on eBay, but only a fraction of eBay sellers have made eBay selling their full-time jobs. Only a fraction of those sellers have reached the top tier of eBay sellers: the PowerSellers. These are the most successful sellers on eBay. To become a PowerSeller, you must maintain at least $1,000 per month in sales for a period of three consecutive months. Many PowerSellers have consistently achieved far more than that, and some maintain more than $150,000 in monthly sales. The question is, how can you become one of them? We're here to tell you.

Now you may be wondering who we are and what makes us such eBay authorities. We're old hands at being online; in fact, we've been online since 1983, when most people didn't even know there was such a thing! Brad was an editorial director for America Online. We've written books about working from home and guides for using the Internet. Finally, we've been collecting things and shopping at garage sales and flea markets for more years than we care to admit, and we've bought and sold things on eBay since 1999. But none of those things qualified us to write this book. It only qualified us to ask the questions.

To *answer* those many questions, we went right to the source. We interviewed scores of current eBay PowerSellers to get their advice and to learn their secrets about how they achieved their status. This book is the culmination of our research.

As a book of secrets for people who are already comfortable on eBay, *eBay PowerSeller Secrets* will not provide you basic information about registering yourself as a seller or teach the basics of buying and selling on eBay. That information is readily available on eBay, and there are many fine eBay primers that cover all that. We didn't think the world needed another one. If you're new to eBay, go ahead and buy one of those basic primers. If you're ready to move beyond the basic, and you hope to become a PowerSeller yourself, buy this book, then pull up a chair. We're here to help.

It used to be that you could sell pretty much anything and everything on eBay. In the early days, the site gained the reputation as the "yard sale" of the Internet. While it's still true that you can sell almost anything at all on eBay, selling stuff on eBay and working toward building a full-time eBay business as a PowerSeller—a business that will support your family and sustain a comfortable standard of living—are two entirely different things. PowerSellers have shown us that today eBay is way more than a "yard sale" of any type. Be prepared to find a niche for yourself amid a world of commerce that spans the globe and crosses into every type of commodity you can think to buy and sell. The possibilities are almost boundless, and we'll show you how to think beyond the old sports equipment, outgrown clothes, and other castoffs that once defined eBay's content.

We've organized this book based on what we believe you'll need to know as you make your eBay business grow. The early chapters will help you define your business goals, begin to locate those all-important sources of inventory, and equip your new business for processing volume orders. Without a constant and steady flow of inventory, you'll be able to sell on eBay as a hobby, but you'll have a hard time achieving PowerSeller status.Without a well-planned business setup, you'll soon be swamped with work that you can't quite keep up with. Rather than having your business thrive, it will actually falter.

Then we'll show you how to create effective, attractive, and successful auction listings. You'll learn how to maximize your every effort to build not only your sales but also the customer base that will keep your sales strong. You'll learn all the ins and outs of processing your customers' payments, shipping out your merchandise, and providing the kind of customer service that distinguishes the PowerSellers. Finally, we'll take a look at what you'll need to do to keep proper business records, and we'll explore branching out from eBay onto the Internet at large as an e-merchant.

In each chapter you'll learn inside tips and advice from the PowerSellers who have already achieved your goal. They once stood right where you are and dreamed the same dream. Now that they've achieved that dream, they've been generous enough to share some of what they've learned with the rest of us.

You'll find the PowerSellers to be a fascinating group of people. They are smart, they work hard, but they also live lives they've fashioned for themselves. While reading this book, you'll find that many of the sellers we interviewed live in Florida. One after another they've told us the same thing, "Since I can work and live anywhere, why shouldn't I live where it's beautiful all the time!" Other sellers have found ways to bring old family businesses into the 21st century. They work in a new branch of an established family business that held no real appeal to them before they could do it on eBay. Still others have been able to reorganize their lives to better meet the needs of aging parents and young children, staying close to home where they're needed most.

They *are* a fascinating group, which has allowed us to write a book that we believe is fascinating too. (You'll have to trust us on this. If you think it's awful to read a boring book, just imagine how it must feel to have to write one!) We've shared a wealth of knowledge with you, but we've also made it fun to learn about eBay and the art of the PowerSeller. We've used a lot of wisdom from the PowerSellers, and we've told you stories about who they are and how they work to illustrate the advice they've given us. Ten of the chapters end with a PowerSeller's profile, including a photo so you can see the real people behind the user IDs that identify them on eBay. We wanted to remove some of the mystique that surrounds this group and show you that these people are no different from anyone else.

Except that they are PowerSellers, of course. And you can be one, too. We, along with the scores of PowerSellers whose strategies and secrets are documented here, will show you how.

Chapter 1

Know Your Business/
Grow Your Business

So, you have decided to run your own eBay business. You are in excellent company, as more than 1.3 million people worldwide are already earning their livings this way. With the proper planning, dedication, and hard work, there is no reason you should not be able to join them. Here's the good news: You don't have to invent this whole thing for yourself. You can learn from others who have gone before. Reality check: You don't have an open field either. Among those 1.3 million eBay entrepreneurs are people who are selling exactly what you want to sell. You'll need to figure out your own place in the eBay world and claim your own piece of it. Don't let that discourage you. Not only do you have all of the power of your own imagination, you also have a community of people who are willing to help you learn your way around. You are not just signing on to a Web site when you log on to eBay, you are joining a community of businesspeople.

In that respect, owning your eBay business is not really different from owning a brick-and-mortar store. You will have all of the same concerns that any business owner must endure. You'll need to plan for inventory. You'll have to develop customer service policies. Cash flow, as with all businesses, will be a concern. You'll need to plan for the inevitable fraud. You will also have all of the same rewards that owning your own store can bring. You decide what to sell and how you want your business to operate. And, of course, your boss is someone you can be sure to get along with. PowerSellers will tell you that in many ways, you can consider your eBay business as a little shop in an enormous mall. That's just how much running an eBay business resembles operating a regular store.

On the other hand, eBay makes your business unlike any other humans have ever known. For one thing, this is a business you can start for as little as $200, according to one Platinum PowerSeller. Plus, your business never closes. Whether you are actively working or not, people from all over the world are conceivably shopping with you at any moment of the day or night. Your customers come from all over the globe, and it is not very likely that you will ever meet a single one of them. Nearly all of your interactions will occur through your computer, creating new challenges in communication and customer service. That's not to say you won't know and care about your customers, because you surely will. After all, people are still the driving force behind every business. And, although you can't easily stop in at the shop next door and talk business with your neighbor, you can certainly become a part of a vibrant business community and find support, advice, and friendship just on the other side of your computer screen.

Know Yourself

Before you can begin to know your business, take some time to be sure you know yourself. Running an eBay business is not right for everyone, and even if you want to give it a try, you may find out that your personality is not really suited to the realities of life as an eBay PowerSeller. Operating your own business requires enormous energy and commitment. You have to be willing to embrace change, since that's a big part of eBay life. There are certainly easier ways to earn a paycheck, and you must be sure you are being realistic about the challenges that lie ahead.

Make Sure Your Personality Is Well-Suited to Sitting in Front of Your Computer

You will spend countless hours day after day listing your products, answering e-mail, tracking your auctions, preparing your shipping, keeping your records, and communicating with other sellers on discussion boards. Know in advance that your work life will be spent intimately connected to a computer. If you require more physicality in your job, you should recognize that before you go too much further. TraderNick told us how his brother teases him every time he steps into his work area, asking him how he can possibly "stand" sitting there all day long. Because eBay is a computer-based universe, you cannot conduct your eBay business without putting in endless hours at the computer. Many of us don't mind, but you might, and it's important to know if you're more like TraderNick or his brother from the very beginning.

» Be a good time manager

Be honest with yourself. If left alone, will you devote the time you need to your eBay business, or will you find yourself tempted to get out into the garden on a nice day, play catch with the kids, or take the dog for a walk? Once you become your own boss, it's up to you to determine your work schedule. Only self-motivated

Be a good time manager

people work successfully from home, and answering this question for yourself is vital to your future success.

On the other hand, do you have a tendency to work way too hard? Will you know when it's time to stop and go spend time with your family and friends? Your eBay business never closes, but you have to be able to shut the door on your time there. TraderNick decided he had to have a brick-and-mortar storefront in addition to his eBay business for just this reason. He said it became obvious to him that he wasn't being a good dad or husband, because he was so focused on his eBay business. Now he has a distinct time each day that work ends and family time begins. That's not to say you have to go to the extreme of taking on a storefront in addition to your eBay business, but you do have to be able to close up shop for the day and get back to the rest of your life.

Selling on eBay Is As Much a Way to Live As It Is a Way to Earn a Living

PowerSellers live a life that is different in many ways from the lives of other workers. They work very long hours, but they choose which hours they work. They work hard to find and list the products they sell, but they get to immerse themselves every day in items they know and care about. There is no such thing as a PowerSeller who is lukewarm about his or her business. There are many people who sell on eBay as a hobby or to bring in a little money, but if your goal is to become a PowerSeller, accept that you will live, breathe, eat, and sleep eBay every day.

PowerSellers often report that they have no vacation days. They can't interrupt the flow of their operations long enough to have a stretch of time away from home and work. Sure, they have the flexibility to take the morning off to see their kids participate in the assembly at the elementary school, but you can be sure they'll work later that night to make up the time they missed. E-mail must be answered every day. Products must be packaged and shipped. Listings must be posted. Any day that is missing these activities is a day that cuts into the profits of a PowerSeller's business. You can be sure PowerSellers don't miss too many days!

On the other hand, this is a business that can still operate when you don't feel well enough to go into an office among other people. You can work in your pajamas if you choose. You can catch up on work during a patch of insomnia. Your freedom is as real as your responsibility and commitment are. That's part of the joy of owning your own business, especially on eBay.

Know eBay

The business you are planning now will exist in a virtual world. This virtual world is inhabited by millions of other people, including tens of thousands of others who are earning their living exclusively on eBay. You can't expect to enter this virtual world and thrive without knowing your way around. No doubt, you already know a good deal about the world of eBay, which is why you are hoping to become a PowerSeller. But, there is still a lot to learn as you cross the line between eBay hobbyist and eBay PowerSeller.

Know What You're Aiming For

What exactly is a PowerSeller? An eBay-designated PowerSeller is a seller who generates at least $1,000 per month in revenue (some generate over $1 million!) and has at least a 98 percent positive feedback rating. To make it easy for buyers and others to recognize PowerSellers, eBay allows them to include the PowerSeller symbol as part of their eBay IDs. They are eligible to have a personal eBay contact, and they have the opportunity to attend special eBay events. For more information about the entire PowerSeller program, go to http://pages.ebay.com/services/buyandsell/welcome.html.

Specifically, here are eBay's criteria for becoming a PowerSeller:

- Be an active seller on the eBay site for a minimum of 90 days.

- Maintain a minimum of four average monthly listings for the past three months.

- Maintain a minimum feedback number of 100 with a 98 percent positive rating (or higher).

- Keep your eBay account current—no outstanding balances.

- Comply with eBay listing policies.

- Uphold the eBay community values, including honesty, timeliness, and mutual respect.

Know all of eBay's rules and follow them

- Maintain a minimum of $1,000 for three consecutive months of average gross monthly sales.

There are five tiers of PowerSellers, distinguished by the level of monthly sales they must achieve:

1. Bronze: $1,000
2. Silver: $3,000
3. Gold: $10,000
4. Platinum: $25,000
5. Titanium: $150,000

If you're going to earn your living selling on eBay, you want to become a PowerSeller—not only because it means you're making a fair amount of money, but also because many buyers are more comfortable doing business with PowerSellers. Their status means they are successful, and they've achieved that success in large measure by delivering good products and great customer service.

Moreover, eBay rewards its PowerSellers with modest perks, with the specific perks tied to the PowerSeller level achieved (though most PowerSellers feel their perks come from their own business success):

Tier	eSupport	Toll-Free Access	Account Manager
Bronze	X		
Silver	X	X	
Gold	X	X	X
Platinum	X	X	X
Titanium	X	X	X

» Know all of eBay's rules and follow them

You have ultimate freedom in defining the nature of your eBay business, but freedom is not possible without a backdrop of rules, and eBay has plenty of those. Violate the rules, and eBay will terminate your business. You'll be investing too much in this endeavor to carelessly lose your place in the market through ignorance of these rules. Just as in the material world, ignorance of the law is no excuse.

Know all of eBay's rules and follow them

Fortunately, eBay makes it easy to find their rules. Go to http://pages.ebay.com/help/policies/seller-rules-overview.html for a complete listing. For starters, here are some basics.

If you list an item for sale and someone bids on it, you have to sell it. You have entered into a binding contract at that point—a contract that's binding for both parties. If you refuse to sell an item you've listed, the buyer has a legitimate complaint, and when your failure is reported to eBay, you will be warned and/or disciplined. eBay will consider you a "Non-Selling Seller" for that transaction. Now you may wonder, why on earth would I refuse to sell something after I've listed it? But, it's not inconceivable that you might feel you haven't received enough money for the item, or you might just regret having listed it once you've done it. This may be especially true in the beginning when you may be listing things from your own personal collection of items. Or, if you grow too fast, you might inadvertently list and sell something you've already run out of! So be sure you really want to sell anything you list!

You may not artificially inflate the bidding on your item by "shilling" it. In other words, you cannot bid on your own item under another screen name, or have a family member or friend do this to drive up the cost of your auction and generate interest in your sale. That's not to say no seller on eBay has ever done it, but it is against the rules, and you will be disciplined if you are caught. In fact, eBay considers this a most serious offense, and many sellers have been removed permanently from the site for violations, as it flies in the face of bidder trust. Just to be safe, don't even let anyone in your family bid on your items because it can appear to be shill bidding!

Remember that you are in this now for the long haul. You are not just trying to sell a few things here and there. You are creating a business. Use good business practices from the beginning to set yourself on a solid footing, and know the rules of the community you are working in.

eBay operates on a basic set of values. Most of these are similar to the ones we learned as children, including "Treat other people as you wish to be treated yourself." It's familiar, wouldn't you agree? To set the tone for your eBay business, check out eBay's community values at http://pages.ebay.com/community/people/values.html.

» Use the site map

You can always spot the tourists in any large city by the oversize tour-guide maps sticking out from their back pockets. The virtual city of eBay also has such a convenient tool, and luckily for you, it is a lot less conspicuous. You've probably been getting by on eBay without much need to navigate too deeply into the site. You know how to find items to bid on and how to do basic listings to sell items too. You may also be using your My eBay page to get quick access to everything you're doing on eBay and verify that any eBay-related e-mails you receive are legitimate.

However, now's the time to learn all about eBay, and the way to start is by using the Site Map. When you click the Site Map link at the top of any eBay screen, you will see the screen shown in Figure 1-1. The people at eBay couldn't have made it

FIGURE 1-1 From eBay's Site Map you can quickly get to just about any part of the site.

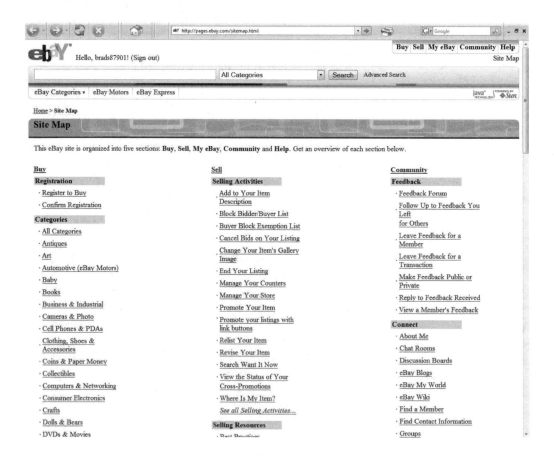

easier for you to find your way around and turn the many little corners of eBay designed to help you learn more and become a more effective eBay user. "My first step when I'm wondering how to do something new on eBay is to start with the Site Map," reports Baronart, a dealer in fine art. Keep it simple and use this great tool eBay provides for you.

Keep Educating Yourself, Because eBay Changes Every Day

You will have to work to keep current with eBay, because it is an ever-evolving entity. "In four years selling on eBay, I literally had to fundamentally change my business model and/or operations every six to twelve months," says PowerSeller David Yaskulka. Once you are familiar with all of the basic rules, stay up to date on the changes that come about routinely. Fortunately, eBay makes that easy for you. Go to http://www2.ebay.com/aw/marketing.shtml, shown in Figure 1-2, for the latest announcements and news features.

» Subscribe to AuctionBytes

If you're like most online veterans, you subscribe to lots of free newsletters, most of which you just delete because you don't have the time to read them. Well, AuctionBytes newsletters at www.auctionbytes.com/ really deliver the goods! They claim to be the number-one source of news on the online auction world, and there's no reason to doubt them (and we're not saying that just because we write for them). AuctionBytes' NewsFlash newsletters, electronically published three or four times a week, are worth every second you spend reading them. They feature insightful news about eBay with no hype. They also include product reviews, a letters section, and a whole lot more. Through the AuctionBytes home page, you can also access "Cool Tools." These include photography tips, a classified section, and reviews of auction-related books. They don't limit their news coverage to just eBay but include information about other online auctions and auction sites, too. You'll learn as you read on that we're proponents of branching out beyond eBay when the time is right. Of course, right now all of your energy is devoted to learning about eBay, but it doesn't hurt to keep an eye on the rest of the online auction world when news is delivered with your e-mail automatically.

Subscribe to AuctionBytes

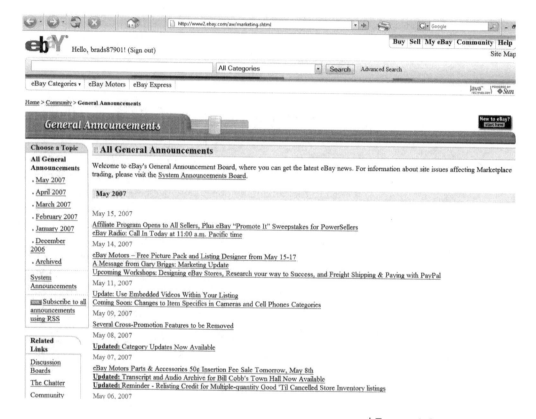

FIGURE 1-2 It's essential to stay updated with eBay news, and the General Announcements page can help you do that.

A Sample Article from AuctionBytes Newsletter

eBay PowerSellers: America's New Celebrity

By Brad and Debra Schepp
AuctionBytes.com
April 17, 2005

The time has long passed since you'd be likely to find someone who'd never heard of eBay. Today eBay is nearly as recognizable a part of American culture as jazz music. Thanks to the rapid growth of the online auction world and the media's devotion to documenting all the odd, bizarre, and famous items that come up for sale, practically everyone knows about eBay. Those among us who buy or sell on the site are so common, that nearly everyone has a personal story to tell about an eBay experience. Until recently, however, the eBay PowerSeller was an individual toiling away outside the media spotlight. Of course, PowerSellers knew about each other. They've formed powerful alliances over the years and created a vibrant business community. But, they've also lived a world apart from the average American. When we began researching our book, *eBay PowerSeller Secrets*, about a year ago, we found the term required definition and explanation to almost all those outside of the PowerSeller community. What a difference a year makes!

PowerSellers are taking their spot in the world of American celebrity, and that spot is a bright one. Stories appear in print ranging from the small local newspaper to the business section of the Sunday *New York Times*. In October, the *Times* ran an article on the topic of eBay PowerSellers that featured Debnroo, also known as Deb and Andy Mowery. Happily, this was just the beginning of the successful couple's touch with fame and glory. Deb and Andy sell home and garden items and pet supplies. What makes them most interesting is that their business evolved over time. They started selling postcards from Andy's father's antique business. Then, like so many other PowerSellers, they found that they liked earning money while incorporating freedom and choice in their lifestyles. They then researched and hustled and did whatever they had to do to build a thriving business. As a result of the article in the *New York Times,* Sony Pictures TV offered to feature the couple on the television show, *Life and Style,* a daily series for women hosted by Jules Asner, Cynthia Garrett, Lynne Koplitz and Kimora Lee Simmons. The offer included a fabulous trip to New York and an experience as television celebrities that Andy and Deb will cherish for a lifetime.

In exchange for coming on the show and sharing with the world exactly what the life of an eBay PowerSeller is like, the couple received a trip to New York, complete with airfare, hotel accommodations, and limousine service. But, first a production crew came to the couple's home office to film them in action. There they got their first experience working with a producer and an audio crew, and even had the chance to do retakes. That's when they began to suspect that this wasn't going to be a two-bit media experience! By the time the experience ended, Andy and Deb had enjoyed a real taste of what life can be like for the celebrity set. A limousine met them at LaGuardia Airport and delivered them to their hotel. The next day, they enjoyed a ride down 5th Avenue in a 40-foot limo, just thrilling at the thought of passersby wondering who was behind the darkened glass. Exiting the limo in front of the studio, they enjoyed the stares of the crowd trying to figure out exactly who they were. Then it was on to their private dressing room and into makeup. They had about 90 minutes to rehearse before the filming began before a live audience. Although the show does include a script, Andy and Deb reported that this was followed only loosely, and they had plenty of time for free-flowing conversation. The spot debuted on April 11, 2005, to the delight of all who know and respect the Debnroo couple.

See a photo of Andy and Deb in New York at http://digbig.com/4debt.

Tune in to eBay radio

Deb and Andy's experience may be the extreme, but PowerSellers are gaining recognition all the time. In the months we've been speaking at public forums and conducting interviews about our book, the term "PowerSeller" has increasingly been bandied about without need of definition. Our radio interview spots now often include a local guest PowerSeller who will share the interview with us to inject a first-hand point of view. People no longer want to learn simply about buying and selling on eBay, they want to get a taste for the life people who are earning their livings by buying and selling on eBay live.

Within the last month, we were guests on one such radio show airing in the Midwest. Not only did the interviewer know about Professional eBay Sellers Alliance (PeSA), he wanted to talk in great detail about the recent PESA conference in Atlanta. He wanted our opinion on how the PowerSellers were going to alter the eBay landscape and what we thought we should expect from them next. That suggests that not only does he have a level of familiarity with the PowerSellers, their issues and concerns, but that he also assumes his average listener does too.

Like we said, what a difference a year makes!

For PowerSellers or soon-to-be PowerSellers looking to make their businesses better known, we have a few tips. Make yourself known. Be active on eBay's bulletin boards and Groups, write for local publications, and make your About Me page interesting, with a dash of personality. We really believe the media is tired of the same old sources, and if you can come across as someone with something fresh to offer, they'll be eager to tell your story too.

Subscriptions to the newsletter are free, so you have nothing to lose. Figure 1-3 shows you an example of an AuctionBytes issue.

» Tune in to eBay radio

Broadcast by wsRadio, the "worldwide leader in Internet talk," eBay Radio is a fun, easy-on-the-eyes way to get up to speed on eBay topics and stay current with important developments within the community. A new show is broadcast every Tuesday from 11 A.M. to 12 noon Pacific Standard Time. It's easy to find at www.wsradio.com/ebayradio/. This link leads you to wsRadio's eBay Radio page, shown in Figure 1-4. If you can't be available during the broadcast time, don't worry. You can easily access recently archived shows or search the entire archives for shows dedicated to subjects that will interest you.

Once you find a show you're interested in, just click the link for it. The radio show then begins playing thanks to streaming media technology. You can also download a podcast (an audio file that's delivered to you automatically) of the show. You can

FIGURE 1-3 The AuctionBytes newsletter is indispensible to all eBay sellers.

listen to podcasts through your computer or any MP3 player. There you have it, good solid information available for you to learn more about eBay any hour of any day, simply by listening to the expert guests and their call-in questioners. You can even listen while you're running your eBay business!

» Sign up for eBay's Seller Newsflash

eBay makes it easy for you to get the news sellers need to stay competitive. Go to Seller Central and click News & Updates. Once you're a PowerSeller, you'll be able to sign up for eBay's *Power-Up* seller newsletter to receive advance notice of events and promotions. You'll learn when eBay is planning to have free listing days and feature discounts, and you'll learn what top items buyers are currently searching for. It's easy to sign up for

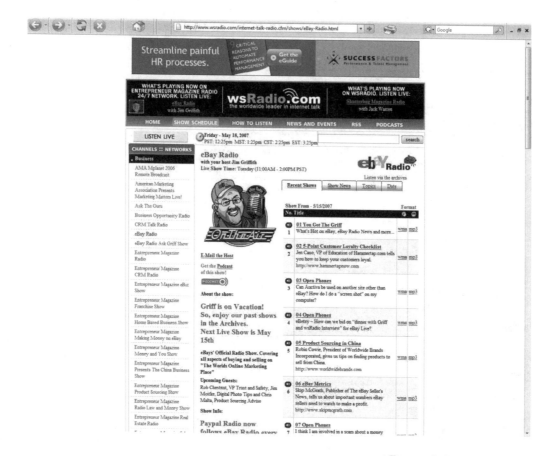

FIGURE 1-4 From wsRadio .com's eBay radio Home page, you can get to Griff's show—a nice diversion.

these e-mail updates, and eBay assures all users that the company will not rent or sell their personal information to third parties for marketing purposes. If you miss out on the *Power-Up* newsletter, your competitors might just scoop you.

» Attend eBay University and stop by eBay's learning center

eBay University is a college that comes to you. Its instructors travel from city to city to bring their wisdom to eBay buyers and sellers across the country. Courses are available for both buyers and sellers. There are two course levels, for beginning and advanced students. The advanced course for sellers ("Beyond

Attend eBay University and stop by eBay's learning center

the Basics") is perfect for readers of this book. It's designed to help sellers build their businesses and move up the success ladder. The cost for attending eBay University is usually $59 for a full one-day seminar. You can also attend online courses or buy the Selling Basics course on DVD for $7.95, or the Beyond the Basics course on CD for $19.95. eBay University's Welcome screen is shown in Figure 1-5.

eBay University is only a small part of the eBay Learning Center. You will find the center at http://pages.ebay.com/ education/. In addition to the eBay University courses, you can come here to listen to or view brief tutorials on basic and more advanced eBay buying and selling topics. The Learning Center also includes links to other resources, such as information about eBay fees and PayPal.

FIGURE 1-5 eBay University offers good courses at a reasonable price, and you don't need to attend in person. You'll find the Welcome screen helpful for learning your way around the campus.

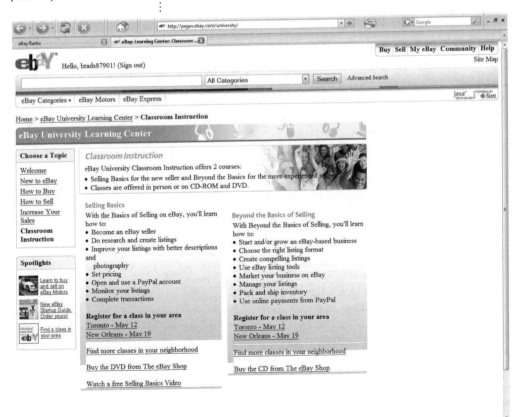

» ## Go to eBay Live!

As an aspiring PowerSeller you must plan to attend an eBay Live!
convention. Every June eBay hosts a three-day extravaganza of
all things eBay. You'll find tens of thousands of other eBay
enthusiasts plus companies and vendors who can help you
identify tools and products to help your business grow. "If you're
just starting out you should definitely go," says PowerSeller
Arthur. "It gives you a great perspective of what's going on, plus
a room full of vendors who might be able to help you."

You can't possibly be on eBay any time after January 1
without finding lots of information about the upcoming show in
June. eBay pulls out all the stops to make sure you know about it
and come join the crowds. Go to http://www2.ebay.com/aw/
marketing.shtml for the latest information on this year's eBay
Live!

Feedback Is Critical

In the world of eBay, nothing is more important to a seller than
a stellar Feedback Profile. This consists of your total positive
feedback score and the percentage of your total feedback that
was positive. Think of it as the face you show the world. It is
the only way buyers and sellers know about each other's
trustworthiness, and it keeps eBay from being totally
anonymous. Sellers with relatively poor Profiles are at a real
disadvantage on eBay. Some buyers won't take the risk in doing
business with you until you've proved yourself in the
community. With a low feedback score, you are even limited to
the number of postings you can make on eBay message boards.
Until your feedback score exceeds 10, you are limited to no
more than 10 postings a day.

As you already know, PowerSellers must maintain at least
98 percent positive feedback. Here's how that works: For every
transaction that happens on eBay, both the buyer and the seller
may leave feedback for each other. Your feedback "score"
consists of the number of distinct trading partners who have left
feedback for you. The percentage of this feedback that is
positive is also part of your Feedback Profile. (Note that an
individual user can only impact your rating by one point either
positively or negatively, regardless of how many transactions
you have with that person.) Unlike in school, an "A" rating is

nothing less than about 98 percent. Anything below that means that shoppers need to examine the feedback comments for this seller carefully and shop very cautiously.

As we write this, eBay has just rolled out "Feedback 2.0," which goes beyond the previous feedback rating system. Buyers still leave an overall feedback rating of positive, neutral, or negative. But they can now also rate sellers on such specifics as how accurate the item description was, communication, shipping time, and shipping and handling charges. Buyers rate sellers on these criteria via a 1- to 5-star scale, with 1 being the lowest and 5 the highest rating. The average score for each rating is shown on the seller's Feedback Profile page.

You must begin to build and safeguard your Feedback Profile from the very first day you start your business. For every transaction you complete on eBay, complete a feedback report as the final step. If you have been casual in leaving feedback, vow to change your ways as of right now. PowerSellers unanimously say that they guard their Feedback Profiles as preciously as they guard their greatest treasure.

The first thing you can do to build your feedback rating is to buy more things on eBay. Now, that may seem like odd advice to someone who wants to sell, sell, sell. But, think of your eBay purchases as part of your startup business costs. You don't have to purchase expensive items. You can also tailor all of your purchases to things you're going to need for your eBay business so that you can get the tax advantages of business expenses. Surprisingly, feedback you receive as a buyer is completely valid in building your feedback score. Many people checking your total feedback score won't dig deeper to review only those comments you received when selling items. They just want to know that you legitimately completed your transactions, you were true to your word, and you conducted yourself as an honorable member of the eBay community. To ensure you receive positive feedback as a buyer is simple. Pay quickly and follow the seller's rules for calculating your shipping and handling. (Either use the shipping calculator that's part of the listing, or pay the flat fee).

Don't Be a Stranger

Remember our comparison of your eBay business to a small shop in an enormous mall? Well, it's time to meet your neighbors. You are not just beginning a new business venture, you're joining a new community. As in any other neighborhood, you'll meet people who rub you the wrong way, people you'll want to befriend, and people you'll simply do business with. The amazing thing about eBay is the community that forms around the globe, across cultural barriers, and beyond the limits of the physical world. People who earn their livings on eBay share certain values and aspirations. They are kindred spirits in their search for better ways of earning a living. They may be all different, and they are, but they also share a common bond. They come to this virtual marketplace to make a life for themselves that previous generations couldn't possibly dream about. Don't be shy, go on out and meet your fellow sellers. The place to get started doing this is at the Community tab from eBay's home page. Click here and you'll find the screen shown in Figure 1-6. It includes links within the following categories: Feedback, Connect (from here you can get to the communications-related areas we'll discuss soon), News, Education, and More Community Programs.

The next two tips focus on the heart of the Connect area: Discussion Boards and Groups. You are standing at the gateway to the eBay community. Go on ahead and jump right in.

» Get involved in the discussion boards

One of the best ways to join the community is to get involved in the discussion boards. At first, you may feel that you should spend all of your time strictly listing and selling your products, but becoming part of the community will help you build your business because it will put you in touch with hundreds, if not thousands, of people who have been where you are right now. It is only smart to learn from them. From the Community page described in the preceding section you'll click Discussion Boards. Here you'll see a screen listing all of eBay's boards. There are boards for Community Help, Category Specific Discussions, General Discussion, Workshops, eBay Tools, and Giving Works, eBay's charitable fundraising.

Seller Central is one eBay discussion board you'll want to visit early and often. Find it from the discussion boards screen, or you can go directly to Seller Central by typing www.ebay .com/sellercentral into your browser. Once you're there, click Seller Central Board under Helpful Links on the right side of the screen, shown in Figure 1-7. You'll see a long list of topics

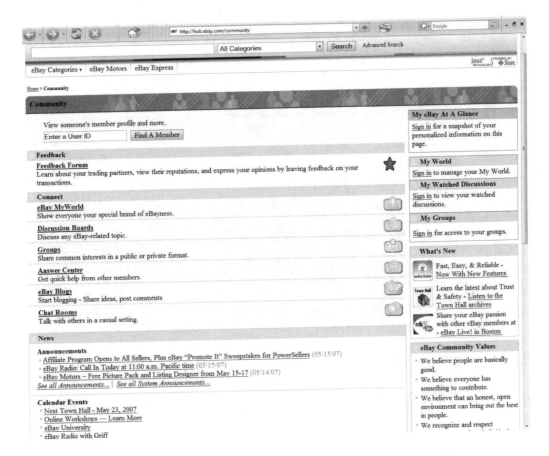

FIGURE 1-6 eBay's Community page should be among your first stops when you want to communicate with other sellers.

under discussion. You can just browse the topic listings and click whatever topic interests you. When we stopped in today, one of the liveliest topics was Seller Tips & Tricks of the Trade, with more than 2,000 postings. If you don't have the time to browse, you can find specific topics you're researching. Just type the topic you're researching into the box at the top of the topic list, and click the Search Board button. All of eBay's boards work this way.

» Get involved in groups

Groups are distinct from discussion boards in the types of information they offer. You will still find discussions in the groups, but you will also find posted newsletters, photos, and polls. Groups are more focused than the boards. Different

Get involved in groups

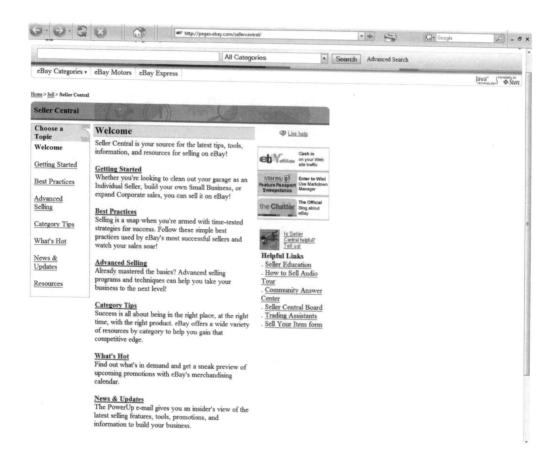

groups are dedicated to specific topics. You can reach all of the groups from the main Community screen by clicking on Groups in the Connect area that you used to find the discussion boards, shown in Figure 1-6.

It won't be long before you discover that some of the groups are private. Unlike the discussion boards, which are open to everyone, groups can be designated as "public" or "private." If you wish to join a private group, you must request membership and meet the criteria for joining. Go to http://groups.ebay.com/index.jspa?categoryID=35 to see a complete listing of groups devoted just to sellers. Or, from the Group Center screen, click View All (just to the right of seller groups).

As of this writing there are more than 400 seller groups! That's not counting any of the groups meant specifically for

PowerSellers and PowerSeller wannabees. There are additional groups for you. To join a private group (private groups are labeled private next to the group name), you'll need to send an e-mail to the moderator explaining why you qualify for membership. To get you started, there are also some groups for aspiring PowerSellers that are open to the public and full of useful information for people like you who are trying to reach PowerSeller status.

Know Your Products

Now, you've explored your personality and found it suitable to an eBay business. You've explored the eBay community with the eyes of a serious seller, and you've begun to learn your way around the neighborhood. Next you must decide what you are going to sell on eBay. No single decision you make will alter your early experiences quite as much as this one will. Fortunately, many sellers who have gone before you have offered you some profound advice.

» Start with what you know

This is the single, most universal bit of advice PowerSellers offer to those who want to follow in their wake. It may seem obvious, but there are practical reasons to follow this piece of advice. "If you sell what you know, you'll start your business with a knowledge base that would ultimately take years to build otherwise," says the owner of Dan's Train Depot. You won't have to be learning the ins and outs of a product area at the same time that you're learning the ins and outs of an eBay business. You give yourself an added advantage right from the beginning.

If you start by selling things you know about, you also gain the added advantage of knowing that you can trust your gut. "Being able to trust yourself to take a risk early on is very important," says Wegotthebeats. You won't do that if you're dealing in a product area that is unfamiliar to you.

This "sell what you know" advice is a sound strategy for new sellers looking to build feedback and gain experience. But as you start transitioning from casual seller to eBay businessperson, you'll want to sell items regardless of whether the items personally interest you. (More on this soon.)

» Don't sell things before you know about them

Now, this may seem like an obvious counterpoint to the preceding tip, but there are reasons to be specific in calling it to your attention. You are not just trying to sell a few things on eBay, you are trying to create a whole new business. You must appear to be in control of your business even if you don't feel terribly confident about what you're doing. Your spouse, your family, and your friends can lend their support to your shaky self-image as an eBay seller, but your customers must not doubt your professionalism for a moment. If you're dealing in items that you don't know, you will never be able to project the self-assurance necessary to create the public image you are seeking.

From a very practical viewpoint, selling items you know nothing about makes you vulnerable to taking losses on valuable items. Many sellers will tell you that items rise to their own market value on eBay. To a degree that's true, but if you don't know what you have, you are likely to place it in the wrong category. This may cut the amount of action you'll get from your auction. You will also be less able to write the kind of powerful item description that brings you top dollar for your item. Don't sacrifice an item out of a lack of education. It's too easy to do the research necessary to learn about what you have. Until you're sure, hold on to it and list things you know about.

Research What You Sell

Fortunately, researching your items could not be easier. You can start by searching for your item in completed auctions. To do this, click the Advanced Search link on eBay's toolbar and enter your keywords and other search options. Check the box for completed listings. Figure 1-8 shows you what your search screen should look like. This will pull up all of the items similar to yours that have sold on eBay within the last 30 days. With this search, you will be able to see what the going price was for items similar to yours and if those items actually sold. You will also be able to compare the condition of your item to items that have competed directly with what you want to sell. Open individual auction listings, and you can get a look at the

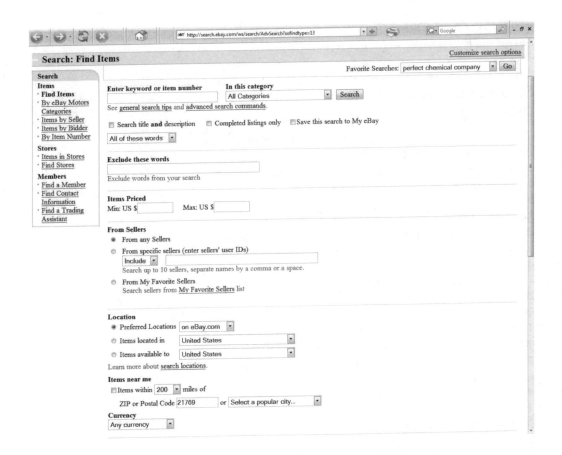

FIGURE 1-8 From the Advanced Search page you can find completed auctions for comparing your items to those already listed and sold on eBay.

different methods other sellers have used to describe the item you have. Look at these descriptions with an eye toward the ones that sold for the most (you can sort them by price).

You'll surely get some tips about what to include in your own descriptions! For an even fuller look at auctions similar to yours, search current auctions as you're searching completed ones. Just open each search (completed, current) in its own screen, and you can easily switch back and forth.

In many ways, eBay has helped cut into the publishing market for collectible guides. Instead of having to purchase a new book every year to reflect changing values, many sellers who deal in antiques and collectibles use eBay searches as their buying guides. Not only is the market value up to date, it is also more realistic. Ultimately an item is only worth what a buyer is willing to pay for it. There is no better place to see what the market will bear than the world's largest marketplace.

» Seek out marginalized niches for your product

Keep the view of the world's marketplace in mind when you are considering what products to sell. Once you open an eBay business, your customers are just as likely to come from across the ocean as they are to come from across town. "I look for things that aren't so popular in the United States as they are in Japan and Germany," says Wegotthebeats. This seller specializes in CDs, and he knows his market well enough to know what products are hot in foreign markets. Not only does this allow him to buy his inventory knowing that he'll have customers for his items, it makes it possible for him to scoop up music that isn't commercially successful here for pennies and sell it overseas for, sometimes, hundreds of U.S. dollars. Now, you can't expect to have that kind of experience right out of the starting gate, but you can expect to ultimately know your product area well enough to identify niches that will be just as profitable to your business.

» Research your own customers

Once you start selling on eBay, check to see what your customers are buying. This is simple enough to do. From the Advanced Search menu, click to Find Items by Bidder. You'll get a screen that allows you to specify that you want to see everything a specific bidder has made bids on in both current and completed auctions. Figure 1-9 shows you a completed search for one particular bidder. Now you know absolutely everything your customer has been interested in during the last 30 days. When you gather your inventory for future sales, you'll know exactly what your customers are shopping for.

» Stay away from contentious items while you're just getting started

It's very important to remember that not only are you beginning a business, but you are also building your reputation. Don't start

Stay away from contentious items while you're just getting started

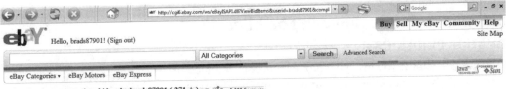

Current and recent auctions bid on by brads87901 (271 ☆) me ☁ Top 5,000 Reviewer

To protect bidder privacy, not all items that this member has bid on may be displayed. When the price or highest bid on an item reaches or exceeds a certain level, User IDs will be displayed as anonymous names. For auction items, a bold price means at least one bid has been received.

Note: Anonymous names may appear more than once and may represent different bidders.

In some cases, brads87901 (271 ☆) me ☁ Top 5,000 Reviewer may no longer be the high bidder.

1 – 8 of 8 total. Click on the column headers to sort

Item	Start	End	Price	Title	High Bidder	Seller
250104891169	Apr-15-07	Apr-17-07 16:51:55	US $9.99	512MB MEMORY Card for Canon PowerShot A630 A640 A520	Purchased on: Apr-17-07 16:51:55 See All Buyers	skakawack
250109488900	Apr-27-07	Apr-30-07 12:36:52	US $12.99	Gillette Fusion Power Razor Blades -8-Cartridges Refill	Purchased on: Apr-30-07 12:36:52 See All Buyers	fullhouse_liquidators
290113002872	May-04-07	May-11-07 17:42:14	US $6.50	Scripto Pen Pencil Set, Liberty Bell symbol, "Freedom"	foxhill3436 (*)	pfacwa
320111917407	May-07-07	May-12-07 15:42:22	US $7.05	Vintage Blue Scripto Mechanical Pencil P360 Sample	wob638 (*)	darcyco
160114961071	May-08-07	May-13-07 10:01:35	US $12.27	(3) "The History of Mystery" by Max Collins 1888054530	scifipaul (*)	collectorspress
160114966036	May-08-07	May-13-07 10:15:25	US $10.04	(5) Come Fly With Us History Airline Hostess 1933112069	chawk60 (*)	collectorspress
160114973660	May-08-07	May-13-07 10:38:33	US $0.99	(5) TV Wonderland television ads from 1950's 1933112050	brads87901 me (*)	collectorspress
160114981391	May-08-07	May-13-07 11:00:32	US $22.38	(3) The Great American Paperback by Lupoff 1888054506	scifipaul (*)	collectorspress

About eBay | Announcements | Security Center | Policies | Site Map | Help

Copyright © 1995-2007 eBay Inc. All Rights Reserved. Designated trademarks and brands are the property of their respective owners. Use of this Web site constitutes acceptance of the eBay User Agreement and Privacy Policy.

eBay official time

FIGURE 1-9 A completed search for a specific bidder's history allows you a quick glimpse of that eBay user's recent activity.

off by selling items the condition of which can be contested. "We built our feedback rating selling vintage postcards," says Debnroo. "Our customers were nice, mostly older retired people, who honored their bids and paid their bills." Debnroo quickly built a strong positive feedback rating even though selling postcards was not ever going to make the couple rich. "Don't start out trying to build your feedback rating by selling china, for example," they explained. "The grading of this item is very subjective. Even if you know a lot about china, buyers and sellers are bound to disagree about the condition of pieces. You want your early sales to be without question so that you can build strong feedback. So, stay away from anything that can be interpreted too loosely." By the time this couple branched out into other product areas, they were well-established and well-respected eBay sellers.

» Sell what you love, but don't be blinded by your emotions

Of course, it helps if you love your product line, but don't let your own feelings and opinions get in your way. "If it were up to me, everything I sell would be green," says Wiccan_Well. But, this seller was savvy enough to recognize that her customers did not necessarily share this passion. Ultimately, you are not shopping for items for yourself, you are shopping for items your customers will want to buy. Wiccan_Well stocks far more blue items than green, because she knows that blue is the best-selling color of items in the United States.

To learn what sells best, simply use Google to search for "best-selling." Then you can enter whichever item or descriptor you are working with. Best-selling handbags, best-selling scent, best-selling fabric, for example, will all show you what most shoppers are looking for. The search results for best-selling yoga mats are shown in Figure 1-10.

You will also find that you can do research everywhere you go, as long as you keep your eyes open. When you are going about your daily business, notice what items people seem to be using, wearing, or buying. Keep in mind which of these may be good for you to add to your stock. The owner of Wiccan_Well took some extra yoga and meditation classes, because she knew those were the types of activities her clients would be interested in pursuing. She said that with each class, she noticed the clothes, scents, and jewelry her classmates were wearing, and she made it a point to include similar items in her inventory.

» Sell quality items

When you are shopping for inventory, ask yourself, "Would I be proud to give this to my best friend?" recommends Wiccan_Well. If the answer is no, don't sell it. Many people go on eBay to sell off the same items they'd sell in a garage sale. They can be very successful in getting rid of unwanted things this way, to be sure. But, this is not the attitude to take when setting out to build a whole business on eBay. Your goal is not to be a one-shot seller or a twice-a-year-clean-out-the-kids'-rooms seller. You're shooting for PowerSeller status, and that's a whole different thing. Your challenge will be to build a renewable and reliable source of inventory that you can sell repeatedly to a

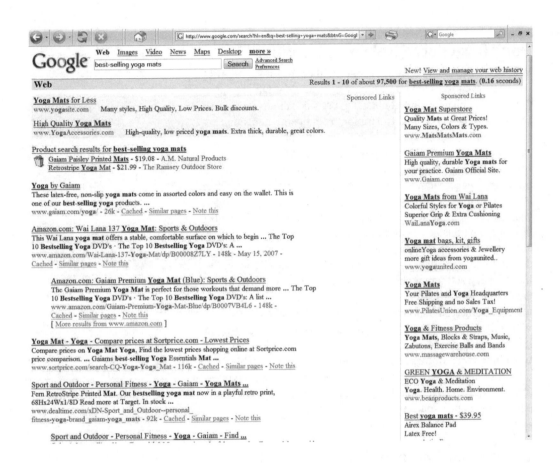

FIGURE 1-10 Google search results for best-selling yoga mats will help you identify the Internet's best-selling mats.

customer base you will build over time. Start from the beginning by stocking high-quality merchandise. It is impossible to effectively sell products you don't believe in, so don't even start with them.

A good part of building any business is building loyal, repeat customers, and that is more likely to happen when your customers know you sell quality goods. Keep this larger goal of building a customer base in mind and you won't even be tempted to scrimp on product. The last thing you want is for someone to open an eagerly awaited item purchased from you and feel disappointed. Disappointment creates a customer you can never get back, plus it is likely to leave you with disappointing feedback, too. In Chapter 2 you'll learn a lot more about identifying product areas and researching sources of products to sell.

» Don't forget practical considerations

Your new life as an eBay PowerSeller will change many things you can't even foresee from where you stand now, but certain things won't change, and you need to consider them. Don't set yourself up for failure and frustration by choosing items that simply won't work with the life you currently have. For example, when you're deciding what to sell, don't decide to stock and sell large items if you live in a small space. You're bringing your job home, and no one will be happy if the kitchen is given up to boxes that you have to climb over every time you want to get to the fridge. Consider all of the practical elements of combining business with home. Will you have a dedicated computer for your eBay business? Do you have a place you can devote to photographing your items? Life is easier if you don't have to keep setting up photo shoots every time you want to create a new listing. Remember all the incidentals that are vital to your business. Where will you store packing material? Where will you do your shipping? Are you equipped to package fragile items for shipping? If not, you may want to rethink what you'll be selling. None of these considerations is insurmountable unless, of course, you don't bother to consider them. So think long and hard. Decide carefully, and be willing to stay flexible enough to change your mind if you need to.

Know What Not to Sell

There are some things that are illegal to sell on eBay, and there are other things that may be legal but don't make for good, consistent business dealings. On your way to making PowerSeller status, don't step outside the boundaries of the law or the boundaries of common sense. Some items may not be totally banned, but they are restricted, and you must meet certain criteria in order to sell them. eBay is a socially conscious company and has banned some items that may be technically legal but not honorable to trade. eBay bans, for example, the sale of items deemed inappropriate or insensitive to the victims of a tragedy such as the September 11, 2001 terrorist attack. That makes some sellers feel better about the marketplace as a whole. "I'm glad to know eBay won't allow such morally questionable things to sell. It makes me feel better about conducting my business with them," says Bidnow5. For a complete list of prohibited and restricted items, go to http://pages.ebay.com/help/policies/items-ov.html.

Don't Break Any Laws

If it's against the law to sell it in the real world, you won't get away with selling it on eBay either. This may seem like plain common sense, but you'd be surprised how uncommon a commodity that can be in the rush to get ahead. Don't break any copyright laws either. You may be tempted to record a popular show that has not yet been released to video or DVD and make a quick sale, but don't do it. You'll lose your chance to build a solid eBay business, and you could easily leave yourself open for prosecution on criminal offenses too.

» Don't sell homemade food or body items

There are very strict guidelines for selling food on eBay, but sellers are allowed to trade in food items as long as they respect the restrictions and follow the guidelines. Every year, especially around the time of the holidays, you'll find homemade goodies and treats for sale. Now, this may seem like a great way to supplement your income, especially if you have a specialty that makes you a favorite among your friends and family. Whether it's fudge, flavored oils, or a favorite body lotion, it's a bad idea. Don't do it. You are likely to leave yourself open for all kinds of trouble, ranging from disgruntled customers to liability lawsuits. Interestingly, when it comes to collectible food items the policy is even less clear. For example, Military MREs (Meals Ready to Eat) were popping up for sale on eBay recently. It turned out these were prohibited items unless they were considered a collectible, or not meant for human consumption (a bit of an oxymoron).

» Include disclaimers and allergy warnings for all consumable items you sell

If you sell items meant for human consumption, don't forget to state very plainly in every listing that you are not recommending the item for medicinal purposes or making any claims about what the item can do to treat or heal any medical condition. Also, be sure to warn potential allergy sufferers not to bid without first checking with you about all of the product's ingredients to be sure they do not include anything that will cause allergic reactions. For example, Wiccan_Well sells herbal teas and Burt's Bees skincare products. Every listing includes such warnings, not only to prevent customers from having unrealistic expectations about the items and their efficacy, but also to protect the seller from anyone who might buy a nice chamomile tea expecting relief from a stomach ulcer. Be very clear that your items are being sold strictly for the purpose of recreation, relaxation, and enjoyment.

Mind Your Business

Not to sound rude, but stay focused on your business and start thinking like a business owner from the very beginning. Now is not too soon. Let's get a little philosophical here. eBay has made it possible for people who may never have once considered operating their own business to have one. That is incredibly empowering, and you must start harnessing that power from the very beginning. It has never been easier to start a business with very little capital risk and watch it grow. Minding your business, there is almost no limit to what you and your new eBay business can do together.

» Start small, start slowly, and don't quit your job

Throughout this book you will read stories of people who discovered eBay one evening and by the next morning they had their first item listed, and they never looked back. Some people almost accidentally stumble upon the right product at the right time and off they go. You are under no pressure to join them. Spend time doing your research. Decide what you want to sell. Learn your way around eBay. Develop policies and procedures for managing your business, and get yourself started.

Unlike the favorite children's method for getting used to the water, your best bet here is probably not to just dive right into the lake. "If you work as a lawyer, you can't expect to quit your job, start an eBay business, and make up for your salary," says TraderNick. It's good advice to remember. That's not to say you won't ultimately be able to quit your job and make up your salary, but starting a business is stressful enough. Why would you want to add risking your family's security to the stress? You'll know by reason of your cash flow when your business has grown enough to support your lifestyle. In the meantime, don't quit your day job!

Every Time You Learn Something New, You Add Another Brick to Your Invisible Store

Wiccan_Well offered this bit of advice to eBay sellers hoping to build their businesses. Keeping this in mind helps you to focus on the task of building your eBay business in a very concrete way. If you were building a brick-and-mortar store, you'd have to spend time physically creating, decorating, and preparing the space. For your eBay business, most of this planning stage is going to happen intellectually as you build your knowledge and competence in a virtual marketplace. You would give yourself the time and devote the energy necessary to physically building your store if you were opening one on Main Street. You must also allow yourself the time and devote the energy necessary to the intellectual pursuit of learning your way around the eBay marketplace. This is not time wasted in building your business, any more than choosing the right décor for your shop would be time wasted. Rather it is time invested in building your business.

Don't Be Discouraged If You Are Not a Businessperson Now

That's the beauty of eBay—you don't have to be a business-person to start an eBay business. The practice is so common there's even a name for these folks—accidental entrepreneurs. "I was cleaning carpets when I discovered eBay," says Bidnow5. "I started selling on eBay, because my dad wanted to get rid of some stuff," noted Debnroo. Many people before you have come to eBay with little or no business experience. Don't let your lack of experience discourage you. You'll do just as they have done. You'll work hard. You'll learn quickly as you go. Next year at this time, you'll sit back in amazement at what you didn't know now. You have lots of advantages that those who have gone before you did not. You have much more help available to you on eBay than the pioneers to the site had. You also have this great book, which will offer you hundreds of tips PowerSellers took years learning. So, chin up, chest out, and no self-doubt allowed around here.

» Be patient. Be aggressive. Be smart

Be patient in giving yourself the time and freedom to learn about your business and set it growing strong. Be aggressive in sticking with your business plan, setting goals, and working hard to achieve them. Be smart in staying flexible with your product choices, acquisitions, and business practices. You'll be much more successful if you continue to question what you know, what you are learning, and what you are doing. Be ready to change and adapt. "They say it takes five years to build a business, and it can take just as long to build one on eBay. You are not necessarily going to step right into a success," advises Jeralinc. Look to the future, but don't be in too much of a hurry to get there. For example, creating your own Web site, separate from eBay's, is a worthwhile goal. But you don't want to put your time and resources into that before you're ready.

Don't Be Surprised If Success Strikes Fast

On the other hand, dozens of PowerSellers tell tales of hitting one right out of the park on their first at-bat. "When I started, my goal was to sell ten wedding dresses a week," reports Bridewire. "Within a year I was selling 100 a week!" This kind of success brings its own set of challenges. No one ever said it was easy to ride a rocket. If this should happen to you, be prepared to work harder than you ever have in your life. Hang on tight, and enjoy the ride. You'll have quite a story to tell a year from now.

» Your eBay business will not work if you don't treat it like a business

You can have a great life selling stuff on eBay as a hobby and working at your regular job. There is nothing that says you ever have to strive to be an eBay PowerSeller. Except that something made you pick up this book, so you must have a drive of your own. Use that drive and make every listing you post on eBay from now on a step toward your PowerSeller status. You will never become a PowerSeller unless you take your business seriously and consider it to be as important as your full-time job. If what you want is to power-sell, then dedicate yourself right now to making every eBay interaction part of your plan to get from casual seller to PowerSeller. Even if you don't seem like a PowerSeller to the rest of the world, present yourself as one in your own head. It may be just a matter of your own perception now, but perception is a good place to start. This may mean that you'll be working two full-time jobs for a while, but no one said this was going to be easy.

» The money you earn from eBay isn't really yours

Very soon your PayPal account will start building and your products will start going out the door. Don't think for even a moment that those checks are your reward for what you're doing, and you should use them to go out to that favorite restaurant of yours to celebrate. Remind yourself with each new sale you ring up that the money isn't yours. It belongs to your eBay business. "I've known lots of people who earn a little money, go out and spend it, then settle in to watch TV. They'll never have a business that way," says Dan's Train Depot. Dan couldn't be more correct. Folks like that may be perfectly happy selling a little here and there on eBay to earn a little extra cash, but that's not a PowerSeller frame of mind. In the beginning, absolutely everything you earn should be put right back into your business. There will be time enough to spend your earnings once you've built your business.

» Pay yourself a salary

When you have achieved a steady cash flow, start paying yourself a salary from your earnings. Just be sure to make it the smallest possible salary you can get by with. That's a legitimate business expense and perfectly acceptable as long as your budget can support it. This will also be a good way for you to determine when you can start scaling back on the job you have now. When your salary from your eBay business is approaching the total of your monthly living expenses, you may just be ready to make the leap.

» Know the value of every sale and go after it

In the beginning, every sale you make increases your feedback rating and builds a potentially loyal customer. Don't underestimate the value of even the smallest sale. Go after all of them. Many PowerSellers will tell you that they no longer feel

Know the value of every sale and go after it

it's worth their time to pursue the smaller sales. The volume they sell is too large for smaller sales to be profitable. You may someday feel the same way, but you are nowhere near that point now. You may find that you just don't want to be bothered responding to the customer who is sending you e-mail after e-mail to get more information about the item that's currently bidding at $4.99. Do it anyway! If you don't do it for the money, do it for the sake of building your business. You never know when that bothersome e-mailer will be the one who becomes your most loyal customer. Consider your profit margins, but don't live and die by them. There will be time for adjusting your business to those margins once it's a flourishing business.

Volunteer to Work and Learn

If, after reading this far, you're beginning to have second thoughts, here's a useful alternative. Find a PowerSeller in your area and volunteer to work for her. In return for your help with shipping, listing, or answering e-mails, she'll most likely be willing to teach you about the ins and outs of the life of a PowerSeller. You'll be investing nothing but a few hours of your time per week (she might even be willing to pay you a little). You'll get invaluable firsthand experience and a real taste for what this life is all about.

Finding a local PowerSeller isn't too hard. Here's one way to do it: Go to the basic search screen on eBay. Enter PowerSeller as your keyword. Be sure to check the box to search by both title and description. Leave the search designated to all categories. Now, in the box for Item Location, use the pull-down menu to specify the geographic area closest to you. Complete the search, and you can scroll through your results and find PowerSellers who are near to you.

Know Where to Find Help

Starting an eBay business now that eBay has matured gives you an advantage. You'll have some help available to you that wasn't available to today's PowerSellers when they first began. With that said, know that, even now, you can't expect much help. The culture of eBay is a little like that of a family with a dozen kids. There are rules, there are people watching and policing the overall comings and goings, but when it comes to the details, you're better off figuring them out for yourself. eBay prides itself on providing a level playing field, and it's up to you to see how you're going to play on it. So, don't expect anyone from eBay to hold your hand, and you won't be disappointed or discouraged when no one does.

eBay has help pages that cover the rudimentary details of using the site. You'll find help at http://pages.ebay.com/help/index .html, shown in Figure 1-11. Since you are not a newcomer to eBay, you probably won't find much here that will help you. Still, the help pages are a place to start. You can also access Live Help, from prominent eBay screens (e.g., the Home page). You'll see a little Live Help button near the top of these screens. Clicking this button will take you to a live chat with someone who can offer you help in real time. "Whenever I'm stumped on

FIGURE 1-11 eBay's Help screen is a familiar stop when looking for quick answers.

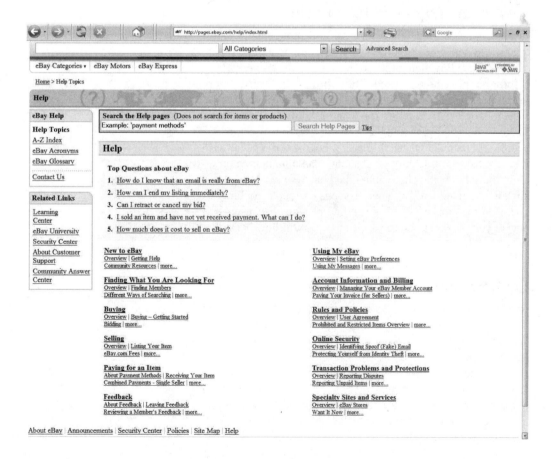

eBay, I just hit that Live Help button," says Baronart. "I always get good results from them." eBay's live help feature is definitely underused. Estimates suggest that most eBay users never press that button. Still, sometimes when you do press it, you receive a message stating that due to volume, you must expect a waiting time before anyone can address your question. Most sellers are too busy to spend much time on eBay's equivalent of "hold." When you achieve Gold PowerSeller status, you will have your own account manager, and then you'll have better access to help. By then, the things you'll need help with will be much more complicated than the things that stump you now; so take heart, you will ultimately have some help. In the meantime, search for help in other places. Fortunately there's plenty to be found.

Most eBay Help Is Seller to Seller

Just like in that family with a dozen kids, if Mom and Dad are too busy to help you, you'll be better off going to a big brother or sister. The eBay community is famous for the friendly, helpful people who occupy it. Start with the Answer Center (http://pages.ebay.com/community/answercenter/index.html). Just click on the appropriate topic and ask lots of questions. There is really no such thing as a stupid question, and the people who populate these discussion boards do so because they like to help. It is only reasonable to assume that among all of the sellers who check in on the board, someone has already struggled with whatever issue is currently troubling you. Don't assume everything is brand new just because it's new to you. Ask, ask, ask, and the answers will flow back to you.

» Get help from auction doctors

Need expert help from seasoned eBayers? Sure you will, at first. Through eBay's Auction Doctors Group, you can find eBay veterans who will review your listings and suggest specific detailed improvements.

Don't be shy. Consider that the Group's charter is to "supply a consolidated forum where users can have their listings personally reviewed by seasoned veterans." Follow the advice here, become a successful PowerSeller, and then become an Auction Doctor yourself!

Don't Forget to Help Others Too

As a community, eBay couldn't function if its members didn't help each other. In the beginning you'll be receiving a lot of help, support, and advice from sellers who have gone before you. When you get yourself established and start feeling like a pro, don't forget to pass it on. You don't even necessarily have to wait until you're an eBay veteran or a PowerSeller.

Go directly to the discussion boards for your area of interest and start sharing your thoughts and ideas with others, even if you don't have a lot to say yet about eBay and its workings. Everyone has something to contribute, and you'll be a better community member if you remember to give back in kind what you have received. Don't allow yourself to feel too busy for this; after all, the people who helped you weren't too busy, were they?

» Search for help outside of eBay

Consider your product area and look for help there. Dan's Train Depot found that the hobbyists he knew offline were more than happy to help him in any way they could. Many of them knew something about eBay, and all of them knew plenty about his product area. Now that eBay is so much more mature, it's almost more likely that you will have trouble meeting people who don't know anything about eBay than you will meeting people who do know something. Don't hesitate to ask around in your particular field of interest for advice and help in getting started.

Work with a Friend

You don't have to do this alone. You may have a friend who is much more comfortable with computers than you are. Don't hesitate to ask for help getting started. You may even have a friend who is also interested in starting an eBay business. You can always work together and share your learning and success. That way, you double your experience level right from the beginning.

Meet a PowerSeller

Dan Glasure

Dan Glasure is the Dan in Dan's Train Depot. You will find him on eBay under the username danstraindepot. He's been selling on eBay since 1999, and today he has more than 20,000 feedbacks, with a positive feedback rating of 100 percent. Not only does Dan have his eBay auctions and an eBay store, but his eBay business has also led him to open his own Web site, www.brasstrains.com, and he is now authoring a book and price guide for brass model trains. But that's getting ahead of the story.

Dan started on eBay by selling comic books. He'd been a collector for years. Later he turned to another of his hobbies, model trains. This is one of the cases when good fortune, good timing, and hard work all come together. Dan soon came upon a single huge collection of H.O. model trains for sale. With the financial help of his father, he bought the whole thing, and he and his dad got busy selling it on eBay. They soon sold the entire collection, and Dan began advertising locally to purchase more inventory. Before long he was purchasing large collections from all over the country. Today he says that locating inventory is never a problem for him.

Dan's operation can be challenging because each item must be individually photographed and described. This makes listing his items very time consuming; in order to manage his volume, he has hired good employees. At one time, he had as many as 13, but he

found his business could be more profitable by scaling back a bit. He currently has 5 employees. One of his staff members does nothing but photography for his listings. That explains why he currently has hundreds of auctions running. Dan recommends hiring staff as soon as you need them. "You can't do this all by yourself," he says, noting that a lot of new business owners hesitate to add the expense of staff. Dan reports that his staff makes his business far more productive and successful than he could make it alone.

It is important to think the costs through and be careful about getting too big too fast. Currently, Dan is one of the largest sellers of model trains in the world—in particular, rare brass model trains. Dan's upcoming book and Web site, www.brassguide.com look to bring this rare art form to a much broader audience. But eBay is still a powerful marketing tool and a great moneymaker for his business.

Know Your Business/Grow Your Business Checklist

✓ I have reviewed and I clearly understand eBay's rules.

✓ eBay's Site Map is now one of my standard tools.

✓ AuctionBytes newsletters now arrive automatically, and I am well aware of the other benefits of using the AuctionBytes Web site.

✓ I'm learning a lot through eBay's Learning Center.

✓ I've found a few favorite new Discussion Boards and Groups.

✓ Completed auctions have become a key tool for my market research.

✓ I'm thinking about products I'm familiar with and which of those I might want to sell.

✓ Now I'm thinking about other products my customers might like.

✓ My eBay business is a real business, and I'm treating it that way.

Chapter 2

Source Products
for Success

We hope you're feeling sparked and energetic after reading Chapter 1. By considering all of the issues we discussed in that chapter, you've had the chance to reassess your commitment as a potential PowerSeller. It's wonderful that you've decided to keep going and join us here in Chapter 2, where we will address one of the greatest challenges PowerSellers face: where do you find all of the items you need to sell to achieve and maintain PowerSeller status? Of course, a few PowerSellers create products for resale, but the great majority—by some accounts 85 percent—buy products that they then resell.

So the question of where you can find products is an important one. Fortunately, you'll find many excellent answers throughout this chapter. How you'll acquire your inventory will vary greatly depending on what you decide to sell. If you're following our advice from the last chapter and starting with something you know about, you already have some ideas about where you can acquire products. That's yet another reason it's wise to start selling things you know about. But, gathering items for your own enjoyment and buying things in the quantities you'll need to stock your eBay business are not the same. You'll have to work to come up with lots of new ideas about where you can get and maintain a steady stream of merchandise.

That little four-letter word, "work," is just what we mean. Many PowerSellers will tell you that they spend the bulk of their time finding, developing, maintaining, and servicing their supply lines. This work is not the kind of task you can do once and consider it finished. It's more like housework, always there, always needing your attention, no matter how much you seem to do. The tips you'll gain from this chapter will help you get started. Then as you work and learn, your eBay business will grow. The good news—and this is encouraging—is that as you do this work, you'll hone your skills and your instincts will sharpen. Everything you learn will make you smarter, more effective, and more able to see the possibilities of new sources of product everywhere you look.

As your trusted tour guides, we wish we could tell you that by the end of this chapter, we will have given you the keys to the vault. You'll have zeroed in on all of the best sources of product, and you'll be well on your way to PowerSeller status. Well, it pains us to admit that this is just not going to happen.

Don't despair. What we will give you is still going to empower you and get you on your way. First we'll help you clearly define your challenges, and that will help you plot your course. Then we'll stock your toolbox for the job ahead. We've spent countless hours researching sources of products and information to get you started. You'll still spend hours researching, but you'll be starting from the next level, not from the bottom rung of the ladder. Finally, we'll help you learn how to distinguish what sources of products and information are valuable and what sources are not so valuable. At the end of this chapter, you will be initiated into the world of sourcing products for your eBay business, and that's a big step on your road to PowerSeller.

First Things First

Before we start down that road, let's set the course. The challenge you face in acquiring your inventory is really twofold. First you have to figure out what is marketable and selling well on eBay. Second, you have to figure out where to acquire these marketable goods in quantity and at a price that allows you to earn a profit when you sell them. Fortunately, we've gathered some excellent tools you can use for these tasks. But, first, you need to equip yourself with one thing that all PowerSellers must have, a tax identification (ID) number.

» Get a tax ID number, now

If your state has a sales tax, and most of them do, you will have to acquire a sales tax ID number before you can legitimately sell your products, even online. This process can take several weeks to complete, so go ahead and get it started now. By the time you're actually ready to be selling, you'll be registered and legitimately in business according to the laws of your state (don't forget to check the laws of your town as well). You will need this ID number for reporting the sales tax you collect from the people who buy from you. For now, don't worry about that; we'll address it in much more detail in Chapter 10.

A tax ID number is often also called a *resale certificate*. Both of these terms prove that you are a legitimate business and registered with your state. Many wholesalers and manufacturers will not sell products to you if you don't have this documentation of your legitimacy. So, don't delay. It's the first thing to do as you go about acquiring your inventory.

Get a tax ID number, now

Getting signed up is not so daunting a task as you might think. You can start by going to Google and entering a search for "Tax ID Number (your state)." You'll at least get some information about the tax ID program, and you may even gain access to forms you can complete online to get the process started.

As an alternative, you can go to http://www.mtc.gov/ Resources.aspx?id=272&ItemId=272, shown in Figure 2-1. From this site, you'll find links to most of the states and the District of Columbia. The link for our state actually allowed us to access the necessary forms and get the process started.

FIGURE 2-1 The Multistate Tax Commission's home page makes it easy to get information about obtaining a tax ID number.

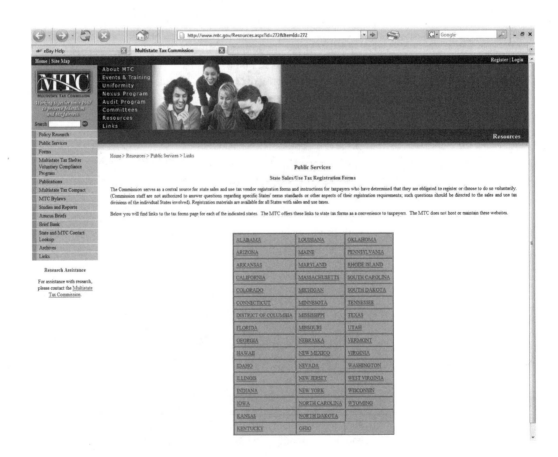

What Are You Thinking of Selling?

Now's the time for you to consider your own ideas and evaluate what you are thinking of selling. If your plan is to sell new products, your road to inventory acquisition will take you in a different direction from the path you'll take if you're planning to sell used items. Either way, you'll have your work cut out for you, but you'll definitely be approaching the tasks from very different angles.

Selling new products means that you need to identify reliable sources of products. Reliable means that the products are of a consistent quality and that the sources you find are consistently able to provide them to you. You will also need to work to maintain a steady supply of products as the needs of your customers and the market for your items shift. You will be working to identify a group of specific sources, and then you'll work to keep them steady, while you continually keep your eyes peeled for more and even better sources of products.

Selling used products means that you will actually spend a great deal of your time going out to acquire products. Unlike when you research new products, which you can accomplish more readily at home, you'll have to physically visit the places where used items are sold. PowerSellers who sell used items claim that most of their weekly efforts are spent shopping for items to sell. Now, there are exceptions to this rule, which we will explore in a bit. But, being realistic, if you are going to sell used items, you should really love the thrill of the hunt and the joy of the chase.

» Think of your products as a total product line

As long as you're building an inventory anyway, consider the totality of your products and think of yourself as providing a product line to your customers. Instead of offering a variety of entirely different types of things you happen to come across, consider building a unity into your product line. Present your prospective customers with a body of products that go together. "The only way to differentiate yourself from other sellers is to give your customers a lifestyle," says a PowerSeller with a feedback number of nearly 14,000. "Combine your products. People want to belong to a group or club." She sells skin care products, but she also sells candles, incense, wind chimes, and decorative items to beautify a customer's space. All of these things can make a person feel pampered, and they are all likely to appeal to the person who would shop for any single one of them.

Not only does this strategy create a cohesive product line for you and your customers, it simplifies your shopping for inventory. You will find many different products you might want to try, but sticking with a genre of products helps you focus your efforts. It keeps you from getting scattered by the temptations you'll come upon. Now, that's not to say you shouldn't keep your eyes open to a great source of new products for your line. That should always be your mindset; but stay focused, and don't chase after every new thing you see just because you've found a place to source it.

On average, only about 10 percent of an eBay seller's business will come from a previous customer (because eBay is constantly driving new traffic to your listings). But savvy PowerSellers can triple that number with not only outstanding service (see Chapter 9), but with a coherent product line that keeps the same customers wanting to come back time and time again.

» Consider the needs of your products and your customers

When you're deciding what you'll sell, don't forget to consider the necessary items that go along with your products. If you decide to sell aromatherapy machines, you'll also want to sell the aromatherapy beads that go with them. If you sell cameras, also stock the batteries for the cameras. The same is true for any item that requires filters, bags, or any other consumable part.

Make yourself the place your customers come to for their initial purchases and their repeat purchases. You may even find companies willing to help you create these product bundles. When we spoke to manufacturers at a recent merchandise trade show in Las Vegas, more than one said they will customize kits for eBay sellers. CPD, which sells wireless accessories, regularly puts together kits for its eBay sellers. "We try to give them more so they can give more," a company representative told us. In fact, many sellers of high-demand commodity items such as cameras report that they make no profit at all selling the cameras themselves, and that *all* of the profit comes from the accessories!

Consider selling something that other eBay sellers may use. This goes beyond the usual packing supplies or shipping labels. As you build your business, see what items you find handy and then consider stocking them. Have you found a reliable scale for weighing your boxes? Do you have a favorite light for photographing your products? How about office products that you find especially useful? Anything you can identify that other eBay sellers might need and want gives you an automatic customer base to address. Remember, back in the mid-19th-century California gold rush, it was often the people who sold supplies to the prospectors who ultimately struck "gold."

» Calculate your budget

Before you start actually buying inventory items, calculate your total budget for your initial costs. Finding products to sell can be very exciting, and you can easily spend more than you should, because you're trying to buy a lot of items at one time. Knowing clearly what your budget is also allows you to allocate portions of it for specific product types. This enables you to spread your money across a variety of inventory items so that you can check on the return of your investment as you see what prices you get for different types of things.

» Always shop with a calculator

In time, you will be able to eyeball an item and know quickly if it will bring you enough money to make it worth your while. But, that time isn't now. When you consider how much you can spend on an item, a vital part of that equation is determining what you'll have to earn from it to make the process worth your while. Knowing the cost of the item includes knowing the true costs.

For new items, those costs can include shipping the items to you, and possibly taxes and fees to the seller, which can be hefty, especially if you import goods from overseas. For used items, those costs include your time in locating and transporting the item, how much work is required to get it ready to sell, and any supplies you might need to do that task. Calculate it all, and then see how much you'd need to earn from that item to give you a comfortable profit margin. Don't forget to include the value of your time, although you may not be able to recoup its full worth until your business is more established. Is that price realistic on eBay for this item?

Find Out What Sells

Answering the question of pricing is both art and science. The artistic part comes from the instincts you'll bring to the task. If you're dealing with items you already know and understand, you'll feel more confident in making this assessment. The science part comes with good old hard work. That means research, research, research, and more research. We wish we could tell you that once you finish this research, you'll know everything you need to know. Although you will be smarter, you'll still have to keep researching so that you can expand your product offerings and keep up with your inventory as it diverges into ever-new corners of your market. Researching will get easier as you find your favorite research tools and hone your research skills, but it will never be finished.

» Start your research at eBay's Solutions Directory

eBay's Solutions Directory (www.solutions.eBay.com) provides listings for companies that offer eBay-related software and services. The Directory covers many things, including auction management software and shipping, but for the purpose of this discussion, we'll consider the sourcing solutions. You'll find listings of products from eBay itself and also from companies that provide data analysis of eBay sales. Information about these products includes links to each company's Web site and user ratings of the product discussed. When we searched the Solutions Directory for "data analysis" we came up with 17 different offerings that could help you identify potentially lucrative products. See: http://cgi6.ebay.com/ws/eBayISAPI.dll?SolutionsDirectory&page=results&subgroup=15.

» Check eBay's "Hot Items by Category"

eBay tracks the hottest selling items and publishes them monthly, in an easy-to-find location on the site. From any eBay screen, click the Site Map link along the top. You'll see the middle column of that map is devoted to sellers. Scroll down until you get to the What's Hot link under Selling Resources. Click that, and you'll come to the What's Hot page, shown in Figure 2-2. These five choices, Merchandising Calendar, Hot Items by Category, eBay Pulse, eBay Pop, and eBay Marketplace Research can provide some useful information as you begin your search for what's selling on eBay. We'll start with the Hot Items by Category list.

The Hot Items list is a PDF file that you'll read using Adobe Acrobat. (We're assuming, of course, that you have this free program already. If not, you can download it at http://www.adobe.com/products/acrobat/readstep2.html). Unless you have the full version of the program (quite expensive) you can't manipulate the information that appears, but you can study it and take notes.

FIGURE 2-2 eBay's own What's Hot page provides valuable links for researching hot product areas.

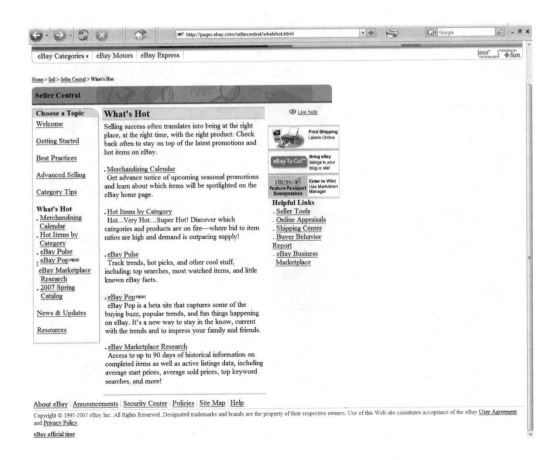

Check eBay's "Hot Items by Category"

Within each product category listings are analyzed for both recent bidding activity and new listing activity. Hot products are ones that show bidding growth that has significantly outpaced new listing growth. Also, these products have a higher bid-to-item ratio than other products in the same category. You can easily see that the traffic for these items has been good. Items are designated as Hot, Very Hot, and Super Hot depending on bidding activity. You can pinpoint very specific products by drilling down a given category (e.g., antiques) to Level 2 items (e.g., Decorative Arts), then Level 3 (say Picture frames), and finally Level 4 (metal).

Let's take a look at the Home & Garden category as an example.

For the month of May 2007, a Super Hot item in the Home & Garden category was Pools & Spas, as you can see in Figure 2-3. A Level 3 hot item would be anything in the general category of

FIGURE 2-3 Using eBay's Hot Items by Category list allowed us to zero in on the most popular items in eBay's Home & Garden category.

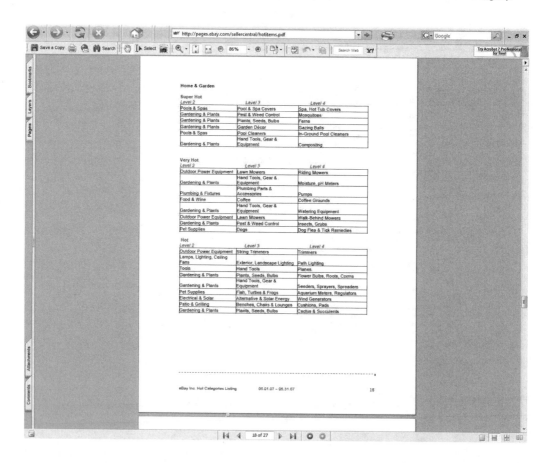

Pool & Spa Covers. Moving over to Level 4, you see that Spa, Hot Tub Covers were hotter than the average listing for the general category. If you were selling those items in May, you probably would have done well.

The Hot Categories Report for May was 27 pages long as of the middle of the month. You can see that there's a lot of available information. You can toggle between the list and eBay searches to see how much money the hottest items were bringing and what kind of bidding action they were generating. Here's how: Let's stick with the level 4 category, Spa, Hot Tub Covers category. With the Hot Items List minimized, open a search page on eBay and do a Completed-Items search for Spa, Hot Tub Covers. Now you can see what prices these items brought in the last two weeks. When we checked, the highest-priced item was sold at $339.95.

When evaluating the sale of an item, always consider the starting price, the ending price, and the number of bids the listing attracted. Combined, they provide the total history of the listing and give you good insight into just how well the product did. "Another critical factor," says Platinum PowerSeller David Yaskulka, "is Conversion Rate, which along with Starting Price, will ultimately be the prime determiners of your overall eBay fees ('take rate')."

» Keep the Hot Items list in perspective

There is no doubt you can gain a huge amount of information from the Hot Items list. It's free, it's easy to use, and you'll get a good overview of everything that sells on eBay by using it. It's a very worthy tool to begin with. But, remember, it's just a beginning. Once you gather the information you can get from the Hot Items list, continue on with your research, so that you can put the information you gathered there into perspective.

First, remember that the information you got is likely to be close to a month old, maybe even older. That doesn't mean it's not valid, it just means it's not the very latest snapshot of what's going on. (Seasonality may also be a factor. Obviously, the demand for mittens will surge during the winter months.) That's fine, as long as you realize that it is almost guaranteed that there will be some variation in the numbers since the information was captured. Don't get caught buying heart-pattern boxer shorts in March because you see they were "hot" in February!

Keep the Hot Items list in perspective

It is sometimes better to do a regular search and also have the current items screen up, allowing you to toggle back and forth between the two screens.

Next, remember that if you have such easy access to the Hot Items list, so do the 200+ million other people who use eBay. If every seller on eBay used the Hot Items list alone to make decisions about what to sell, there would never be a single item on the Hot Items list twice. If researching what products are likely to sell well on eBay were really this easy, everyone would be a PowerSeller. Now that you know how to identify what has sold well on eBay, move on to finding products that you believe will sell well in the future.

Use eBay's Merchandising Calendar

Another choice from the What's Hot screen featured in Figure 2-2 is eBay's Merchandising Calendar. This shows you what eBay will be promoting on its Home page for a three-month period. Let's consider a calendar for the month of March. As you might expect, that calendar would feature items for spring as well as the annual "March Madness" college basketball tournament. There may also be something you may not have anticipated though, such as a promotion for National Crafts Month, which happens to be March. That's a promotion that you may be able to take advantage of since it's more obscure.

Review eBay Pulse

Click this link to get a quick fix on the most popular searches people are conducting on eBay. The default shows you the most popular products across all of eBay. However, by using the drop-down menu (see Figure 2-4) you can select a particular category (e.g., Books) and see the most popular searches within that category (Harry Potter). eBay Pulse also lists the eBay stores with the largest inventories. From a trend-watchers' perspective though the best area may be "Most Watched Items," which will show you which auctions the most people are tracking through their My eBay pages.

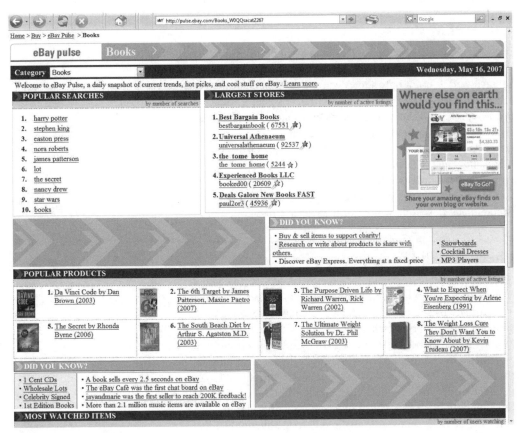

FIGURE 2-4 eBay Pulse allows you to find the most popular specific searches buyers are using to find products in a given category.

Nonprofits in the Spotlight

eBay's nonprofit partner MissionFish and thousands of nonprofit organizations get promoted on eBay through the eBay Giving Works program, which we'll describe fully in Chapter 6. eBay puts its charity promotions on a calendar called "Spotlight on a Cause." Predictably, the Spotlight is on health and fitness in time for the New Year's resolutions in January and February, on the environment for Earth Day in April, on education for back to school in August and September. Not only can you choose a nonprofit to support based on this calendar, but you can also merchandise into it. Fitness equipment with 10 percent donated to the American Heart Association will get great exposure in January/February. Have a chance to source some pink items? Consider listing them with a donation to the Susan G. Komen Foundation during the Spotlight on Breast Cancer Awareness in October.

Check eBay Pop

If you're a numbers person (and as an aspiring PowerSeller you'd better be!) see eBay Pop, a newer service in "beta" when we reviewed it. It not only shows you the most popular items on eBay, but it gives you specifics like numbers actually sold, average price, and even more important what the trend for that item has been over the last two weeks (such as up 5 percent, or down 10 percent). Other areas include timely articles about merchandising ("Prepping for St. Patty's Day) and pop culture–related news headlines.

The final category in the What's Hot area is eBay Marketplace Research, which we'll cover in Chapter 6.

» Check out BidThumbs.com

Here's a Web site (see Figure 2-5) that will literally give you a thumbnail look at what is currently selling on eBay.

This site lists items with reserves that have been met, or which have no reserves, scheduled to end within a day. You'll find items in a broad range of categories from collectibles to electronics to clothing and cars. Simply roll your mouse over the thumbnail for a quick look at the item, its current high bid, the number of bids it has received, and the amount of time remaining in the listing. If you find something intriguing, simply click on it, and you'll go directly to the auction listing for complete details.

This is a great way to judge exactly what's selling right now on eBay. The site creators only include information in these particular formats, because they believe this is the only true way to judge what is actually selling. Every item listed on this site will result in a successful sale. So, the guesswork is gone from the analysis. The site is updated frequently throughout the day. Because all listings will close within 24 hours, when you check back tomorrow, you'll find all new listings to explore. Checking this site routinely will allow you to have a clear idea of products you might want to look at, and it will help you spot trends over the course of days and weeks. Plus, it's free!

» Explore the world of blogs

Blogs, or Web logs, are informal Internet newsletters that take the form of dispatches from the front. Blogs have taken the

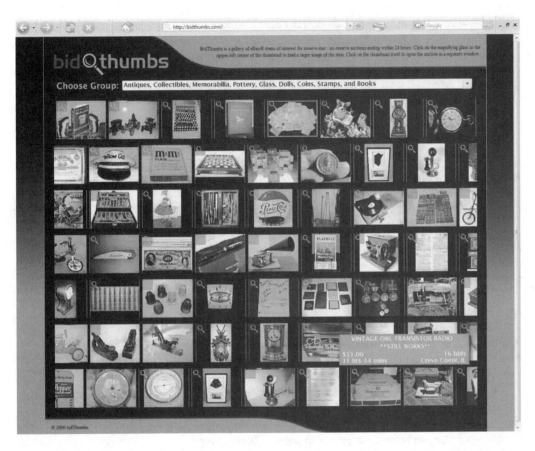

FIGURE 2-5 Use the BidThumbs.com Web site to see pictures of items for sale in the group you specify.

world of publishing out of the hands of the big guys and put it directly within the reach of all of us. Anyone can have a blog, and for that reason, blogs vary greatly in quality and content. But, one thing is for certain, reading blogs can help you discover what other people are thinking about, hoping for, and dreaming of. They can be a great way to spot emerging trends, and therefore product ideas that others aren't tapping into yet.

You can search for blogs through Google just by clicking on the "more" button from the main Google page. Select the "blog search" option. Now, your search results will only include blogs. You can also use a blog directory to find relevant blogs. A good example of this type of directory is blogcatalog at http://www. blogcatalog.com/. Finally, you can go to http://www. weblogawards.org to view a list of award-winning blogs. Each

December a vote is held to determine the best blogs in more than 45 categories. In December 2006, more than 525,000 votes were cast! Starting with these blogs makes it a little easier to get your feet wet in the world of blogs, which is so broad, that getting lost and losing hours of valuable time are both easy and likely. Still, if you want to get a glimpse of up-to-the-minute insight into what concerns people who are your potential customers, blogs are a fascinating place to start.

» What's hot from Andale

Andale provides tools and services for eBay users. You'll learn more about the counters Andale offers for your auction listings in subsequent chapters, but in addition to those, you'll also find some wonderful tools for evaluating potential inventory items directly on Andale's Web site. Go to www.andale.com for a tour of everything the company offers. One service, Andale Research, provides data on the price and sell-through rate of specific items.

Andale's information is recent, specific, and reliable. Using it to help you define your product line is an excellent choice. You can have a one-month free trial period for this tool. After that, the price for using it is $7.95 per month.

Andale's What's Hot tool provides detailed information about eBay's categories and the hottest items in those categories. You can use it to search for items you are thinking of selling, or you can browse categories to see which are doing well and what items within those categories are selling. Figure 2-6 shows you just a sample of the information you'll find. The numbers to the right of each category show you the number of hot auctions for each category. Now you can see which categories are generating the most traffic. You can study each category to find individual items that are selling well. You can also use a Smart Clustering tool that finds the hottest product groups.

Reports available to you through Andale's What's Hot tool rate how much demand there is for specific categories and items within those categories. You can also check individual products for average sale prices, auction successes, average hits, and the number of bids each auction attracted. All of this information can be exported to Excel for your own deeper analysis. The What's Hot tool costs $3.95 per month to use, but that price brings you unlimited use of the service.

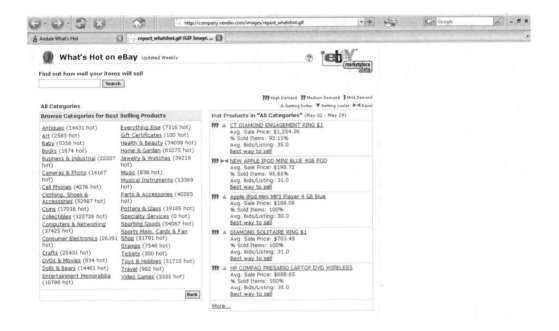

FIGURE 2-6 Andale's What's Hot tool allows you to see sales activity across eBay's categories and to evaluate sales within the categories too.

» Check yourself against shopping aggregators

Since we wrote the first edition of this book "shopping aggregators" have become available all over the Internet. These sites, like Shopping.com and Google Product Search (http://google.com/prdhp?tab=wf) let you compare the cost of any one of millions of items across many retailers. Some even include product reviews as well as reviews of retailers. As an online merchant, you need to become very familiar with these aggregators because your customers may already be using them to assess your prices. So when making decisions about what inventory to buy, and how to price your items, cross-check your math against an aggregator to make sure you can expect a reasonable return on your investment.

You may want to pay special attention to Shopping.com, which is owned by eBay. We don't know yet what plans (if any) eBay has for further integrating eBay listings into Shopping .com, but it's certainly the first place you should look.

This is not to say you should try to compete on price alone. We discuss pricing strategies at length in Chapter 5.

Where Will You Get Your Inventory?

Now you've gathered some tools for determining what's selling well on eBay and evaluating what you may want to add to your inventory. Next challenge: where are you going to find those products at prices that will allow you to make a profit? We'll provide some ideas to get you started, and then you'll need to do your own research. At first, you'll find many different sources for your products, and then you'll begin to see which ones are the best. Where you'll find your inventory depends largely on whether you sell used merchandise or new merchandise. The channels and methods for acquiring merchandise in each of these categories vary greatly, but you can use some basic strategies for learning about sources for both. Don't forget to keep your antennae up and your eyes open. You never know where a new source will appear, and you want to be ready to jump on it when it does.

» Think locally, sell globally

No matter where you live, there are things that are native to your location that other people in other places may never have heard about. If something is very popular close to home, consider it for sale to a global market. In our little part of the world, there is a wonderful, local producer of jellies and preserves. You'll find them at every tourist stop and attraction within 30 miles of our home. These might also prove to be favorites to people who don't live close enough to pick them up locally. Maybe your part of the world has a particular craft item, jewelry style, pottery line, or glass manufacturer. Start looking around for the things you may just take for granted and consider what appeal they may have to a wider audience.

You may also tap into local wholesalers, manufacturers, and liquidators. You'll save money on delivery of their products to you for resale. You'll also gain access to items that may not be readily available to others outside your geographic area. This not only provides you with sources of unique products, but it also lessens your competition once you get your product to market on eBay.

» Turn to your local reference librarian

If you need a jump-start on your research, don't overlook your reference librarian. Librarians are trained researchers, and most

are more than happy to help you research a topic they may
not often get called upon to explore. Stop by the library at an
off-hour when your librarian may not be too busy with other
patrons. Introduce yourself, and get to know each other. Tell the
librarian that you are researching market trends and products.
Ask for help in locating wholesalers and manufacturers and in
defining good search terms for Web searches. Don't forget to
ask about local associations and organizations of businesses,
auctioneers, and estate planners.

» Do it yourself on the Internet

"I spend hundreds of hours online searching for new sources,"
says a PowerSeller who sells only new products. Just as this
PowerSeller devotes time every week to the search, you will too.
We'll get you started with some sites to explore, but in the end
you'll spend a lot of time tracking down sources for yourself. Be
persistent, and don't allow yourself to get discouraged. Most of
the PowerSellers who are now successful on eBay had to do this
same thing for themselves. Your distribution channels won't
appear overnight, and the task is never really ended. You'll
continue to refine your sources and explore new opportunities
just as long as you operate your business. In addition to the
person-to-person opportunities for help we've already
mentioned, many libraries offer online reference services via
their Web sites, including databases that would otherwise cost
money to access. Some larger libraries even offer live reference
help 24 hours a day, 7 days a week.

» Don't expect to find help on eBay

Remember those friendly discussion boards we told you about
in Chapter 1? Well, the sellers you find on those boards will
be more than happy to lend you a shoulder to cry on and a
sympathetic ear, but they will not give up their sources of
products. Sellers guard their sources very carefully, and you can
easily understand why. The hard work ahead of you was once
ahead of them, too. They remember your pain, but they're not
going to sacrifice their good, reliable sources of products to ease
it. Will you when you've got your sources in place?

That doesn't mean they won't answer questions about specific
sources if you ask them. There are often lively discussions of

Don't expect to find help on eBay

sources that have fallen out of favor with sellers, and these discussions include valuable insights about why certain sources aren't what they once may have been. Just remember that asking other sellers overtly about a specific product source puts you at the risk of revealing a potential jewel you may have found for yourself. So, don't be too up front in your requests for information. It's better to hang back and read the discussions for educational purposes. The things you learn from them can help you in evaluating your own research. Aside from the boards, be sure to see if eBay has hosted any sourcing workshops that would help.

There are other discussion areas you can visit outside of eBay for this type of research, too. For example, AuctionBytes.com has forums where sourcing is discussed. These are good places to visit to help you identify sources. However, you should also look at these public forums as a way to avoid problematic sources.

"While I've seen professional sellers help new and aspiring PowerSellers time and time again," says David Yaskulka, "in so many ways, asking them about their sources is generally considered 'crossing the line.' Once you cross it, you likely won't get good advice from that seller again."

Sourcing Used Items and Collectibles

If you've decided to sell used items, you'll have to get very specific. You don't want to start acquiring under the general category of "used," because you'll likely end up with no product consistency. You'll be too easily swept up into buying quantities of stuff that you simply can't sell on eBay. So how are you defining "used" for your eBay business? Will you sell high-quality children's dress clothes? Do you mean refurbished electronics? Are you thinking about kitchenware and gadgets? What about secondhand sports equipment? What you decide to sell will determine the places you should start looking for your inventory. As we've said before, be prepared to spend many hours shopping if you're going to sell used items. That means lots of driving, lots of hauling, and many early mornings getting the scoop on the best markets.

Garage and Yard Sales

In the early days, eBay was much like an electronic garage sale. This really isn't true anymore. As the site has matured, and the whole electronic commerce phenomenon, too, you are just as likely to find luxury items for sale on eBay as you are to find secondhand goods. It's impossible for you to stock your eBay business solely from garage sales and yard sales. You'll need to make these only a small portion of your shopping efforts. You can supplement your inventory this way, but you really mustn't count on this a source for building your inventory. For one thing, in most parts of the country, yard sales and garage sales are seasonal. You can't depend on any product source that disappears for months at a time.

When you do go for the garage sale/yard sale method of inventory acquisitions, be prepared to start early. If you're not out driving by 7:30 on Saturday morning, you're late. Now, let's be a little crass. Start with the most affluent neighborhoods you can find. You're more likely to find items of higher value there. Move on to the less expensive neighborhoods when you're done with their wealthier counterparts. But before you do, go to the older neighborhoods, because there you're more likely to find older residents who have had years to gather and collect stuff they now consider junk. You're more likely to find a valuable collectible among the belongings of people who have been keeping house for forty years than those who have been at it for four.

Before you set out, read the ads, so you can plot your course. Often these ads list individual items or groups of items up for sale, and you'll be able to map your route to fit what looks promising. You don't want to lose valuable shopping time by wandering around aimlessly. If the ad lists lots of baby items and toys, you'll know you're dealing with a relatively young family that probably hasn't had the time or resources to gather enough valuable stuff to be able to sell it off at a garage sale. You can skip them altogether, unless, of course, you've decided to sell used baby items.

Moving Sales

Moving sales are more promising than garage and yard sales. First, people move throughout the year, so you don't lose whole seasons of shopping because of weather. Also, when people move, they're in a frame of mind that tells them to dump what they own rather than to move it. Moving is often the impetus to get rid of things they'd otherwise keep. So, not only are you likely to have a greater range of items to buy, but you're also likely to get a better price. When the option is dump it or pack it, people are often willing to dump it for less than they might otherwise expect to get for it.

Estate Sales

Estate sales can be even better than moving sales. Estate sales generally happen because a family is faced with divesting itself of the contents of an older relative's home. We know it seems a little ghoulish, but this presents you with the opportunity to buy a broad range of things that have probably been around for a good long while. Keep in mind that the cream of these things will most likely already be gone to family members as keepsakes and family heirlooms, but most estate sales still include lots of good, valuable items. Also remember that in some areas estate sales offer 20 to 50 percent discounts on the last day of the sale. So it sometimes pays to go back and see what's left over.

Professionals often run estate sales on behalf of the family. If a professional is involved, you'll pay slightly more for collectibles, because this person will likely recognize the value of the item almost to the extent you will. In fact, the professional will likely already be handling the eBay sales for the family.

Church Rummage Sales and Local Charity Fund-Raisers

Rummage sales and the like are not constant enough for you to count on them to stock your business, but they are often great sources of things to use as supplements to your product line. Know the seasons for them in your area, and try not to miss them. Again, it's good to target the more affluent church communities if you can, but overall, you are often likely to find good items available at any church rummage sale. These events are usually planned within the church community well in advance so that the congregation members can plan for them and be prepared. Members are likely to save some of their nicer things to donate, because they are using these items to support a community that they truly care about. While you're acquiring your goods, you can also be doing good by supporting a charitable cause.

Local charity fund-raisers can include yard sale–like events or even much bigger events that resemble flea markets more than yard sales. Our local library has a wonderful book sale every year as part of our small town's Heritage Festival. We never miss this sale, and we get there early. All year long, the library accepts donations of books from its patrons. Dozens of volunteers sort, organize, and stack these books for the sale. On the first morning of the weekend-long event, we are always astonished at the wonderful books there are to buy. They range from hardcover bestsellers that were popular throughout the previous year to wonderful old collectible books that must have been Christmas presents in decades gone by. Nothing at the sale costs more than $1.00, and many of the books are in excellent condition. The library benefits from the proceeds, and we can scoop up some great items to be resold on eBay.

Auctions

Auctions are divided into two categories, private and government. These can each be divided again into online auctions and auctions that take place at physical locations. Auctions can be good sources of products. Some PowerSellers acquire almost all of their merchandise this way.

Private Auctions

Private auctions are generally operated by auction professionals. They may occur at the site of the property, much like an estate sale, or they can happen at the auctioneer's establishment. The ones that happen at the auctioneer's site are generally made up of goods gathered from many different estates or other sources. Check your local phone directory, or ask your librarian about local auctioneers or auction houses and get on their mailing lists. That way, you'll have advance notice of upcoming sales and you can prepare for them.

When you go to the auction, have in mind the types of items that you're shopping for. Don't go there with nothing specific in mind, because you're too likely to impulse-buy that way. On the other hand, don't close your mind to an unforeseen bonus item either. Just don't allow yourself to get carried away. The same is true when it comes time to bid. In the live auction setting it's easy to get caught up in the thrill of the bid and pay more than you should for an item.

Don't expect to find help on eBay

We suggest getting a heads-up on the auction during the preview period, held either early on the day the auction actually begins or up to several days prior. This way, you can scope out all of the items up for bid.

Be sure you've registered with the auctioneer so that you'll be eligible to bid, and make sure you know if there are added buying fees for the items you win. Make a clear list of the items you'll pursue, and designate your highest price for each. Then, do your best, but be prepared to let things go if you must.

 You don't always have to be present to win—you can leave bids and sometimes even bid by phone. Some auctions have catalogs, and some do not. Once you develop favorite houses, try to get on the mailing list for advance catalogs and review potential items and research prices before you go.

At auctions, you're likely to find someone who simply wants the item more than you do. You must always bid with your potential resale price in mind, and don't chase an item someone else wants more. If you find this is a problem for you, enlist the help of a friend or partner who can help keep you in line, or pursue other sources of products. You can't stay in business long if you can't control your acquisition costs.

Government Auctions

Government entities ranging from the federal government to your local municipal government hold periodic auctions for all sorts of items, both at physical locations and online. Your local and state police may also have periodic auctions. You'll find different types of items at these auctions than the ones you'll find at public auctions. Radio equipment, office equipment, and electronics are commonly sold. You can often get great deals at these auctions, but you really have to know about the products being sold. Many of them will require some repair or refurbishing. Also, there are often seemingly slight differences in pieces of equipment of this kind that can dramatically alter their resale value.

Items sold through these auctions are not always guaranteed to work, and there are no refunds or returns if you're not satisfied with what you've purchased.

Flea Markets

We bet you already know if your area has good flea markets to explore. Flea markets can be good for secondhand items and collectibles, and some flea markets are targeted to these markets. In that case, you'll find many of the same types of items that you'd find at garage and yard sales, but you won't have as much driving around to do, since they'll all be in one place. At the same time, remember that flea markets are also seasonal in many parts of the country, so you can't depend on even the good ones to be consistent throughout the whole year.

We don't recommend that you pursue flea markets for new items, however. If you're going to sell new items, you want to be buying your inventory from the same people who sell it to the flea market dealers. Why should you pay the flea market person for acquiring it and dragging it to the market for you to buy? Cut out that middle person and keep the profits for yourself.

Thrift Stores

Thrift stores can be spotty places for finding inventory, but since selling used items on eBay means consistent and routine shopping, you're wise to add them to your list. Thrift shops often benefit from the goods that belonged to people who wanted to clear things out of their homes but didn't want to be bothered with a garage or yard sale. On the other hand, you'll also find they are the final resting place of things that were already offered at a garage sale and rejected.

Introduce yourself to the manager of the local thrift store and get to know this person. Once the manager knows you and what you shop for, he or she may just be willing to call you when your type of item arrives. If the manager knows you stop in regularly, you may even find it held aside for you the next time you stop in. Know when the truck arrives with new loads of goods for the thrift shop, and plan to be there soon after the staff has had enough time to sort through the delivery. Knowing the manager will go a long way toward your gaining this type of insider information.

Newspaper Advertising

Place ads in your local newspaper for items you want to buy. Don't overlook the little free supplement newspapers that serve nearly all communities. When you place your ad, be sure to include your e-mail address as well as your phone number. While you're checking on your ad in the paper, peruse the other listings of items in the "Wanted to buy" category. You may spot

Don't expect to find help on eBay

a competitor, or you may get some new ideas of the types of things people are shopping for. You may also get some copywriting ideas. Online communities, such as craigslist, are related to newspapers in that they offer classified ads. We know several PowerSellers who place ads in their local craigslist to acquire some of their eBay merchandise.

Collectors Are a Special Case

Collectors have a special home on eBay, so if you're coming to eBay to deal in collectibles, you'll be in good company. There are thousands of different categories of collectibles for sale on eBay, so as you might guess, you'll have a lot of competition. That shouldn't dissuade you, but just remind you that you'll need to work hard and stay focused to make dealing collectibles your path to power-selling.

The first thing you must decide is if you'll be selling collectibles or antiques. Antiques are legally defined by the U.S. Customs Department as any object that is more than 100 years old. Collectibles, on the other hand, are generally mass-produced items that are less than 100 years old. Collectibles can actually be anything that people like to collect, from 45 RPM records to Star Wars figures to Beanie Babies.

eBay owes its very existence to collectibles. In turn, eBay has changed the collectibles market. It is now so easy to trade in collectibles that collectors who may never have had the opportunity to complete a collection can do that through trading on eBay. Where it used to take a lifetime to gather the more esoteric parts of a collection by traveling locally and seeking out sources of collectibles through publications devoted to the genre, today's collectors can travel the world for their missing pieces and never leave home.

At the same time that eBay has opened up the world to collectors, it has also made the market for collectibles that much more challenging for sellers. Whereas sellers used to operate in a field occupied mostly by people who came to know each other over the years of pursuing their collections, today's eBay sellers serve the world market. That means that they compete on a much larger scale for the same finite body of collectibles. At the same time, eBay has helped popularize collecting, and that has opened a whole new market for reproductions, which adds yet another challenge to the collectibles seller. "When people can pay $50 for a reproduction of a Fire King rolling pin, that depletes the market of my customers who are willing to pay $1,000 for the real thing," noted a collectibles PowerSeller from the Southeast.

Still, as anyone who has ever been bitten by a collector's bug can tell you, once you've got the itch, nothing can stop you. Plenty of PowerSellers deal in collectibles, and they wouldn't have it any other way, because by doing so they can immerse themselves full-time in something they truly love and enjoy. So, if you've got your heart set on power-selling collectibles, don't be discouraged. Just get ready to work.

Since you're already pursuing your collectibles hobby, you have a pretty good feel for where you can get items for sale. In addition to your own sources, you will pursue all of the venues we've already discussed for buying used items, and there are a few more you may not have already thought of. The challenge for you will be to create and maintain a steady enough stream to keep your inventory solid.

» Advertise in ways you may not have tried yet

In addition to advertising in newspapers, local supplements, and your local craigslist, consider advertising in national markets for your products. If your area of collecting has national journals, magazines, or newsletters, you may find you actually get a better return on your advertising money through these publications than you do by limiting yourself to local markets. You will also want to consider Web sites where other collectors gather.

Make yourself a presence on these and post your requests for products. You may be able to glean the doubles and extras from the collections of others. You probably won't find real bargains here, since you are shopping among people who know what they have, but you can still swap and trade items for resale with these educated partners.

» Search on eBay

Don't discount finding collectibles to resell on eBay. Search for your items under common misspellings, because those listings are likely to have been placed by someone who doesn't know much about your area of expertise. If you can scoop up something from a less savvy eBayer, you can make that seller happy, and you gain a bargain for yourself. When we were new eBay sellers ourselves we acquired a collection of "Big Little Books" (small format hardback books created mostly for kids and popular in the early part of the 20th century) through a classified ad. We knew almost nothing about these and as a result (we're not ashamed to admit) made a few mistakes in pricing and in our descriptions. We're sure some sellers scooped up bargains as a result. We want *you* to be like those sellers!

» Be prepared to travel

Every PowerSeller we spoke with who deals in collectibles travels—a lot. Know where and when your regional collectible shows are and be ready to go and build your inventory. You will most likely have to travel beyond your regional boundaries too, especially if your collectible area has big annual gatherings. Plan for these and adjust your budget so that you'll be prepared to spend money on inventory, knowing that as a collectibles dealer, you don't have the luxury of consistent shopping spread evenly throughout the year.

» Get to know your customers and what they buy

You can sharpen your collectibles sales by getting to know your customers. Then you can shop with them in mind. When you travel and uncover new product offerings, you can buy with the confidence that you know people who will be interested in your purchases. That's a huge benefit, not only because you can have quick turnover of your products that way, but also because it allows you to spend a little more, if you have to, in order to get the product. "I know which patterns of Roseville my customers shop for," said one PowerSeller from New Jersey who sells this art pottery. "I know if I find nice pieces in those patterns that I've got customers who are likely to catch my auctions and bid." Once your customers get to know you and you get to know them, you'll start to recognize pieces that they may need to complete their collections. Now you can tailor your purchases even more.

You'll have to give yourself time to establish this type of presence, but the collectibles world, in spite of the numbers, is still a limited universe, and people can still carve parts of that universe out for themselves with good products and customer service.

Finding a great niche can really pay off for used items. Used kids stuff, used sporting goods, even the "right" used books are tried-and-true niches. Take a narrow niche (ideally the one for which you have passion and expertise) and go deep!

Sourcing New Items for Sale on eBay

If your plan is to sell new products on eBay, your sourcing experiences will be very different from those of the sellers who deal in used products. Instead of spending much of your time driving around and scouring for great items to resell, you'll spend much of your time scouting around for reliable sources of products to resell, but you can do much of this scouting right from your home. The goal in finding products to resell is to get as close to the original source of those products as you possibly can. Every set of hands that pass the product from its creator to you takes a chunk of your profit margin for the effort.

When you're looking for sources, go for quality. Anyone can find and sell junk on eBay, but you won't build repeat business that way. The days of eBay as the world's electronic yard sale have long passed. People come to eBay now for all types of purchases, from pet supplies to computer equipment, from baby strollers to fine jewelry. Your customers may well think of eBay first whenever they need to shop for a particular item, as eBay is the world's most popular online shopping site. Decide early on that you're not going to operate strictly by price. Figure what your profit goals are, and then go for exceptional customer service and great products. Together they will justify the price you need to get to earn your goals.

Avoid buying unchecked returns, damaged goods, and rejected products in lots. You will find so many items that are not fit for resale that what may have first appeared to be a good deal will prove more trouble than value. You don't want to have to sort through piles of junk so that you can glean the few items you can resell. Not only does that make those few items more expensive than you first thought, but it's a big waste of your time and energy.

As you start your research, you'll find lists of wholesalers for sale online, even on eBay, itself. Don't spend your time and money on these. If these sources are so easy to find that you can simply pay for them, don't you think the thousands of other people who want to sell on eBay can buy them too? Every story has a moral, and so does this one. If something really is a great, secret bargain, why is the person offering to tell you about it? If those lists were really what the sellers claimed them to be, they'd keep those secrets for themselves and go on to make money by selling things more valuable than the list they're offering.

At the same time, don't forget to shop on eBay itself for new products to resell. Just as you might be able to scoop up deals on collectibles from less savvy eBay sellers, you might be able to find bargains on new items. You can also sometimes get good deals from sellers who only accept very limited payment options. Also, consider making some purchases from eBay sellers with no feedback or low feedback ratings. These new sellers—and you may be among them at first—often can't get as much for their products as more experienced sellers can, because people hesitate to risk shopping with them. Their auctions often don't generate the bid activity that drives their prices up. Here's an opportunity for you to scoop up something at a good price, and help a new eBayer at the same time. Just be careful. Try smaller purchases at first until you test the seller. Spend some extra time communicating with the seller before you bid so that you're both clear on what the product is and what the terms of the sale are. Be sure you understand this inexperienced seller's shipping and return policies. Then, give it a try.

You should expect to try many different sourcing channels as you build your inventory. The more channels you open to yourself, the more likely you are to develop a good solid stream of inventory. You will eventually zero in on the ones that you like best, but in the beginning, be prepared to test out your different options. We'll help you not only learn where to find sources but also how to protect yourself as you do your exploring.

» Buy at the end of the season

Not to sound too immodest, but we are two of the best shoppers we know. If it wasn't a deal, we simply don't own it. When our kids were small, we did all of their clothes shopping at the end-of-the-season clearance sales. Watching the papers, we hit the

finest department store in our area on the first day of their
clearance. In February, when others were sick of the cold, nasty
weather, we were scooping up snowsuits, sweaters, and corduroy
overalls by the handfuls. In August, when others were thinking
"back-to-school" we were thinking of next summer's trip to the
beach, and we were gathering bathing suits, sun dresses, and
little shorts. We made most of these purchases at 75 to 80
percent off the regular department store prices. At the beginning
of the next season, when other parents were whining about the
high cost of clothes and having to drag around to complete the
season's wardrobe, all we had to do was cut the tags and run the
stored items through the wash. The kids looked great in clothes
we simply could not afford at full price, and we saved a bundle.

This same shopping strategy works not only for children's
clothing, but also for many other items. Just stick with things that
are not too trendy or faddish. One season's hot item can easily be
next season's reject, so shop for classic style and good quality as
well as value. Also remember that you'll have to have a good
place to store the things you buy in August that won't be sold
until April or May. The basement isn't a good choice, because
you don't want your merchandise to smell musty. You also can't
use this strategy if you smoke, because even if you don't realize
it, everything that comes out of your house will smell of smoke.
Watch for pets too. You don't want to invest in new inventory that
is no longer salable because it carries an odor. Ask a friend to be
honest and let you know if your storage area has a smell. You
can't usually detect the smell of your own place, in the same way
an unbiased nose can. If you have to factor in off-site storage for
your end-of-the-season bargains, you'll take a chunk of your
profits out of this sourcing option, and you may want to consider
selling more "forgiving" items instead.

Safety Checks for Testing Sources

Whether you start working with liquidators, wholesalers, or
manufacturers, you'll want to protect yourself from spending
too much money on the wrong items. Don't expect to build your
inventory sources without making mistakes. Every successful
PowerSeller can tell you stories of deals that didn't work out as
they'd hoped. You'll learn a lot from the mistakes you make,
and that's okay. Just be careful not to get sucked into deals with
dishonest, disreputable sources that are more interested in
fleecing you than they are in selling you fleece.

Buy at the end of the season

Make sure the company you're working with actually exists. Get the physical address for the building that houses the company. Don't be satisfied with just a post office box as an address. If the company has nothing but a post office box, don't do business with them. They may be on the level, but they may also be nothing more than an individual who has nothing to sell you and only a box at the post office to collect your payment. Don't risk it, because there are too many other sources that can be documented. Don't waste your time and money this way.

Get a telephone number for the company you're considering buying from and get in touch with a person there. Making contact with a human not only goes toward establishing a relationship with the source, it also allows you to clarify the company's product line, return policies, and shipping practices. You can tell a lot about a company by talking to an employee, especially when that employee is interacting with a potential customer. Evaluate how easy it is to get through to someone, how responsive this person is to your questions, and how enthusiastic this person is about doing business with you. It's information you can't gather without the human touch.

Now get information about how this company operates within its industry. Find out if the company belongs to its trade association. If they don't belong, find out why. Check with the Better Business Bureau to make sure there are no complaints filed against the company. That doesn't necessarily mean that you can count on the company to be reliable, but you will find a red flag if customers have been taken before. Don't stop with the Better Business Bureau. Go on to see what accreditation the company has. Look for backing from such sources as VeriSign, Dun & Bradstreet, Hoover, or other reputable companies that provide credit-checking services. This tells you that the company has met standards of operation that put them in reliable company.

Liquidation Sales

There are liquidation sales and then there are liquidators. Liquidation sales are one-time sales that go along with a business closing its doors, while liquidators are companies that sell off the inventories of other businesses. You will find liquidators both offline and online. When searching for liquidation sales, you can work locally. That makes it possible for you to actually inspect the merchandise personally, and you'll save shipping charges too. Just be sure that the liquidation sales offers are true. There is a great deal of misleading advertising here. When a business closes, it generally starts discounting merchandise at smaller percentages off, and the percentage increases as the last day of business approaches. Timing can be everything here. You want to strike when the percentages have increased so that you'll really get bargains, but you don't want to wait so long that all of the good things have been scooped up before you can buy.

If you learn of a pending store closing, consider approaching the owners with an offer early in their liquidation process. If you offer to buy in bulk, they may be willing to shunt some of their merchandise to you and not include it in the general liquidation sale. Liquidation sales are tightly regulated by state and local business and tax laws, so be sure to know what those are for your area. Your local reference librarian can help you get this information and can also help you locate local liquidation companies.

Liquidation Companies

Don't be discouraged if there are no liquidation companies in your area. You can easily find liquidators online. Buying liquidations online can be a little trickier than shopping locally, since you can't inspect the items you buy, but many PowerSellers use online liquidators for sourcing products. You just have to educate yourself and be careful about what you buy and which companies you shop with. Know in advance that the products you receive might include damaged goods mixed in with the salable items. This will alter the price point you pay for your merchandise. You may also find that what you ordered and what you got are not the same. But, those are some of the pitfalls of working with liquidators whose merchandise often includes items returned to stores by customers who were dissatisfied with them, items that have been damaged, and items that simply didn't strike a chord with their intended market.

When we did a Google search for liquidators, we got nearly 3,000,000 responses. Near the top of the list was Liquidation .com. This means that you're not the only one who will stop by this site in your search for product sources. You're bound to hear about this site quickly, once you start using the discussion boards. Liquidation.com is the online branch of Liquidity Services, Inc., and it's actually another online auction site.

Buy at the end of the season

The merchandise offered for sale here ranges from clothing to electronics, and from building materials to cars. Liquidation.com doesn't actually own any of this. The site is for auctions that bring buyers and sellers together to swap products. So, the format is familiar to eBayers. Each auction listing includes details about payment and shipping and what the "buyer's premium" is. This is a percentage, often 5 to 10 percent of the purchase price, that the buyer must pay in order to complete the transaction.

Sellers often complain that their Liquidation.com purchases come with very high shipping rates. They also have told us that, since Liquidation.com doesn't own the merchandise, there are some quality control issues associated with the products they've received. Stiff shipping charges and spotty quality are a dangerous one-two combination, and we urge you to use caution in buying products here. "I still use Liquidation.com," said a PowerSeller from South Carolina, "but not as much as I used to. I've found other sites I like better."

Another online source of liquidated products is Speedyliquidators.com. This is a Canadian-based firm that specializes in selling off the undersold items from retailers. They accept only new products, never used ones, so you won't find any items here that have been returned or are defective. You also can't easily see what you're buying, because there are no images stored on the company's Web site. You do have easy access to customer service and convenient hours for calling to get more information about purchasing. It's a good alternative to try, and it's proof that there are plenty of other liquidation sites available to you online.

Wholesalers

When you buy wholesale to resell on eBay, you really have to watch your costs carefully. Not only will you pay more for wholesale items than you will for liquidated ones, but you have to add in the same costs whether you buy them wholesale or as liquidations. Those costs include shipping, storage, and sorting through the order to remove damaged goods. Wholesale goods often come in large volumes. Finally, you cannot shop with most wholesalers without a tax ID number, so aren't you glad you've already started that process?

eBay has a wholesale category right on its site, so stop by and check it out. The wholesale category is the last category listed under the categories head on eBay's Home page. When you click the Wholesale link you'll see the screen featured in Figure 2-7. As

FIGURE 2-7 eBay has its own category for wholesale items.

you can easily see, just about every category of wholesale item is for sale here. It's a good place to start your online wholesale search, but remember, everyone else on eBay has access to this same source. So stay focused on finding other sources, too.

When you start searching for wholesalers online, use common search terms that wholesalers and their customers would use. Some of these include payment terms such as "Net 30 days" or "Net 60 days." Others to consider are "Purchase order" and "Letter of credit." You'll get a lot of hits from these, so be prepared to be patient.

» Wholesale tricks to try

When you buy wholesale, you generally have to purchase in bulk. As you approach wholesalers, ask them about buying their

Wholesale tricks to try

Worldwide Brands

If you spend any time at all researching wholesalers among PowerSellers it isn't long before the name Worldwide Brands comes up. That's because in an area that's rife with fraud and exaggerated claims, Worldwide Brands is as close to a sure bet as there is. Worldwide Brands sells information, carefully screened information, about liquidators, wholesalers, and other suppliers. It compiles this information with small-to-medium-sized sellers in mind and updates it daily. All of the companies listed through Worldwide Brands have agreed to work with home-based businesses.

The company's one-stop shopping service, OneSource, offers easy access to more than 9 million products from 7,000 suppliers. To use it you simply select a category, enter the product you're interested in, and then start writing and printing as OneSource provides a list of companies for you to contact. Market research data is also built into OneSource, providing insights into whether the product you're researching may sell well online, how many people are searching for it, and details on sellers who are selling it on eBay. That's a whole lot of information you can get with one or two clicks. We hate to sound like a commercial, but WorldWide Brands is the only company of its type that's eBay-certified. At $249.00 for lifetime access OneSource doesn't seem inexpensive, until you consider how much time and effort it can save you.

---

fringe items. When a wholesaler fills a large order, there are often dribs and drabs of product left over. These lots are too small to make up another complete bulk order. Ask about buying them. You may be able to scoop up great products in the smaller quantities that are right for you anyway.

Here's one of our favorite tips. "Whenever I get a box of goods from a wholesaler, I peel back the label," revealed a PowerSeller who specializes in gift items. "Sometimes the wholesaler reuses boxes, just like I do, and some of these are from the manufacturers. Even if a manufacturer's label isn't complete, I've gotten enough of the manufacturer's name and address to find them online. Then I can approach them and try to buy from them directly. My family knows that every time this happens, we get to celebrate!" So, be vigilant, and never give up. You just don't know when a little tidbit can become a great new source.

Manufacturers

Manufacturers are a PowerSeller's cause for celebration, because buying from the manufacturer puts you directly at the source of your product. This reduces your acquisition costs and directly affects your profit margin. As you remember, this was your original goal, to get as close to the source of your product as you possibly can. Unfortunately, this is not that easy. Many manufacturers have distribution channels in place that do not include sales to individuals. They are selling in bulk directly to the wholesalers, who then sell to retailers and you. You can't expect to approach the biggest, most well-known manufacturers and have them welcome your individual business. You'll also need that tax ID number to work with manufacturers. You did start that process, right?

Although the situation has improved as eBay and online commerce in general has become more accepted, you may meet with some bias among manufacturers as an eBay seller. Unfortunately, some manufacturers consider it demeaning to see their products for sale on eBay. It's all part of the (dated) eBay-as-garage-sale image. It's no longer true, and it's certainly not fair, but you will find that some manufacturers will refuse to sell to you once they know you're planning to sell on eBay. So, just to begin with, don't make it very obvious that you are an eBay seller. In the next chapter, you'll learn about why you'll want to have your own Web site, and here's another reason you can add to that discussion. Once you have your own Web site, you can simply say that you operate an e-commerce business. It's the truth, even if you only have your business on eBay, but with your own Web site, you also have an Internet address that backs your claim. So, play it close to the vest while you're trying to get started with a new manufacturer.

Being familiar with eBay Giving Works can create a huge advantage here. When a manufacturer is worried about eBay, consider offering to only sell their items as part of a 10 percent for charity campaign—and consider choosing the manufacturer's favorite charity! You can even ask them to participate as a donor, so that you don't have to be responsible for the entire 10 percent donation.

Online Sources of Manufacturers

Searching for manufacturers online is not unlike searching for wholesalers. Some of the search terms you'll find useful for finding manufacturers include "manufacturer rep," "wholesale application," and "independent representatives and distributors."

Wholesale tricks to try

We have located two of the best sites for you to explore as you start your search.

Thomas Global

Thomas Global, shown in Figure 2-8, offers you direct access to 700,000 manufacturers and distributors from 28 countries. Through this online service you can research sources for products and services in 11,000 categories from companies worldwide. Most of these companies sell industrial products for business-to-business sales, but with millions of listings, you may just find something you'd like to source. Products include scales, halogen lamps, and even nails. Compare the items here to eBay's "Business & Industrial Category." You'll see that a lot of the same material is available in both places. If this is your line of interest, you've got a great source to start your research available right now.

FIGURE 2-8 Thomas Global is a good site to visit if you're thinking of selling industrial types of goods.

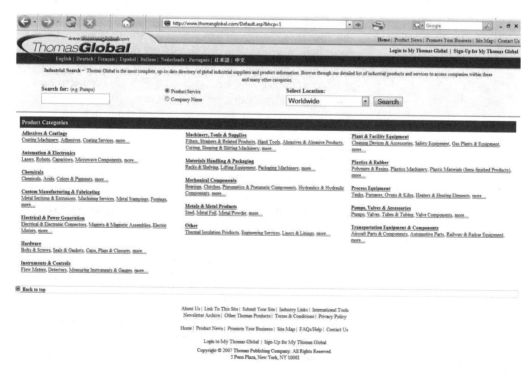

» Try TDCTRADE to locate international trade contacts

TDC, which drives global marketing for The Hong Kong Trade Development Council has a very useful Web site you can find at http://www.tdctrade.com/.s. Here you will find online sources of products and resources for contacting manufacturers and companies that operate not only in Hong Kong, but also in Mainland China and Taiwan. The site lists more than a dozen different categories of products available, ranging from jewelry to electronics and toys, from gifts to housewares, and from garments to "entertainment." Because the Council is based in Hong Kong, language is no barrier to English-speaking buyers, but services are also available in other languages,

TDC's sole purpose is to bring business contacts together, and it boasts a database of 700,000 international contacts. Look into its PremierConnect business matching service if you're interested in importing products. While that particular service is expensive, there's also a lot of free information available through TDC.

"I use TDC all the time," said one PowerSeller who specializes in apparel. "Not only is the site a great place to source my products, but I've used the TDC to arrange escorted trips to China to visit and tour factories I'm thinking of working with. They take care of everything, making it possible for me to visit Mainland China and feel both secure and comfortable."

» Go to manufacturers' trade shows

Actually going to manufacturers' trade shows is a great way to make contacts directly with manufacturers. Get your reference librarian to help you find the dates and locations of shows that will work for you. When you go, focus on the small- to medium-sized companies. These are companies that are just building their own reputations and establishing themselves in their marketplaces. You may find they are more eager to work with individuals, and they are not as likely to be able to afford any anti-eBay bias. You may just be able to help each other grow by providing them with a good distribution channel while they're too small to have established channels of their own. Also, you are more likely to meet a high-ranking employee of a smaller company, since owners of smaller firms are more likely doing much of this work for themselves.

Don't miss the ASD/AMD trade shows

While you focus on the small- to medium-sized manufacturers, don't discount the larger companies all together. You may find you're happier with the smaller firms, but if you're interested in something offered only by a larger company, don't be intimidated. Sometimes just making personal contact with someone and letting them see who you are is enough to get you through the gate with a larger company. They may even be looking for an eBay distributor for their products, and you could provide that service. In doing so, you'll be establishing a new sales channel for them. You handle listing and sales, and they provide inventory, which can reduce your inventory costs.

Just be sure to have professional-looking business cards ready. Include your e-mail address and your Web site, if you already have one, but don't mention eBay right away. Make a good impression and see where the conversation goes from there. You don't need to hide your eBay status, but your first meeting may not be the place to advertise it either.

» Don't miss the ASD/AMD trade shows

There's probably no better opportunity for you to meet face to face with manufacturers than the ASD/AMD shows (merchandisegroup.com), held several times throughout the year. These are the largest shows of their type and are likely your best opportunity for general product sourcing. They're open to the trade only (you'll need that sales tax ID number or a business license), but there's no charge for buyers to attend. This is a show meant for smaller businesses, and it features thousands of manufacturers all there to sell you products. The show we attended was a smorgasbord of opportunity for eBay sellers. Imagine walking through a variety store the size of five Wal-Marts, and you can start to appreciate what walking the floor of this show is like. Instead of dealing with only one company, you have the chance to forge deals with thousands.

We asked dozens of the companies there whether they currently sell to eBay sellers, or if they don't, whether they would. The answer was almost unanimous—almost every one would love to do business with eBay sellers. More than a few were already working with PowerSellers. And some wanted to pick our brains about how they could locate eBay sellers to do business with! So much for manufacturers who sell to small businesses being difficult to track down.

❯❯ Tag-team trade shows

PowerSellers Debnroo have come up with a great way to work trade shows. One of the partners goes to the trade show while the other stays home in the office. Using a cell phone and a portable communications device, in this case a T-Mobile Sidekick, they communicate about the items at the trade show. Partner Number 1 finds an interesting product and sends details about it back to the home office. Partner Number 2 is waiting and ready to search eBay for sell-through information. Together they work to determine not only what looks like an interesting product, but also how much they're likely to be able to get for it, and how well similar items are selling on eBay. By the end of the show, they have a good, clear idea of how well the items they chose are selling, and they have established clear sources for getting those products. No wonder these two have such a successful eBay business going. You'll learn more about them in the profile at the end of this chapter.

Don't Discount the Big Discount Houses

Sourcing your products through wholesalers and manufacturers will allow you to buy items for sale in bulk. That's how you can ensure a steady stream of products once you've focused on the items you want to sell. But once you have your distribution network in place, don't discount the chance to supplement it when an interesting opportunity comes along. Many PowerSellers do this through local shopping. You'll hear chatter about sourcing products through dollar stores on the discussion boards, but we don't recommend that. Generally, the items sold at dollar stores just won't generate high enough prices to warrant your time and energy pursuing them. The large discount houses and buying clubs in your area are a completely different story and often provide great supplemental sources of product. Just because you may have a Sam's Club or a Costco conveniently located near your home doesn't mean that everyone does. The same is true for sellers who live near outlet malls where many bargains can be found for reselling.

If you come across a great buy at stores like these, scoop it up and sell it to eBayers who are more geographically challenged than you are.

Are You a Special Case?

By now you've probably gotten the idea that sourcing your inventory will be a big part of the work that lies ahead of you as you build your eBay business. For most of us, that's entirely true. It will be the single most time-consuming, challenging part of operating your eBay business. You may be surprised to learn that some eBayers don't have this problem at all, and if you're lucky enough to be one of them, you begin with an automatic head start.

Do You Own a Store?

If you already own a store, you have absolutely no reason not to be selling on eBay. You already have your sources in place for finding your products, so selling on eBay just opens new markets for you, gives you a new revenue stream to tap, and allows you to broaden your customer base. Plus, you can use eBay to sell your own end-of-season clearance items or the items customers return. This is bound to be better than sending them to a liquidator or paying the overhead to store them for next year, when they may not sell any better than they did this year.

Does your merchandise lend itself to a trade-in/trade-up program? One North Carolina PowerSeller owns a store that sells youth sports equipment. This gets outgrown long before it wears out. He used eBay to start a trade-in/trade-up program for his customers and their parents. He buys back their used equipment and sells it exclusively on eBay. His manufacturers objected when he started selling their new products on eBay, but they don't have a problem with his selling their used products there. So, he actually earns money the first time he makes a new customer, the next time that person upgrades the child's equipment, and again when he resells the used equipment to another customer on eBay. This is a smart eBayer.

Are You a Wholesaler?

Just as store owners have no reason not to sell on eBay, the same is true for wholesalers and their families. One PowerSeller from Kentucky came to eBay to sell inventory from her father's wholesale shoe business. She claimed she never would have entered into her father's business as it was, but she was so fascinated by selling on eBay that she's gone on to train others in her area about selling on the site. In turn, her father's wholesale company has never been more successful now that a whole new world market has opened for him. If you're lucky enough to own a wholesale operation, or have a relative who does, you won't have any trouble getting all the items you need to become a successful PowerSeller.

Are You a Manufacturer?

Now it may seem obvious, but manufacturers also have opportunities as PowerSellers on eBay. Yeshosery is a manufacturer of socks for men, women, and children based in North Carolina. They started selling on eBay to eliminate their leftover inventory from their big orders. (In other words, their fringe items, as we talked about before!) They moved on to selling things they had left over from their production efforts. For example, they have auctioned huge bags of bows that they used on little girls' socks one season. Now crafters scoop them up as quickly as they get listed. Yeshosery moved on to producing their own items specifically for sale on eBay, and now they also source items from other manufacturers. Representatives of the company told us they had no idea when they started that their little effort to clean up the warehouse would explode for them into a whole new branch of their business.

Are You an Artist or a Craftsperson?

If your life's work is producing beautiful things, you have a year-round business opportunity on eBay, and you'll never have to worry about finding sources for your products. You already search for markets to feature your items, so you have no reason not to turn to eBay as a new market just waiting to be tapped. eBay makes it possible for artists to be more independent than ever before, as they no longer have to depend on the middleman to help them market their creations.

It's All a Balancing Act

Okay, now that you've gotten all of this advice about finding great sources of items to sell on eBay, be careful. Your efforts

Tag-team trade shows

are not over, because you're entering a very fluid business. Just when you think everything is in place, you have to be prepared to keep going and continue your searching. Remember those "Hot Items by Category" that we studied all those pages ago? Well, once your items start selling well, you'll end up helping to put them right into that same list that others are studying to learn what's selling well on eBay. Once other people see how well your items are doing, they'll start selling them too. Once that happens, the simple law of supply and demand will devalue your items.

Don't allow yourself to build your inventory to the point that you get stuck with a huge volume of devalued items when the market floods. While your product is doing well, keep researching and searching for the next great trends and products you'll pursue. That way, when the market drops for the items you already sell—and it most likely will—you'll be ready to move on to other more profitable products. Remember the sad tale of the Beanie Babies!

Meet a PowerSeller

Andy and Deb Mowery—Debnroo

Debnroo, Inc., is a privately owned S-Corporation retail seller of home, garden, and pet products. With over $1 million in sales for 2006, Debnroo enjoys 30 percent annual growth, and employs four to six full-time and part-time employees. The company's evolution went from a small mom-and-pop collectibles operation to a nationally recognized retailer of many popular brand-name items.

While all entrepreneurial paths are unique, Debnroo's path shares many of the common characteristics, challenges, anxieties, and successes of those pursuing their dreams through their own small business.

Deb and Andy met in 1987 as college students, and by 1997 they had left the corporate world behind in frustration. They chose self-employment as their path to success.

In 1999, Andy's dad Jim asked them to help him sell antiques on eBay from the inventory of his large store. Little did the couple know where that would lead! It only took the couple a few months for them to recognize the power of eBay to make their hopes of self-employment real. They named their business "weauction4you.com" and hoped to one day open a retail drop-off store. While collectibles offered the pair significant profit margins, they soon recognized the long, labor-intensive process of creating unique listings would make scaling the business to any significant size difficult. They would need a sizeable staff, and the pair didn't want to become primarily managers.

They spent the next couple of years developing a solid product line of home, garden, and pet items. By 2003, they were selling over 250 products from 15 manufacturers and coordinating 200 to 400 transactions each week. They built their business by selling their products at reasonable profit margins and charging shipping and handling fees based upon the premise that their shipping was a service they provided for their customers. They also enhanced their sales by selling internationally.

By the end of 2003, they'd changed the company name to Debnroo, eliminating the auction element of their first name choice. The name change helped them build their credibility with potential suppliers, by eliminating the prejudice some felt against eBay sales at that time. The couple also discontinued selling collectibles in favor of the new inventory items. Throughout most of 2004 and 2005, the couple worked to fully equip their warehouse and train their staff. By 2006, they were formalizing their training and employee compensation programs.

"In some ways, we have found the challenges we faced in recent years have been far more difficult to overcome than those of our early years, when we were just trying to build enough sales to support a company," noted Andy. He commented that other big sellers on eBay have echoed this same idea. "It's one thing for two self-motivated people to build a business to the point where it sustains them," he said. "But, it's entirely another to change that arrangement to one that sustains others' livelihoods and requires a team of individuals who may not feel the same type of motivation."

When we spoke, Deb and Andy were enjoying their eighth year in business. The couple was looking forward to continuing to build their business, both on and off eBay. They were planning to build an Internet presence that will lessen their vulnerability to the changing tides of eBay itself. But, instead of planning the final destination on this road, the pair have decided to stay focused on the short-term growth of their company. "We focus on building a quality company that acts responsibly to the community and provides good opportunities for employees," noted Andy. "We remain grateful that we can still do all this from the swing in our backyard, enjoying every day with our cats, Wilson and Sunshine." And to think that it all started with just a few collectibles!

Tag-team trade shows

Source Products for Success Checklist

✓   I've applied for my sales tax ID number.

✓   I'm considering my products as a total product line.

✓   Before sourcing products I'm calculating my total budget.

✓   eBay's Hot Items by Category, Merchandising Calendar, eBay Pulse, and eBay Pop are part of my arsenal.

✓   I know the benefits of participating in eBay's Giving Works program.

✓   Andale's Price Finder and What's Hot are now familiar to me.

✓   When sourcing products I'm thinking locally to sell globally.

✓   Are there creative ways for me to advertise for products?

✓   I've learned the right time to buy products for resale.

✓   I won't completely discount wholesalers but I know to tread carefully.

✓   I'm going to focus on working with manufacturers whenever possible.

✓   Can I create my own items for resale?

Chapter 3

From Mom and Pop to PowerShop

Automate from the very beginning and plan for growth

Before we get started building your seller's PowerShop, let's take a quick survey. Do you already have a computer with Internet access? Are you already registered as an eBay seller? If we've done our market research correctly, everyone holding this book in their hands will answer "yes" to both these questions. Good. You have the foundation we'll need to build your new PowerShop. You've probably been doing just swell with your Mom-and-Pop setup, but now that you've set your sights on a genuine business, you're going to need to beef up your systems. No longer will you be able to get by with the basic tools that have let you buy and even sell a little on eBay. If you want to move up to PowerSeller, you simply must plan your PowerShop.

Fortunately, we've gathered a lot of help for you from PowerSellers. They've told us all about their computer hardware and software. We've learned how they manage their auctions, inventories, and communications. They've told us the best things they've learned about dealing with their photos and shipping their products. They've given us the benefit of their years of trial and error, so that you can build your PowerShop while avoiding some of the pitfalls they've experienced.

As you read through this chapter, don't allow yourself to be overcome with a sense that you are going to spend all of your time and money building your business before you can even earn a dime. You will find that we describe many different products, and most of them cost money. We're not suggesting that you purchase everything you learn about in this chapter. We're offering you a buffet of items from which to choose. Some of them are really not negotiable, such as a high-speed Internet connection. Others are going to be more useful to you once you've gained a bit more experience. Some you'll need right away, and others you can plan to add in the future. They are all tools that will make your eBay business more efficient and professional, but you don't need to purchase them all right now. Remember, PowerSellers are a creative lot. You'll find ways to tap into your own creativity as you build your PowerSeller's operation.

» Automate from the very beginning and plan for growth

You may be thinking that you just don't see yourself as needing too much automation right now. You may think you're doing just fine managing the sales you've had so far, and you'd rather spend your time making more money instead of building systems that seem too complicated for you. Don't allow yourself to be victimized by this shortsighted thinking. "Automate from the very beginning," advises a PowerSeller from Kentucky. "It's so much easier to build onto a system you have than it is to have to go back and retrofit your system to meet your needs when you're also busy." So, start your research, make your choices, and build your automation into your business. You'll be very glad you did once the sales start pouring in!

As part of this planning for your future, add automation with an eye toward "scalability." By that we mean, as you add something new to your operation, have a clear idea of how you will expand that new element when the moment becomes clear that you've outgrown it. You want to build a PowerShop that will grow with you, not one that will need to be replaced as you grow.

Your Computer

So, as a budding PowerSeller what sort of computer and peripherals do you need? This may come as a surprise, but unless your computer is more than four years old or so, you probably already have in place just what you'll need to get started. PowerSellers told us that they started their businesses with the computers they already owned, adding more computer power only when they needed it. Most people probably have all the horsepower they need in their current computer. It's the things you use in conjunction with your computer—especially a high-speed Internet connection and a digital camera—that you may have to buy.

Consider what eBay sellers use their computers for. You'll be spending a lot of time doing the normal office tasks such as creating letters and documents, e-mailing, and running accounting software. Even when you add auction management software to the mix, you're not doing things that are especially system intensive. Most newer computers are more than up to the task.

We do have some recommendations though. (You knew we would, didn't you?) To make life easier, it's best to have a computer with USB ports right in the front, as in most new computers. This makes connecting peripherals, such as a digital camera, as easy as possible. A large hard drive is important (this is no place to scrimp) for storing those big photo files,

Buy the best technology you can afford

especially until you start using auction management software and image hosting services. Making sure you have a lot of memory (1024MB is now the standard) is also smart. You'll especially appreciate that when you're multitasking, which as a PowerSeller you'll be doing a lot as you check on your auctions, evaluate your sales numbers, and respond to e-mail. If you have an IBM-compatible computer, it's also a good idea to be running an operating system at the Windows XP level or better. This software will have built-in networking capabilities, which you'll need when connecting your computer to a home network.

Aside from these things, any newer computer has the processor speed you will need. If your computer is more than a couple of years old, you can always add memory if you need it, and even an external drive, etc., but new computers costing what they do, it may just make more sense to buy a new one. They're so inexpensive now that it almost doesn't pay to spend too much on upgrades. However, it will almost certainly pay to add more memory to an aging computer as long as the hard drive has enough capacity, and the processor is still fast enough to handle newer versions of your favorite applications.

With regard to a high-speed connection, unless you live in an area that simply doesn't offer cable, DSL, or satellite service (increasingly rare), there's no question about it; you must have one. You are spending too much of your time on the Internet to use dial-up. Uploading your pictures alone is reason enough to go with the high-speed connection. It boils down to the simple question: what's your time worth? Does it make sense to sit and wait for Web pages to load, or should you go from page to page as quickly as you can? Waiting even an extra five seconds for each operation might not seem like much. But, do the math: you'll be doing hundreds or even thousands of operations a day. A faster connection can add hours to your week! If you're serious about your eBay business, you must have a high-speed Internet connection.

» Buy the best technology you can afford

If you do upgrade your computer setup, buy the best technology you can afford. Not only will this give you extra speed and power, but it will help you put off the time when your new computer is obsolete. "We keep our eyes open for good deals, and add computers in clumps as we find a good buy," says a PowerSeller specializing in apparel. That's excellent advice. If you keep your eyes open, you'll find you can get the equipment you need on a nonemergency basis and actually acquire better equipment at a lesser cost. Start your search right on eBay.

» Network your computers

As your eBay business grows, you are likely to add more computer power. When you do, network your computers. Not only will this allow you to share the high-speed connection, but it will also allow you to have ready access to all of your records and software too. You don't want to have to keep switching back and forth between machines so that you can process different parts of your transactions. So wireless networking is a must these days if you have more than one computer in your home or office. The requirements for this are very basic—a router and a network card. If you are buying a new computer, please do so with wireless networking in mind. A network will keep your business operating smoothly. As an added bonus, when you add employees, you'll have your systems in place to allow them to be most efficient.

Stay Healthy to Get Wealthy

As a prospective eBay PowerSeller, know that your livelihood depends on your computer. You need for it to be not only operating but operating as close to its peak as possible. And you certainly don't want to let unsavory characters get the personal information about you that resides within it.

Of course, you want to protect your computer from viruses. You are probably already using an antivirus program; now you'll need to make sure it's up to date and set to operate automatically in the background. It's no secret that an investment in a program such as Norton Antivirus, which you'll find at www.symantec.com/nav/nav_9xnt/, is better than money in the bank, especially these days. Buy it or a similar product, update it regularly, and keep those viruses at bay.

It used to be that all you had to worry about were viruses getting to your computer. But now there are other threats to your computer's health (and your own, if working to relieve your computer's sluggish performance gives you headaches). These new problems come from the Internet, specifically those fast broadband connections to the Internet made possible through cable, DSL, or satellite technology. You need to have one of

Network your computers

these high-speed services, but you also need to treat them with respect. The first thing to remember about them is that they're always on. As long as your computer is turned on, you are connected to the Internet, whether or not you happen to be using it at the time. While this gives you immediate Internet access, it can also allow potential hackers or other unauthorized people to access your computer to nose around and wreak havoc or worse. The best way to protect yourself from these intruders is with a firewall, usually a software program that stands sentry between your computer and outside computers and creates a "wall" of protection. The firewall software filters the information that comes into your computer and goes out of it.

If you are using Windows XP or Vista (we're sticking to IBM-compatible machines in our examples just because those are the ones we're familiar with), enabling its built-in firewall is as easy as can be. In fact with Vista, the firewall should already be "on." See the documentation that came with your computer or access the help files that are most likely available under your Start menu. If you use another operating system, you may want to buy a separate firewall program. Also, be sure that access to your wireless network is password protected (check your router software for how to do this).

The second threat that comes from having a constant connection to the Internet is that Web surfing leaves behind "spies." These often track your Web surfing (where you surf and for how long), or they serve up annoying ads. These intruders can even hijack your browser and take you to sites that you had no intention of visiting. Even worse, while they're there, they can gather personal information about you from the keystrokes you enter when filling out online forms. Plus, they often do this without your knowledge and permission. They just do. This can easily lead to that nightmare, Identity Theft. Finally, they are the cause of computer slowdowns and even crashes.

These programs are almost impossible to find and get rid of on your own. The best solution (and it's an easy one) is to install special programs that can sweep your computer's innards to find this stuff and get rid of it. Here aboveboard shareware comes to the rescue in the form of Ad-Aware, which you'll find at http://www.lavasoftusa.com/index.php and Spy Sweeper, at www.spysweeper.com/. Download, install, and follow the simple instructions to run these programs. They'll unearth enough nasties to choke a horse or a computer. Ad-Aware takes only a few minutes to run, whereas Spy Sweeper takes a bit longer and apparently does a more thorough job. The first time you run these programs, you may be amazed at what they turn up. Run them periodically to keep things humming.

Managing Your Business

Despite the fact that you probably have an adequate computer to start building your PowerSeller business, the same is likely not to be true of the systems you have in place for managing your auctions and operating your business. When you sell as a hobby, you can get by with the basics. You are most likely using your My eBay area, and this will provide all the necessary organizational tools a casual seller might need. That changes quickly once you increase the volume of your listings and sales. The consensus is that once you've moved beyond 15 to 20 listings per week, you're ready to automate. You'll need much more power for storing your digital images, processing your orders, keeping your records, and running your operation.

Fortunately, there are a variety of tools and services available to you to support your business. We'll look at auction management software in Chapter 4. For now, we'll provide you with a shopping list of other tools you'll need. We'll explore image hosting for your photos and tools for hosting your Web site. We'll take a quick look at accounting software that will help you with your record keeping. (You'll get a more detailed tour of these products in Chapter 10.) Then we'll introduce you to tools that will help you analyze your sales and determine your best routes to higher profits. We'll help you determine which products you want to use now and which you might keep in mind for adding in the future. Let's get started with those images.

Image Hosting

Image hosting services provide one of the best ways to distinguish your auctions from those created by sellers without your PowerSeller aspirations. You can always tell the difference between an auction listing that has incorporated image hosting and one that has not. The pictures are clearer and bigger, much bigger, so every detail is clear to your prospective buyers. And there are likely to be more of them too.

Using image hosting is simple. You just upload your pictures to the company (called the *host*) Web server where they will be

Network your computers

stored (there will be onscreen directions). When you're ready to incorporate your hosted picture within your listing, you simply enter the URL address for the picture(s), instead of the filename. You'll do this from the Sell Your Item form, just where you previously entered your photos stored on your own computer. eBay will then snatch it off the Web, as shown in Figure 3-1.

There are image hosting services that handle only this sort of thing. Some are even free to the user, because they are supported by advertisers. Figure 3-2 shows the home page of one such service, Village Photos. You'll find them at http://www .villagephotos.com/. Keep in mind, this service is free, but you cannot store your images there indefinitely and there are limits on the number of images you can upload. In fact, your own

FIGURE 3-1 Input the URL address for your hosted pictures into this form, and eBay will automatically add your photo to your listing.

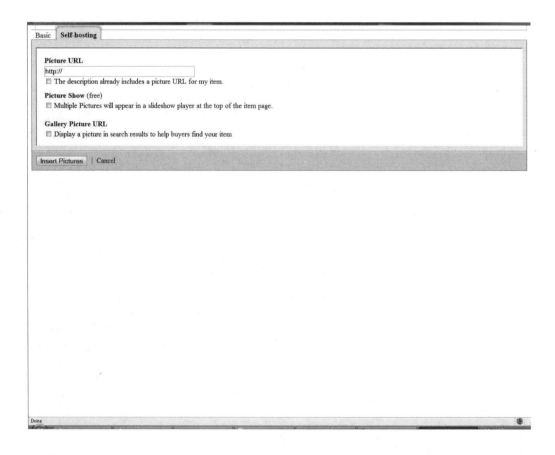

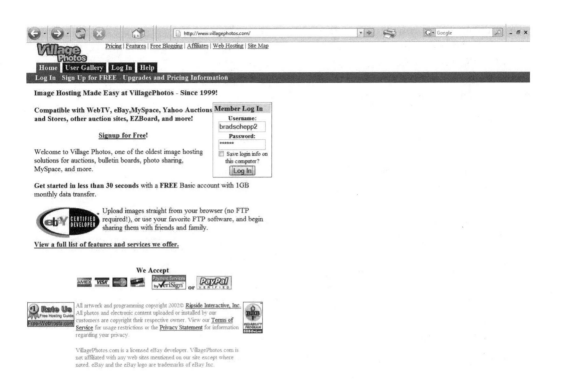

FIGURE 3-2 The home page of the image hosting service Village Photos shows you a free hosting option you can try.

Internet service provider might also provide a significant amount of free data storage, and you can use that to host images also.

As you'll see in Chapter 4, auction management programs include image hosting among their features. Uploading your image is just as easy with auction management software as it is with the dedicated services. Plus you get the use of all the other features the software offers. In fact, one of the best reasons for using an auction management program is the image hosting. Once you upload your digital pictures to the company's computers, you can also use the auction management program to create your listing. Just browse your computer for the digital image, and the software will take it from there, assigning a URL and placing it within your auction.

Whether you use auction management software or an image hosting service, if you prefer to use your stored image with eBay's selling form, you can still do that.

From the Create Your Listing form you only need to click the Pictures button to get started if the image resides in your own computer. If it's with a hosting service you'll need to first click "Show/Hide Options" from the right-hand side of the page and follow the prompts from there. Why would you prefer to use image hosting rather than to store your images on your own computer? There are several reasons:

- Even if you use eBay's "Supersize" feature, a hosted picture will still be much larger. Often this results in more bids, because buyers appreciate being able to more closely inspect your item. It's also cheaper this way, since you'll pay $0.75 extra for supersizing your images through eBay, but only a fraction of that in storage fees through your image hosting choice.

- You will free up valuable disk space on your own computer, leaving space for other tasks that can't be so easily stored elsewhere. If you ever use the same image in more than one listing (e.g., if you have more than one of the same thing to sell, or if you have to list it more than one time), your savings quickly multiply.

- Your pictures will load more quickly from an image host and save you valuable time when you're creating listings.

» Use accounting software

As you build your PowerShop, you'll need to give yourself the necessary tools for managing your records and keeping your books. Chapter 10 will give you all the information and advice you'll need to get started, but while you're gathering your tools, add accounting software to your shopping list. PowerSellers use accounting software in conjunction with their auction management software. The latter keeps track of their daily and weekly business transactions, and the former produces monthly, quarterly, and annual records that their accountants use to figure their taxes, profits, and losses.

QuickBooks

Many of the PowerSellers we spoke with use QuickBooks to manage their accounts. Intuit, Inc., the producer of QuickBooks, is accurate in describing their software as a full-featured accounting program that will easily meet the needs of your small business. We found, however, that not everyone agrees with Intuit that the program is "easy to use."

With QuickBooks, you can manage all of your basic accounting tasks, including printing checks, paying bills, and creating reports. You can produce standard profit and loss, balance sheet, and cash flow statements along with sales reports. You can use the software to keep income, payroll, and sales tax records. QuickBooks also has a tax alerts feature to keep you informed about upcoming deadlines for quarterly, estimated, and monthly tax payments.

Seller after seller reported frustration in getting started with QuickBooks. Once you're up and running with the software, you won't have any trouble with it, but getting to that point can be a challenge. "QuickBooks setup can be tricky for a novice, but it's smooth sailing once that is done," says a seller based in Southern California. "You have to have a basic knowledge of double entry debit/credit systems to set up your files and to understand how to enter certain entries."

QuickBooks Pro 2007 costs $199.95. We recommend that when you buy the software you also buy *QuickBooks 2007: The Official Guide* by Kathy Ivens (McGraw-Hill/Osborne, 2007). It is the only official guide to the software, and it will be very helpful to you as you get started. Also, see Chapter 10 for more information about educating yourself in using the program. Finally, don't forget to follow our previous advice, and lean on your fellow sellers through groups and discussion boards to get help along the way.

Excel

Excel, from Microsoft Corporation, is a spreadsheet software program that many PowerSellers use to keep track of their expenses and earnings. A spreadsheet is a valuable tool because it allows you to input your data and then manipulate it to create and explore "what if " scenarios. Because changing the data in any one cell automatically changes all the relevant data in every other cell, you can quickly explore the ramifications of raising your starting price, changing your listing fees by adding listing upgrades, or lowering your product acquisition costs. Using Excel, you can create charts, tables, and graphs to visually represent your data for clearer analysis. Excel comes bundled with Microsoft's Office software suite, but you can also buy it separately for $229 (but discounted through many online retailers).

Use accounting software

Analyzing Your Auction Data

Once you start completing listings, you also gather a wealth of data that you can use to judge the success of your selling and the areas of your operation that you can enhance for greater profits. You have tools available to you for analyzing the data you'll soon be collecting, and you should try some of these to see which ones you should add to your PowerShop tool chest. Chapter 6 will tell you more about using these tools to your best advantage, but we'll give you some advice right now about which tools you'll want to consider while you're building your PowerShop.

Counters

You are, no doubt, already familiar with the most common and simplest auction analysis tool of all, auction counters. These little tracking devices are used in 80 to 90 percent of all eBay listings, according to Scott Samuel (who created the first counters for online auctions). To understand how useful they can be and why it's important for you to add them to your listings, let's take a look at why Scott created them in the first place.

Like you, Scott sells on eBay, and he has for years. When he first got started, eBay was much different from what it is today. Back then there were only a fraction of the items for sale as compared to now.

Scott created counters because he wanted to be sure eBay was for real and that people were truly buying and selling things on the site. With a counter, you can track how many times your listing has been viewed. If you're not getting many hits, you'll need to try to figure out why. Have you put your item in the wrong category? Is your description lacking?

An estimated 20 percent of all people who use counters use hidden counters to keep buyers (and other sellers) from knowing how much attention their items are receiving. That keeps buyers at a slight disadvantage, because they can't easily judge how much competition they're facing. Also, from the seller's viewpoint, counters that show a lot of hits may discourage new customers from bidding. They may think the high numbers mean the item will sell for more than they want to spend, so they'll move on to someone else's listing. eBay makes it simple to add free counters to your listings. Just use the drop down menu under "Visitor Counter" on the Create Your Listing page to select the type of counter you'd like to include.

» Use auction analysis tools

Auction analysis tools go farther along the path of tracking the data your bidders bring your way and analyzing it to your best advantage. These programs can give you a wealth of information about your bidders' shopping habits, their reactions to your product offerings, and the success of your operations. We'll review two of the most well-known programs in this chapter. We've also saved one other for Chapter 6, where we share more details with you about using these tools to enhance your online auction business.

Vendio

Vendio has long been recognized as a major player in the auction automation arena. Recently, Vendio purchased Andale, long known for its listing counters and auction analysis tools. That means a wealth of great tools are now available under one roof (begin at http://www,vendio.com). Andale's Research service, which Vendio, at the time of this writing, planned to incorporate into its own product line, is one of the most respected in the industry. Here are some of tasks the service can help you with:

- Finding which category will yield the best price for your item
- Learning the price at which you should start your auction
- Determining the best time of day and day of the week for getting the best price
- Learning which eBay listing upgrades, such as bold and highlight, work the best
- Seeing what's actually selling on eBay

Because Andale hadn't been fully incorporated into the Vendio product line at the time of this writing, pricing information was not available for us to include. Please check the Vendio Web site for current pricing information.

HammerTap

HammerTap (www.hammertap.com) offers a suite of auction analysis tools and services to help you succeed as an eBay seller.

Use auction analysis tools

Its primary product is called PowerDesk. With PowerDesk you can perform in-depth research on HammerTap's huge database of closed eBay listings in three category areas: products, eBay categories, and sellers. This research can tell you:

- A product's chances of selling and what it might sell for
- How you can increase your auction listing's likelihood for success
- Ideas for boosting your profit on each listing
- Trends in the market for the products you sell (or are considering selling)
- How big the market is and how formidable your competition currently is

One of the best ways to improve as a seller is to evaluate how the leading sellers in your product category operate their businesses. By using PowerDesk you can research an eBayer's seller history to see how much your competitor is making in gross revenue, the average selling price per item, and the listing success rate per item. You can also view the end day and time, listing type, category, start price, etc. to know how your competitor is listing, enabling you to list better and more efficiently. Finally, you can also know what keywords the seller is using in titles and which ones bring in the greatest profit.

You can use this data to see where you fit into the crowd. If you find you are consistently being outdone by other sellers within your own category, you have a real opportunity for studying their auctions and learning what may be distinguishing them from your own.

HammerTap provides more than a product. It's a university of sorts with online courses, a newsletter, a blog, and even a regular spot on eBay radio. All of this information can help you become proficient in the use of its products. HammerTap is available by subscription for $24.95 per month (although they were offering a discount rate of $19.95 when we checked). You can take it for a free test drive for 10 days.

Your Web Site

These days it seems almost everyone with something to sell has a Web site. As someone who is building a Web-based business, there's no question about it—eventually you must have a Web site. Once you have a Web site, you can move into the e-commerce big leagues, using your eBay listings, in part, to drive people to your site and therefore maximize your profits. You can also drive people to your site through your own advertising, whether this advertising is to your eBay customers or the Web at large through Google ads or some other method. Through search engine optimization (SEO) techniques you can make sure your site appears high up in search engine results. There's no need to get too worked up over needing to know about all these options just now. We'll cover Web site marketing in detail in Chapter 6, and we'll tell you what you need to consider to make your Web site into a store in Chapter 11.

As with so many things, you can either create your own site or pay someone else to do it. Whole books have been written on the subject of creating and maintaining your own Web site. As you might guess, we're not going to be able to provide you with all of the information you'll need to accomplish this task. But, we can give you some advice to get you started, and we're confident you can take it from there.

» Pick your Web address

You'll need an Internet Web "address" (domain name) for your Web site so that people can easily remember it and find it through Google and other Internet search engines. It's not difficult to sign up for a domain name. Your challenge will be to create one that accurately describes your business, catches the attention of your customers, and sticks with them. To illustrate, we'll discuss how Go Daddy, a popular choice for domain registration among PowerSellers, makes it an easy process.

To start, you'll complete the following steps from their home page at www.godaddy.com, shown in Figure 3-3:

1. Type in the domain name you would like.

2. Specify the extension you would like (probably .com for a commercial site).

3. Then search the database of domains to see if the one you want is available. If it isn't, you'll have to try another name. Go Daddy will offer some close alternatives to keep it simple. You might also want to consider one that's less likely to be taken. Try to make

Pick your Web address

FIGURE 3-3 Getting your own domain name can begin with a stop at Go Daddy.com.

it part of your overall branding. Think of how it will relate to your eBay username and try to keep as much consistency as you can. You may have to go with something a little offbeat. Say you're selling hula hoops. In that case, you might want to consider something like www.loopyhoops.com, which was still available when we checked!

The cost for just registering a domain through Go Daddy is about $8.95 for one year. This isn't an ad for Go Daddy! You can register a domain name and get other services similar to these through many other companies these days. For more information, including a list of companies, visit the InterNIC site at www.internic.net/index.html.

❯❯ When looking for Web design, think young

Hiring a professional Web designer can be expensive. These professionals can create awesome sites that offer all types of functions and options for the businesses who hire them. Those features are not cheap, and neither is the labor or expertise necessary to produce them. For your purpose, you need a clean, functional, attractive Web site, but you don't need that site to be too fancy. For a basic, yet attractive, site you can find a competent Web designer close to home. Start with your local community college. Hundreds of students study Web design at these schools. The instructors are sure to be able to recommend one of their students who would be glad to earn some extra money. If you don't have a community college nearby, consider the local high school. Many of these students, who have grown up using computers, are more than capable of helping you build the Web site you're planning.

❯❯ Keep your search local

Another good way to find a Web designer is to search for the Web sites of local businesses, charities, and government offices. Look at the different sites and decide which ones you find most attractive and appealing. Then, search the site for the name of the Web designer. It's usually there. Now you can meet with this person and discuss your Web design needs. Selecting a local Web designer makes it easier for you to work together and customize your Web site.

Photography

As you will see in Chapter 5, great photos are a vital part of your eBay listings. PowerSellers agree that the better your photos, the more likely you'll get bids, and the higher your final prices will go. That doesn't mean you need to become a professional photographer. It just means you need to plan for the supplies and equipment you'll need for taking good, clear, sharply detailed photos. Fortunately, that's never been easier or less expensive than it is today.

» Set up your studio

The size and type of area you'll need to set aside for photography depends on what you're selling and how large your items are. If you are planning to sell items that you can easily lift, you'll want to start with a solid platform, bench, or table on which you can place your items. It saves a lot of stress on your back if you can operate from waist level, and it makes it easier for you to focus directly on the item too. Framing your shot is very important for featuring its details, and you want to be comfortable while you work. It's wise for you to place this flat holding surface against a wall or in a corner, if possible. That helps ground the surface and helps you with your photo backgrounds.

You'll want to use background drapes to highlight your items. You'll need two, one light and one dark. That way, you can create contrast to your items no matter what their colors are. That doesn't mean you must use stark white or deep black. Consider a soft pastel that will barely show, such as light blue or pale pink. Just make sure the color doesn't detract from the details of the item you are photographing. Using a piece of black velvet for your dark drape adds some texture and depth to the background of your photos, and that can be very pleasing to the eye. Just be sure you don't use a strong pattern in your drape. You want it to be a subtle stage for your item, and you don't want anything that will draw the viewer's attention away from the object you're selling. You don't have to spend a lot of money for your drapes, either. You may have some sheets or an old blanket that fits the bill just right. If you do decide to shop, go to your local fabric store and look through the bin of remnants. These pieces of leftover fabric often sell for just a few dollars, and there's generally a large variety of pieces from which you can choose. Test a few to make sure they don't overreflect your lighting and create bright spots in your pictures.

You may need some other accessories for your photos beyond just the drapes. If you're selling clothing, shop around for a mannequin. Clothing never looks as good on a hanger as it does on a body. If you can't use a human model, choose an artificial one. You can even purchase adjustable mannequins that allow you to adapt them to different sizes of clothing. If you can't find an adjustable one, just be sure to carefully and discreetly pin the item so that it doesn't look like a sack draped over the mannequin you have. Consider how you can best show the lines and features of the clothing, and adapt from there.

If you're selling jewelry, consider a stand to feature your necklaces or a model hand to show your rings. Think about your favorite stores and the things they use to display their products, and then try to re-create them in your own photography studio. Also, start to collect different-sized boxes and even cans to lift your drapery and support your items. You can do a lot to emphasize your products' details by featuring them as the center of a landscaped design of fabric and supports.

One last piece of equipment you'll want to consider is a tripod. It's very important that your pictures are sharp and clear. That clarity can be hard to achieve when you're holding the camera in your hand. You'll need to be very steady in your grip to ensure that you don't end up with fuzzy and muddled shots. If you've got a very steady hand, you may be able to get away without a tripod, but for most of us, it's a good piece of equipment to add. It allows you to frame the shot, set everything up, and snap your pictures quickly without having to reset the camera position from the start each time.

» Light up your listings

You'll learn a lot more about lighting your items for photographing them in Chapter 5, when we get down to the details of creating your auction listings. For now, while you're building your PowerShop, keep in mind you may need to buy some photography lights to show your items to their best advantage. Photographers' lighting includes spotlights on stands that allow the lights to be raised and lowered, and umbrellas that rest above the lights for diffusing the beam of light and making it softer. You can buy these items piece by piece, or you can purchase them in kits that usually include two spotlights and umbrellas. But, keep in mind, you'll be investing hundreds of dollars in lighting equipment that is actually designed for use by experienced photographers.

You can also find less expensive and more ingenious ways to light your items for photographing them. Many of the PowerSellers we spoke with prefer natural light, so they prefer to create their photo area near a window, especially a north-facing one where the light is more diffused than the stronger southern exposure. Go to www.bulls2.com/indexb/ lightinghelpfortakingpictures.html to view some ingenious ways to light your photos using very inexpensive equipment. Figure 3-4 shows you how you can use a plastic water jug to diffuse the light when shooting small objects. Seller NKTower, who sells model trains, created a tutorial that completely explains his clever technique. A pin is under the jug, and the top of the jug has been cut to allow the camera lens to poke through. NKTower uses the camera's flash and its self-timer so that he doesn't accidentally shake the camera. The plastic surrounding the pin diffuses the camera flash so that light comes at the object from every angle instead of striking it straight on. The softer light eliminates shadows and doesn't wash out the details of the pin.

» Get a digital camera

This is the one piece of equipment (besides their computers, of course) that all PowerSellers agreed was absolutely essential to

FIGURE 3-4 This ingenious method for lighting small objects is both effective and inexpensive.

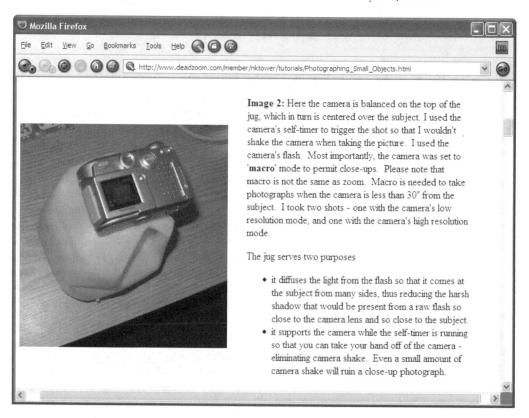

Image 2: Here the camera is balanced on the top of the jug, which in turn is centered over the subject. I used the camera's self-timer to trigger the shot so that I wouldn't shake the camera when taking the picture. I used the camera's flash. Most importantly, the camera was set to 'macro' mode to permit close-ups. Please note that macro is not the same as zoom. Macro is needed to take photographs when the camera is less than 30" from the subject. I took two shots - one with the camera's low resolution mode, and one with the camera's high resolution mode.

The jug serves two purposes

- it diffuses the light from the flash so that it comes at the subject from many sides, thus reducing the harsh shadow that would be present from a raw flash so close to the camera lens and so close to the subject.
- it supports the camera while the self-timer is running so that you can take your hand off of the camera - eliminating camera shake. Even a small amount of camera shake will ruin a close-up photograph.

their eBay businesses. You've likely discovered for yourself that digital cameras are simple to use. You can easily preview your image as soon as you've captured it. If you don't like what you see, you've wasted nothing but a moment's time. Even that wasn't a waste, since you can use your mistake to improve your next shot. You'll be able to ensure that you have exactly the shots you want, and you'll do it instantly. Contrast that to your efforts with a film-based camera. You can carefully set up each of your shots; snap the pictures; finish up the roll with shots of the dog, cat, or baby; and trundle off to have the film developed. When you get it back, whether that's an hour later or a couple of days, you may just discover that you didn't quite catch the feature you were hoping to highlight. Then you'll have to start all over again. You have spent money on film and processing, plus the cost of your travel back and forth to the film processing spot. But, more importantly, you've lost valuable time. In the time it took you to go back and forth with the first roll of film, you could have finished your listings and have had your items up for sale! Now, days have passed, and you're no closer to profits than you were when you began.

So, obviously, you need a digital camera. Fortunately, the digital camera you need is nowhere near the fanciest, most expensive, and full-featured camera on the market. Many of the PowerSellers we spoke with didn't even know which brand of camera they owned, although all of them owned one. Only one PowerSeller could tell us, off the top of his head, which brand he used. He sells jewelry, and he chose the Sony Mavica, because he liked the sharp detail it captures for his smaller items. So, don't overload yourself with the whole concept of digital cameras. If you happen to have one already, that one should be just fine for your business. If you don't have one, keep it simple when you shop for one.

Digital images are made up of hundreds of thousands or even millions of tiny squares known as picture elements, or pixels. The more pixels captured within each image, the more detailed that image will be. Different cameras are capable of capturing different numbers of pixels. For your purpose, posting images to online auctions, you'll do just fine with a four or five megapixel camera. (A megapixel is 1,000,000 pixels.) This is currently at the lower end of the scale of digital cameras, and it is quite possible to also purchase ten-megapixel cameras. These will provide you with beautiful images, but you don't need that

Inexpensive Lighting for Your Photos

Adam Nollmeyer is both a professional photographer and an eBay PowerSeller. Because he knows the ins and outs of photography, he's been able to create some excellent and inexpensive methods for lighting his photographs. He was kind enough to share his expertise with us.

Adam remarked that for the inexperienced photographer, using photographers' strobe lights can be difficult. He recommends using sunlight instead. Here's what Adam told us about using the sun for your strobe: "Do not shoot in direct sunlight. You need to diffuse the strength of the light, so look for an area where light is bouncing off of a building and into your nice, soft open shade area." Adam uses his patio to create the photo area shown at right. He creates the background niche for his products using white cardboard or foam-core.

"I use white for a background because it creates a nice 'high-key' image. These images really pop when you use the gallery feature on eBay and the user is viewing a small thumbnail photo." Adam also uses a "bounce card," shown next. This reflects the sunlight back onto your item centered in the white background. "This will make the shot less flat and give the product some dimension," advises Adam. "The bounce card throws light on the product, and then the white background bounces the light back onto the side away from your bounce card." Take a look at the fine example of the scanner Adam shot using this set up, as shown here. You'll see why following the advice of a professional can really pay.

much power, and you don't need to spend that much money to get the camera you'll need for this task.

Lower-resolution cameras, those that provide fewer pixels, are actually preferable for Web publishing, according to www .shortcourses.com (a fabulous source for more information about digital photography). That's because the higher the resolution, the greater the number of pixels in each file, and the longer it will take you to upload your images to your listings. If you keep your images near a resolution of 640×480 pixels, you'll achieve the clarity of detail you need and still have reasonable-sized files when it comes time to upload them and store them through your image-hosting service. Likewise, when your customers open your listings, it won't take as long as the higher resolution image to show up, leading them to move on in frustration. If you're planning to use eBay's picture services, keep your photos near 400×400 pixels in size, if you're not planning to supersize them. When you choose your camera, be sure it has a macro, or close-up function. This will be very important to you when you're trying to capture the detail of an item or when you're photographing smaller items. Most digital cameras offer this feature now, but some low-end cameras may not. Just one more warning: some lower-resolution cameras can also be more cheaply made. Although low resolution is fine for your purposes, low quality isn't. Be sure your camera is made well. Not only will that pay off in durability, but it will also show up in better image quality and color.

A Scanner? Well, Maybe

The whole subject of digital photography should not intimidate you in the least. The industry has grown very rapidly, and that's largely because digital cameras have come to be so simple to use. But if you have a scanner that you've grown very comfortable with, you may be able to get by with it alone for a while, depending on what you choose to sell. If you're dealing strictly in paper goods such as comic books, magazines, postcards, photographs, books, and sports cards, you may never need anything more than the scanner you've got, unless you want to sell a group of your items all at once. Your scanner will capture a digital image of any flat item as well as a digital camera will. It's just that using a scanner ties you to handling only flat items. PowerSellers generally like to give themselves more options than that.

Get a digital camera

For the latest information on using digital photography equipment in your eBay business, visit eBay's terrific member-to-member board that's specifically for photos. There you will find Community members sharing many helpful hints and suggestions. It can be found at http://forums.ebay.com/db2/forum.jsp?forum=99. eBay's Reviews & Guides area (which you can easily get to through eBay's site map) can be of great help also.

Your Shipping Station

Before too long you'll be packaging and shipping dozens of items each week. Chapter 8 will provide you with everything you'll need to know about efficiently packaging and shipping your products, no matter what their size, shape, or weight and no matter what their final destinations may be. For now, as you plan your PowerShop, you'll want to keep in mind some of the basic needs of this part of your operation. It's wise to plan a space for packaging your sold items and to plan for the materials you'll need to protect them, package them, label them, and get them on their way.

Just as you set aside a place to do your photography, you'll also want to set aside a place for packaging your sold merchandise. This space will probably be larger than your photography area, and you must also factor in some storage space for your packing materials. You'll need a table or other platform large and sturdy enough to support the item you are packaging. If you're wrapping one or two items, most of us can comfortably operate on the floor, but when you're doing bulk packaging, you need to take your poor back into consideration. You'll be more comfortable working at the level of a table or counter.

Determine what types of packaging materials you'll need for your items while you're getting everything put into place and stock them in enough quantity to get you started. That way, you don't have to interrupt your flow to run around finding just the right boxes, packing materials, tapes, and labels while orders are coming in and e-mail is waiting for your attention. Basic supplies include but are not necessarily limited to:

Boxes or mailing tubes

Padded envelopes

Bubble wrap

Packing peanuts

Tape, either clear or brown

Labels

Scale, preferably digital

In addition to these things, you'll need scissors and markers; a utility knife is often handy. Plus, you'll need adequate storage to allow you to keep all these materials handy, but neatly tucked away too. Don't panic at the thought of acquiring and keeping all this. Chapter 8 is full of great tips about shipping your items, including a lot of suggestions for getting free or very inexpensive materials.

You'll Need a Digital Scale

A digital shipping scale is a must-have seller's tool, especially if you're planning to sell a variety of items. Couple a digital scale with a service such as Stamps.com, explained in Chapter 8, and you may never have to go to the post office again (well almost never). Newer models have large readouts, special slots for letters, and a hold feature that lets you remove your parcel and still view the weight. Figure on spending between $45 and $100 (price varies with features and capacity).

As you might guess, one of the best places to buy a digital scale is eBay itself. Type in Postage Meters, Scales as eBay search terms, and you're likely to get hundreds of products to choose from. Some have remote displays, can handle items that weigh hundreds of pounds, and can process hundreds of pieces of mail at one time. Your needs are likely more modest, and a simple scale with a capacity of 50 pounds or so is probably all you need, depending, of course, on what you're planning to sell.

» Consider a thermal printer for your labels

Just to whet your appetite, we'll share with you one great shipping tip now so you don't have to wait all the way till Chapter 8. Get yourself a thermal printer for your labels. You can either rent one of these from the USPS or UPS, or you can buy one. They often appear at dramatically reduced prices right on eBay. The real advantage to using a thermal printer for your labels is that you eliminate the need for toner, since the printers use heat to mark the labels. As an extra bonus, both UPS and the USPS will provide the labels to you without charge. Once you pay for the printer itself, you eliminate the costs of the consumables necessary for all your label printing tasks.

Miscellaneous Tools

You will certainly come up with your own tools and gadgets that you find useful to your individual business needs. All PowerSellers have their own little systems to make things work for them. One PowerSeller who operates high up in the Rockies needs a notebook computer. He simply has no high-speed access available except for a "hot-spot" at the closest Starbucks. He goes there to do all of his major uploading and downloading, so for him a notebook is a necessity of life. Another seller told us he uses a T-Mobile SideKick so that when he travels to buy inventory, he can easily stay in touch remotely with his home office. Still other PowerSellers told us they'd be lost without their cell phones or mobile Web devices. You'll find your own special loyalty to the devices you come across, and then you'll be able to give advice to less-experienced sellers too.

» Pick up the phone

In the beginning, you'll probably find the phone line you have now is all you need. You may actually be able to eliminate a phone line, if you've had a separate one installed for your computer dial-up. Once you have high-speed access, that phone line will be obsolete, so close it out; or better yet, use it for your business phone line. Whether you use your family's phone line or keep a separate one for your business, you want to present a businesslike manner when you answer that phone. If a customer is trying to reach you, it makes a much better impression if you answer in a businesslike manner. Likewise, if you're waiting to hear back from a potential supplier, you don't want your toddler to pick up the phone for you. It just doesn't make a good impression.

After working from home for decades, we've learned the best approach is to answer with a "business" voice and greeting. Not only does this send a clear signal to prospective business partners and customers, but it also lets your friends and family subtly know that you're working. It's much easier to get right to the point and then ask the caller whether you can call back in a little while if you've made it clear to them they've reached you while you're at work. Remember, as a PowerSeller, you'll be putting lots of hours into your job, and helping the other people in your life adjust to that in big ways and small will make life better for everyone.

It is almost difficult now to remember when phone lines didn't include voice mail or answering machines. Once it was a big deal to be asked to leave a message, but now it's uncommon to find someone who doesn't have the ability to let the machine get the phone. If you don't have voice mail or an answering machine, get one. You'll have times when you're busy and just don't want to interrupt your concentration to pick up the phone. You'll also have messages you simply don't want to miss from suppliers and customers. Knowing that a message can still get to you while you run to the post office will reduce the stress in your daily life.

Finally, provide yourself with unlimited long-distance calling. These plans vary from area to area, so you may have to do a little research to find which one is best for you. But, you want the freedom and comfort of knowing you can pick up the phone and dial long-distance any time of the day or evening without worrying about how much each call is going to cost. You need to have this level of comfort, especially when you're researching suppliers. That's a part of your business that may require a great deal of phone time. You don't want to worry about the meter running, and you don't want to have to pay exorbitant long-distance charges either. Your best bet may be your long-distance provider, or you may actually do better with a cell phone company. Either way, do what you have to do to make it no problem at all for you to pick up the phone and dial.

Nick Boyd—TraderNick

TraderNick was already a coin and collectibles dealer when he discovered eBay in 1995. He had a full-time job and pursued his business only as a sideline, when he started selling online. In 1997 he was able to begin working for himself, from home, selling his items exclusively on eBay. Within four years, he was ready to answer his "itch" and open a brick-and-mortar store of his own. Now he operates both his offline store and his online eBay business. Within the last few years, Nick has also developed a thriving wholesale business, selling to other coin dealers. So, as of now, his business has three main focuses: his eBay sales, his wholesale business, and the coin shows he attends every other weekend.

Nick calls eBay a "natural extension of what I already do for a living." Today, he ships between 150 and 250 packages per week. His feedback number, when we spoke, was nearing 11,000 and he still had a positive rating of 99.9 percent! He currently has two full-time employees and a staff of part-time workers who step in on an "as-needed" basis.

Nick has been actively buying coin collections from all over the United States for more than 10 years. He buys from private collections, estates, other dealers, and coin shows. He also visits coin shops and antique markets. He said he doesn't have much luck with garage and yard sales, so he doesn't use these as inventory sources. He travels throughout the Southeast a lot to buy his inventory, and he always drives so that he can stop along the way when he finds antique markets and coin shops. Nick has begun to fulfill yet another dream of his within the last few years. Now he travels internationally to attend coin shows. "My favorite show abroad (so far)," Nick told us, "is the Hong Kong Coin Fair." International travel is something Nick hopes to continue in the future.

He said the biggest change he's seen in the last 10 years of selling coins is the same problem that has befallen the hobby of coin collecting itself. When he began his business, he said, he had plenty of coins and too few buyers. Now he has the opposite trouble to contend with. He has plenty of buyers, but keeping his inventory fresh is a challenge. Fortunately, he enjoys both the hobby and the travel.

When he began on eBay, Nick had a friend who showed him all about using the site. They worked together while Nick built his eBay skills. In return, he has happily helped other people come on to eBay as sellers. Today, Nick says that eBay itself is your best marketing tool for your eBay business. He attributes his marketing success to his descriptive auction listing titles and his accurate descriptions. His PowerSeller status and near-perfect positive feedback rating help assure his customers that they're in good hands and also provide good advertising and marketing for his business.

When we asked Nick about his goals three years ago, he said his dream was to have one or two employees to run his eBay business and one employee to run his shop. Then he could spend 100 percent of his time traveling to build his inventory. Today, not only does he have a well-trained and independent staff, but he is also planning to open a second shop. When we spoke, he was just looking for the right location. Now, he has a goal of pursuing more personal time, including the chance to enjoy some further advanced training in Tae Kwon Do, since last year he earned his black belt!

When we asked about what he's learned from his years on eBay, Nick said he really wishes he had started to integrate all of the aspects of his auction business much earlier than he did. He said his goal has been to make everything seamless, and that's not as easy as one might think. "I'm constantly working at trying to make the 'flow' a little smoother." As of 2007, he chuckled, his operation still isn't quite seamless, but it's been a good long time since they had to endure any major "tweaks."

Nick is now living his life in beautiful central Florida with his wife and three children. He's earning his living by working at the thing he loves the most. He's a member of the American Numismatic Association and the Florida United Numismatists, and he's a well-respected member of the eBay PowerSeller's community. He enjoys his travels and has every reason to believe the goals he's defined for himself are achievable. It sounds like an excellent life to us!

Pick up the phone

From Mom and Pop to PowerShop Checklist

✓ I'm planning to automate my business from the start and keep scalability in mind.

✓ I've reviewed my computer equipment. I am networking my computers. I have a broadband connection to the Internet.

✓ I'm checking into using QuickBooks for my accounting.

✓ I have added counters to at least some of my listings.

✓ I've started planning for my Web site.

✓ Auction analysis tools can increase my effectiveness as a seller, and I've starting researching products from Andale and HammerTap.

✓ I've set aside space for photography and will consider lighting and background.

✓ I've bought or plan to buy a digital camera, digital scale, a thermal printer, and perhaps a scanner.

✓ I've set aside space for my shipping station and considered organization.

Chapter 4

Automate Your Auctions for Smooth Selling

Know what's important when you go shopping

Now that you have your PowerShop ready to go, we've got one last tool to recommend, your auction management (AM) software. Although you can live a whole lifetime using eBay for fun—and maybe even a little profit—without auction management software, once you've really started on your way to PowerSeller status, you're going to need this tool. Trying to be a PowerSeller without it is almost like trying to be a carpenter without a level. You may be able to make it happen, but you'll be making life more difficult than it needs to be.

Auction management tools will provide the efficiencies you'll need to process your listings and sales in the volume you'll experience as a PowerSeller. Of all the PowerSellers we've worked with, only two were not using an auction management program. Those two sold only very high-priced items. This allowed them to qualify as PowerSellers with only a few sales each month. If that describes your intended operation, go ahead to the next chapter. But if, like most PowerSellers, you'll be processing dozens if not hundreds or even thousands of sales per month, you will very quickly need to get automated to stay on top of your work. eBay recommends you consider an auction management program once you're selling more than 10 items per month on the site. Many sellers would say you could wait a bit longer (but not too much longer)!

What can you expect from auction management software? You can expect the software to support you in every step of your transaction. From creating the listing and managing your images, to e-mail communications with your buyers, shipping support, and feedback services, all of these features should be part of any well-thought-out program. There are several dozen auction management programs from which to choose, and finding the one that's right for you will require research on your part, but we'll help.

» Know what's important when you go shopping

Scott Samuel, who created the first counters, and who we introduced in the last chapter, has been online for many years. In 2000, his company, Honesty.com, was sold to Andale, one of the largest providers of auction management services. Scott obviously knows what's important when you're shopping for an auction management product. He recommends that when you are evaluating an auction management program, you should consider these four most important factors:

1. Simplicity
2. Learning curve
3. Problem resolution
4. Customer service

To this list we would add that you consider what the software actually does for you and how it will fit in with your operation.

Which of these factors is the most important? Ultimately it's customer service. If your software freezes up, what are you going to do? Who are you going to call? When you deal with hundreds of transactions a day, maybe thousands per week, problems are going to occur, and you will need someone to stand behind you.

To try out the companies whose products you are considering, send test e-mails to them. See how quickly they respond. Look at the "About Us" page on their Web sites. How many people are behind the company? Who are they? E-mail some of those people. Test out how quickly and how well they respond. "You have to have access to someone at the company who you can trust," says Scott.

What Should Your Auction Management Program Do for You?

The most basic requirement of your auction management tool is that it keeps all your information in one place and makes it simple for you to use and manipulate that information when you need to. Your goal in choosing auction management tools is to be able to have a system that allows you to input your data only once. Every keystroke you save equals time you can spend on more productive efforts in building your business. So, go for a system that allows you the power and flexibility to input your data and then make it work for you.

Auction management companies offer similar services, so what should you look for when you go shopping for your own system? We'll step you through the features you'll be most likely to need and give you some tips for learning more about the tools that might be right for you.

Know what's important when you go shopping

Create Your Listings

The system you choose should make it simple for you to create your auction listings and do it quickly and in bulk. That means it should offer you templates for your listings that will allow you to create multiple auction listings without keying in every piece of information. A variety of templates will allow you to alter the look of your auction listings easily and without the need for you to know or use or hypertext markup language (HTML), which is the computer language in which Web pages are written. We assume you're familiar with it, but if you're not, in reality it sounds a lot more imposing than it is. It isn't difficult to incorporate basic HTML instructions (defining treatment of headings, colors, and other elements) into your listings. They can be as simple as inserting <p> to indicate where a new paragraph should begin. Your auction management software will have a built-in HTML editor that allows you to incorporate the HTML codes using the equivalent of a word processing program.

The program you choose will allow you to import your already-existing auction listings into the new management tool, seamlessly so that you minimize the effect switching your system has on posting your auction listings. There's no doubt, however, that for large sellers especially, choosing a new auction management platform will consume a lot of time, so you must plan and allow for that. You will want to avoid, for example, adding a new system at the same time you're trying to integrate a whole new product line.

You will want your program to offer you image hosting services or to make it simple for you to import your photo files from a separate image hosting service. Your auction management software should also allow you to schedule your listings to start when you determine you want your auctions to begin. This way, you can create all of your listings at one time and then have them automatically begin on a schedule that you determine. For PowerSeller David Yaskulka his first serious foray into a non-eBay auction management solution resulted from measuring what he was paying for eBay scheduling and image services. "These two items alone can pay for non-eBay AM," he said.

Automate Your Communications

You will spend a good amount of time reading, sending, and answering your e-mail. A good deal of this work can be automated to cut down on the amount of time and energy you need to spend on this task. You cannot replace the good quality of customer service that responding individually to a customer's question will bring, but you can automate the more routine forms of e-mail that you must send for every transaction. Your auction management tool should allow you to automate your winning bidder e-mails, your payment reminder e-mails, your "thank you" e-mails, and your feedback responses. The most flexible programs offer you choices of forms for these functions so that your e-mails and feedbacks don't become too robotic. For example, it's not unusual to have a selection of different positive feedback responses available, with the system automatically rotating them to give your feedback a less automated feel.

Manage Your Inventory

Using your auction management tools, you should be able to quickly determine which of your items have sold and which have not. Then the software should make it simple for you to relist any items that haven't sold. You should also be able to see the status of all your sales to determine which ones have been paid, shipped, received, and noted in feedback. Some programs, but not all, will track your inventory and notify you when your supply of a particular item is running low. These may also help you track the expenses you incur for sourcing your products so that you can compare your sources for their cost-efficiencies.

Track Your Expenses

Your auction management software should allow you to quickly determine all of your operating fees, including your eBay fees and your PayPal expenses. You should also be able to export all of your accounting information to your accounting software, whether you choose QuickBooks, Quicken, or Excel. Further, the program should offer you graphic views and charts to help you see exactly how much money you are spending and earning.

Complete the Sale and Ship Your Item

Choose an auction automation system that will allow you to integrate with the USPS, UPS, and Fedex. This will make it easier for you to complete the transaction, calculate your customers' shipping charges, print shipping labels, and track shipping expenses. Or, if your business model squarely aligns you with one carrier (e.g., if you sell cheap, light items), drill down especially carefully on how the auction management software works with that carrier. The devil is in the details here.

Sell through Several Channels

More and more successful PowerSellers are eventually moving beyond eBay to sell through other venues too, including their own Web sites. This is a theme we'll come back to again and again throughout this book. The question for this chapter is: "When you're ready to expand beyond the familiar confines of eBay will your auction management company be able to handle your listings and transactions, etc., or will you have to start looking around for another one?" If you've been relying on one of eBay's tools, the answer is undoubtedly no off-site selling, start new research.

Once you start to move away from eBay, you may want to send data feeds of your product line to comparison shopping engines, such as Google Product Search, Shopping.com, Shopzilla, and others. Auction management companies can help there too. You'll find that many auction management companies have retooled and broadened their services to help you make the transition from eBay seller to e-commerce maven.

How Do You Choose?

You will find that there is a great deal of competition among companies that provide auction management tools. There is also a wide range of features and functions available with these products, and pricing among the different products is very competitive. You may just find the program you like best here in the descriptions we'll offer you, but if you're still not sure, you should continue your own research.

» Start with Auction Software Review

One place to start your research is Auction Software Review at www.auctionsoftwarereview.com, shown in Figure 4-1. This site was created and is maintained by Andy Geldman of the United Kingdom. In researching auction management tools for his own

FIGURE 4-1 The Auction Software Review is a good place to start researching auction management and related software and services.

use, he realized there was no central source of information about these products. He set about creating one of his own. The site breaks eBay software down into about 20 categories including management, promotion, market analysis, business tools, image hosting, and ad creation.

In addition to auction management software, you'll find information about auction analysis software, sniping tools (for placing last-minute bids automatically), and buying tools and also about consultants who can guide you through all this.

For a quick fix on what's available, program features, and company contact details, there's no better source of information. As we write this, Auction Software Review describes about 300 products from well over 100 companies. The biggest change since we last reviewed the site is that there's no longer any

Start with Auction Software Review

charge to access all this great information. You can view all the content without even registering for the site.

Many people who use the site aren't shy about sharing their opinions in its thriving forums. The site is overflowing with priceless input from your fellow sellers. There are three categories of forum postings: Software and Services, Ads and Announcements, and eBay and Online Selling Chat. But that's only the tip of the iceberg. You can drill down these categories to get to some very specific areas, such as book reviews, digital camera discussions, and debates about listing times. What's more all the forum content is searchable.

Of course, not all posters are created equal. Some will be there primarily to promote products, so you have to be aware that they have an agenda. But we did find many helpful knowledgeable people posting for nothing more than the chance to share their considerable knowledge. We can't think of a better place to start your research into auction management software than this site and its forums in particular. When the time is right, calling people who actually use the software is a good idea also.

The product reviews on the site should not be taken at face value. (Who are the reviewers? Why aren't some popular programs getting more than a couple of reviews?) But, there's no doubt that you can use the site to explore software you may not have thought of and to locate companies you may not be familiar with.

Andy Geldman, the affable Brit who provides access to all of this information, is one of the most knowledgeable people we know in the auction automation field. The biggest development he's seen in the last couple of years may be that eBay now shows programmers how its brain works at no cost. Um, that is, it makes its "API" free (API stands for application program interface). Software developers need access to a company's API to create customized applications that work with its software, or in eBay's case, site. Now that this barrier to use has been dropped, a lot of formerly "unofficial" auction management programs have converted to the API, Andy told us. As a result they have greatly improved the quality of their applications without increasing prices. Recent years also saw the launch of MarketBlast, "a well-featured AM program for a one-time off fee of $149," Andy noted, and "Auctiva's completely free (but a little basic) Web-based AM tool." We'll share more on these tools and others in the pages to follow.

Some Suggestions to Get You Started

Because there are so many different auction management programs from which to choose, and because they can all seem very similar in their features, we've decided to give you a boost in your decision-making process. We've chosen a few different programs to describe here. You may be wondering why we chose the ones we did, so we'll briefly explain. First of all, to be included in our discussion, the program had to have been recommended to us by a PowerSeller. That's the only way we could begin to assess a tool's efficiencies—by talking to someone who actually used it. Next, we chose the programs that came up again and again in our research. If more than a few PowerSellers were using it, we thought that was meaningful. Finally, we decided to start our discussion with the auction management tools eBay itself offers. Many of the PowerSellers we spoke with never went farther than eBay in finding a tool to manage their affairs. Sticking with eBay seemed easy and comfortable for them. And unless you're selling more than a few dozen items a week or branching out to other channels, eBay's solutions may serve your purposes just fine. But once sellers ventured out to third-party providers they were generally glad they did. We'll leave the final choice to you—as you're the only one who really knows what you want.

To organize this discussion, we're splitting the auction management world into three camps: eBay's home-grown tools, companies that provide services mostly for small to mid-level sellers, and finally the two companies in a league of their own: ChannelAdvisor (CA) and Marketworks (MW). We're not saying this list is complete and that there aren't other companies out there who could meet your needs. For example, among the larger PowerSellers especially, Infopia (http://www.infopia.com/website/) is becoming increasingly well respected.

» Consider eBay's auction management tools

eBay offers its own suite of auction management software. And again, many of the PowerSellers we spoke with who started with these tools never migrated beyond them. Not only do they tend to be less expensive than "outside" solutions, they are also guaranteed to work seamlessly with eBay. There

Consider eBay's auction management tools

are four different tools you can choose from: Blackthorne Basic, Blackthorne Pro, Selling Manager, and Selling Manager Pro. (Another program, TurboLister, is strictly for listing.) We'll focus only on BlackThorne Pro and Selling Manager Pro, because these two offer the most power and are most suitable for the PowerSeller you will soon be. Blackthorne Pro, shown in Figure 4-2, is a desktop-based tool, while Selling Manager Pro is Web-based. Among the tasks these tools can automate are:

- Listing creation and scheduling
- Inventory management
- Sales information tracking
- Postsale information and management
- Monthly reporting

FIGURE 4-2 eBay's own Blackthorne Pro auction management software offers a desktop solution to your auction management needs.

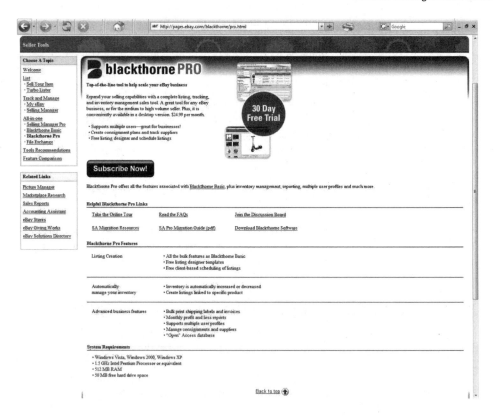

Consider eBay's auction management tools

Selling Manager Pro, shown in Figure 4-3, offers robust features for automating your customer communications, and monthly reporting features. With Selling Manager Pro, you will have:

- Automatic notification e-mail for both payments received and items shipped
- Automatic feedback left when buyer pays
- Printer-friendly views for printing your records
- Tracking of your buyer communication and whether your items have been paid or shipped in bulk
- Records of all your buyer communications to help you process Nonpaying Bidder reports

FIGURE 4-3 Selling Manager Pro is eBay's Web-based auction management software.

Selling Manager Pro seems to offer more features than Blackthorne Pro, but there are also some disadvantages of

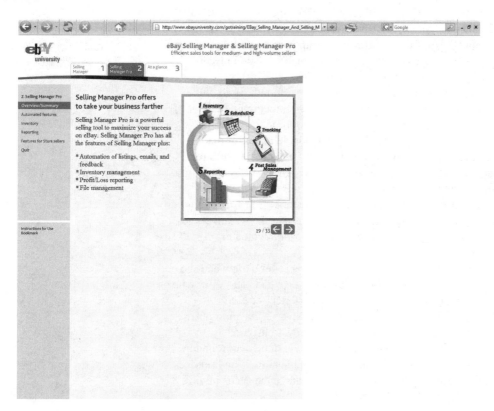

Consider eBay's auction management tools

choosing the tool with more features. For one thing, Selling Manager Pro does not allow you to create your auction listings offline. If you want to create your listings without being connected to the Web, you'll have to also use eBay's separate Turbo Lister program. Turbo Lister is free, and the sellers we spoke with who use Selling Manager Pro do couple it with Turbo Lister. They prefer the convenience of creating their listings offline and then just going online to upload them. They also find the Turbo Lister tool to be a more efficient way to create their listings. Some PowerSellers never move beyond the combination of using Turbo Lister and Selling Manager Pro.

Keep in mind Selling Manager Pro will store your data for only 120 days, after which you can no longer access your records. And should you cancel your subscription, your data will only remain on the system for 30 days. You can work around that by downloading your records monthly, which is a good plan anyway; but if you're not always conscientious, you could lose some of your older data. Blackthorne stores all of your data on your own computer, so files are maintained indefinitely. You'll still have to back up your files, and possibly store them on an external device eventually, but no one can make your data inaccessible. Selling Manager Pro costs $15.99 per month; Blackthorne Pro is $24.99 per month. Both come with a 30-day free trial, plus (and here's something interesting) Selling Manager Pro is free with Blackthorne Pro!

By now, it's completely understandable that after reading these descriptions you're still unsure of which eBay solution may be best for you. Fortunately eBay's Tools Wizards at http:// pages.ebay.com/sell/toolrecommendations.html steps you through the process of evaluating these tools. You simply answer the onscreen questions about your needs and the wizard comes back with specific recommendations. Aren't computers wonderful!

There likely comes a time in a PowerSeller's life when she or he is ready to move beyond eBay's low-cost tools and work with something more robust. That time is different for each PowerSeller. You may decide to move beyond eBay into other selling venues, or your business may grow tremendously, so you're listing say dozens of items per day. Here's our roundup then of other, non-eBay, auction management tools and services. The companies that follow can easily handle the needs of all but the largest PowerSellers.

» Auction Hawk

Employee-owned Auction Hawk is one of the few services that charges a flat fee, with add-on services (like gallery and e-mail managing) included in one monthly price. This leads them to claim that their services cost 50 to 80 percent less than competitive products. You would expect that as a smaller company, it would offer better customer service, and that seems to be true.

One of the real advantages of Auction Hawk is that the company keeps their services simple to use. Here are some of the features of Auction Hawk:

- **Listing Capabilities**   The Auction Hawk 1-Page Lister offers one-click listings. You can schedule your listings, create bulk listings, and manage repeatable listings. With 2,000 template designs for your listings, you have a huge variety of looks to choose from.

- **Image Hosting**   Auction Hawk allows easy integration of images into your listings. With 1-Page Lister, you can crop and edit your images. It also includes watermarking, to safeguard your photos from being lifted by other sellers. The different pricing plans for 1-Page Lister offer you between 50MB and 500MB of storage, depending on the plan you choose. Either is enough so that you don't have to worry about running out of space.

- **Inventory Management**   The At-a-Glance inventory list page lets you see how many listings are pending, current, sold, or unsold. You can also list items separately and not have them put into your general inventory.

- **E-mail Handling**   Tracks e-mails sent. Automated winning-bidder e-mail is sent immediately at auction end.

- **Postsale Features**   With Auction Hawk, you'll get automatic invoices sent, bulk feedback delivery, feedback monitoring to track the status of all your feedback, and feedback alerts to be notified of unfavorable feedback received. Badly Behaved Bidder is a feedback protection service that helps you keep your positive percentage as high as possible. It does this by scouring all bidders for all feedback to determine their negative feedback history. It then mails you a report, as often as every day of the week. This way you can block the more "mischievous" bidders from buying from you. Another feedback-related service is called Email Tracking. With this service, Auction Hawk sends winning bidder notifications with a pixel so sellers know if and when the buyer reads the email. Auction Hawk then sends the seller this information, so that the seller can prove that the buyer received the e-mail should the buyer claim he or she did not. The program also offers bulk-relist support and lifetime archiving for all your listings.

- **Customer Service/Education** A free monthly e-mail newsletter for eBay PowerSellers features tips, tricks, and tactics for business management. Discussion boards provide help from other users, and e-mail support brings you customer service help from the company.

- **Pricing** Auction Hawk features flat fees with no extra listing fees or percentage charges. The Basic plan is for posting up to 220 listings per month, and you have up to 50MB of image space for $12.99. The Power plan offers up to 440 listings per month and 100MB of image space for $21.99 per month. The Professional plan offers up to 880 listings per month and 175MB of image space for $29.99 per month. Finally, the Unlimited plan offers unlimited listings per month and 500MB of image storage for $44.99 per month. For further information go to www.auctionhawk.com.

» Auctiva

One of the biggest recent developments in the auction management field, according to Andy Geldman, was the launch of Auctiva's completely free, Web-based AM tool. While a bit basic, this seller solution runs in your Web browser whether you use a PC or a Mac and, truly, you can't beat the price. But first, some background.

Jeff Schlicht, the founder of Auctiva, was once an avid online auction seller himself. In the course of trying to create hundreds of auction listings, including lumps of coal from the wreck of the Titanic, he realized that there had to be a way to automate the process and make it easier to complete. That's when he created Auction Poster (Auctiva's predecessor), which allowed him to triple his listings.

Auctiva, shown in Figure 4-4, targets small businesses and individuals selling to consumers. It has been featured in many publications and has won many awards for previous incarnations of the software. Here are some of Auctiva's features:

■ **Listing Capabilities**   One Page Listing Tool is a simple-to-use tool for creating professional-looking auction listings. You can choose from over 500 professionally designed templates. And you can also schedule your listings in bulk using campaigns, which can save you a lot of money. You can create profiles with boilerplate information that you tend to use all the time, allowing you to eliminate the need to rekey it. You can load your profiles directly onto the Listing screen.

FIGURE 4-4 Auctiva provides auction management services targeted to small businesses and those who sell to consumers.

Auctiva

- **Image Hosting**   Unlimited Image Hosting is just as it says—it's *free*. The company also helps you manage your images with its folder organizational scheme.

- **Inventory Management**   With Store and Store Window you can choose to have a store window run in all your auctions to help you cross-promote your items to potential buyers. The Auctiva Store showcases all of your currently running auctions in one format, including pages for information about your business, contact information and blogs (which may improve your rank in Web searches). The Auctiva Store is customizable and includes its own Web address that you can drive traffic to. You can even choose to purchase a personalized domain name for your Auctiva Store.

- **E-mail Handling**   You can create custom e-mails to send to your customers that brand your business and lead them to your other listings. You can also automate and customize your feedback process making it fast and easy to leave feedback for your customers.

- **Postsale Features**   Auctiva boasts a "revenue sharing insurance system," which allows you to offer insurance to your customers for less than what it would cost through the USPS. Plus Auctiva shares with you the revenue it receives for each sold insurance policy. Auctiva Checkout makes it easy to add Auctiva Shipping Insurance to earn extra revenue quickly, and your listings are featured in ads at the bottom of the checkout page to encourage repeat purchase.

- **Customer Service/Education**   Auctiva, based in Chico, CA, offers e-mail support and online forums where you can exchange information with other Auctiva users.

- **Pricing**   Auctiva's relatively recent move to make its product free seems to be paying off quite well. The company claims on its Web site to have over 125,000 registered users, and to "facilitate nearly 500,000 listings per day on eBay, nearly 1 in 20 of all eBay auctions." For further information go to www.auctiva .com.

» inkFrog

An important focus of inkFrog's business is image hosting. The company prides itself on having the most reliable and fastest-loading images on eBay. Image hosting is as important to them as their auction tools. Targeting both small- and large-volume eBay sellers, the company's marketing displays a sense of fun, as shown by their home page featured in Figure 4-5. Their frog-based logo is both appealing and omnipresent on their site and in their materials.

Greg Sisung founded BayPal, an online auction management service that then became inkFrog. The company claims that it is now growing by leaps and bounds. This group seems to have created a great sense of customer loyalty. You'll see what we

FIGURE 4-5 inkFrog brings a sense of fun to their auction management software and their home page.

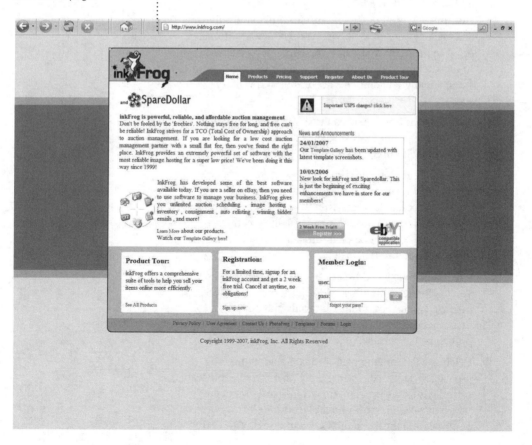

inkFrog

mean if you check out their message boards, which are full of enthusiasm. Here are some features of the inkFrog program:

- **Listing Capabilities**   inkfrog's Lister options and settings enable you to build your auction on a single page. You can schedule, launch, track, and manage your eBay listings from this page. Through inkFrog's Gallery Showcase feature you can display your other active listings on any page. Its Sonny tool allows you to create your own templates.

- **Image Hosting**   inkFrog views its image hosting capabilities and tools as the thing that sets it apart from its competition. Just upload your images to their servers, where they're stored in your account. From there, you can view and edit them with inkFrog's "image magician" tools.

- **Inventory Management**   With inkFrog, you can track and manage your inventory so you know when it makes sense to list items and when you should order them. In fact, thanks to its auto listing feature you can automatically launch items according to inventory levels.

- **E-mail Handling**   You can manage winning-bidder e-mails, create auto e-mails, and send payment reminders with inkFrog.

- **Postsale Features**   inkFrog's Sales Manager is now integrated with eBay's checkout procedure and is no longer a separate feature. After eBay's Checkout system kicks in, inkFrog's Sales Manager helps you track which items need to be paid for, shipped, and then ultimately require feedback.

- **Customer Service/Education**   Active forums allow you to interact with other inkFrog users, as well as inkFrog employees. Online tutorials and e-mail assistance help you learn to use the tools and solve any problems that surface.

- **Pricing**   Two pricing plans are available for inkFrog products. The Image Hosting Only plan is for people who use eBay's listing programs or a third-party lister and who only need image hosting. The cost for this service is $6.95 per month, and it allows you to post up to 4,000 images per month. The Unlimited plan, at $9.95 per month, includes image hosting of up to 4,000 images. Its Lister boasts more than 300 prebuilt templates. Plus, thanks to its recent acquisition of former competitor SpareDollar, you have the option of using the more than 200 "classic" templates, formerly available only through that company. Or, you may create and save your templates with Sonny. You can view and manage your current eBay listings, archive your auctions, and add images to existing auctions. You can schedule your auctions and bulk-list them at intervals, manage your closed auctions, automatically relist unsold auctions, and resubmit duplicate or edited closed auctions. It will also permit automatic winning bidder e-mails, inventory tracking, and automatic feedback. You can add Gallery Showcase to either one of inkFrog's offerings. With this add-on, you can include a flash previewer in each of your current auctions so that customers can see your other items up for sale. This also includes a Web page that shows all of your current auctions with a thumbnail picture next to each. For further information go to www.inkfrog.com.

» MarketBlast

Founded only in 2005, MarketBlast (Figure 4-6) has made quite a splash during its short life. Unique in the industry, MarketBlast's software can be downloaded for a one-time fee, then it's yours to use forever. It's geared solely to eBay sellers, and offers a free 30-day trial so we definitely recommend you at least try it out for yourself. Its feature list is really quite impressive, and we have room here only for the highlights:

- **Listing Capabilities**   With MarketBlast you can update your listings in bulk mode, all at once; easily organize and search your listings; duplicate and schedule your listings and retain complete access to all your information whether or not you're connected to the Internet. MarketBlast includes 50 templates, with "more available for download."

- **Image Hosting**   Image storage is through flickr.com. You can automatically upload your images, and watermark them.

MarketBlast

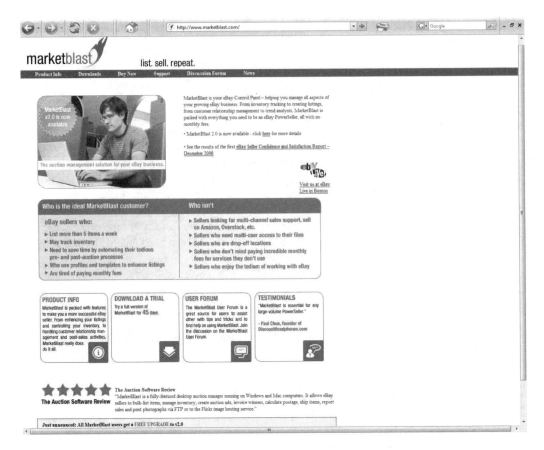

Inventory Management MarketBlast allows you to easily import your data; receive alerts when it's time to reorder merchandise; manage multiple sources for inventory; track sales data, including sales per day and your average fees per sale. A consignment feature helps you manage and track your consignors, manage your communications regarding the status of the auctions you're running on others' behalf, and simplify mailings.

E-mail Handling MarketBlast can handle all of your e-mail communication without needing any add-on software. You can use it to create and mail newsletters and manage your mailing list.

Postsale Features With MarketBlast you can know at a glance the status of an item that's been sold,

FIGURE 4-6 MarketBlast is a new player in the auction management field. Unlike most of its competitors, you download their software for a one-time fee.

create invoices, easily specify your shipper and whether or not insurance is included. You can easily communicate with your winning bidder postsale, all the way to feedback. MarketBlast also helps you to organize and mine your customer database for the information you need, and business reports help you to track your business against the goals you've set, view your performance by category, and do "what-if" analyses.

- **Customer Service/Education**   MarketBlast provides e-mail support, discussion boards, online learning opportunities, and documentation right on its site.

- **Pricing**   There is a one-time fee of $149. For further information go to www.marketblast.com.

» Vendio

Silicon Valley–based Vendio (see Figure 4-7) was one of the first companies to provide third-party services to eBay sellers. It has grown continuously since its founding in 1999, and in November 2006 it acquired one of its largest competitors— Andale. Servicing tens of thousands of customers each month, Vendio now claims to be the largest auction management company in the industry. Each month, Vendio-supported merchants sell more than $100 million in merchandise. Here's another way to measure the company's significance: one topic on its message board, "The eBay Outlook," had more than 400,000 posts when we checked. Now that's a community!

Vendio services include sales management, image hosting, Vendio Stores, Gallery, tools for customer management and Web hosting, and some new services, which we'll describe here. Sellers should start by subscribing to one of Vendio's two Sales Manager programs.

- **Listing Capabilities**   Sales Manager Inventory Edition (SMIE) is for sellers who sell many of the same items (e.g., electronics, books, clothing, jewelry) on a repetitive basis. SMIE was awarded the eBay Star Developer Award in 2005 as the most innovative application for the eBay platform. Vendio feels the most important part of running a business like this is the

Vendio

FIGURE 4-7 Vendio has been offering auction management and related services since 1999, and recently merged with Andale.

ability to automatically keep a continuous supply of inventory on the market at all times while keeping tight control of inventory.

Sales Manager Merchandising Edition (SMME) This version is more for sellers who specialize in selling unique items, such as collectibles. For these sellers, the ability to create attractive and professional-looking listings is what's paramount.

When sellers think of Vendio, it's usually their Gallery service that comes to mind. Vendio Gallery, which is live on over one million listings at any given time, allows sellers to showcase and display all the other items they have for sale on each of their eBay listings. If you use Vendio Gallery you can increase your sell-through rate by an average of 18 percent, based on a study conducted by the company. You can also double the number of people who view your listings.

Vendio contends that many sellers don't revise listings when they're live, opting instead to make changes only after the listing has closed. Vendio Reviser is a new product designed to make it easier to tweak your listings in response to market feedback, while they're live. Making changes in this way can increase your sell through and maximize your item's visibility. You can change listings individually or in bulk, and make changes manually, or automatically according to rules you establish (for example, to decrease an item's Buy It Now price by 2 percent every day until it's sold).

- **Vendio Stores**   With Vendio, you can create your own Web store ("in as little as three minutes"). Vendio Stores provide a cross promotion vehicle if you are using Vendio Sales Manager to list items to eBay. As an example, you can offer complementary items at checkout from your Vendio Store on eBay purchases (e.g., paper and ink cartridges with a printer purchase). Buyers can add these items to their shopping cart with each eBay sale, but you do not have to pay the extra eBay selling fee (because the extra items sold are coming from your Vendio Store and not eBay). Each day, Vendio also sends a data feed of your items to Google's comparison shopping site, Froogle.com, for increased visibility. The service helps with creating mailing lists and promoting your store. Vendio can also help you select the right domain name and will host your store as well.

Vendio's Inventory Publisher is a new service that enables you to send data feeds for your product lines to shopping sites such as Shopzilla and Froogle. This is a free service for Vendio Stores customers.

- **Image Hosting**   Image Hosting is free with either of Vendio's Sales Manager plans or its Vendio Stores service. Otherwise you can use Vendio's Image Hosting on an à la carte basis for a monthly fee from $2.95 to $49.95 depending on the storage you'll need (from 3MB to 10GB).

- **E-mail Handling**   Customer Manager allows for automated invoicing, Final Value Fee refunds, and Nonpaying Bidder alerts. It includes response templates and built-in message filtering and prioritization. Customer Manager allows you to maintain a customer

Vendio

database, to help you serve your existing customers. You can track your customers' histories to see how much and what they've bought from you. You can even track all the e-mail messages you've received from each customer. Every listing you close, customer record, and e-mail automatically gets imported into Customer Manager.

■ **Postsale Features** Vendio's complement of Reports services give you a snapshot of your sales activity, helping you to determine your best marketplaces, see which items are most successful, and track your costs. Basic profit-and-loss reports are free; more detailed reports are available for a fee.

The Buyer Appreciation Service is a free service that allows you to send automated "thank you" notes to both bidders and buyers. The e-mails provide a visible showcase of your other listings to keep bidders and buyers coming back to your listings.

■ **Customer Service/Education** Vendio makes some great tools available to help sellers become more effective.

Wholesale Index: This free service helps sellers acquire new inventory by providing lists of wholesalers or companies that specialize in tracking wholesalers such as Doba. You just click on an item category that interests you to learn about the services that can help you source relevant items.

Shipping Tools: Through this area you can learn more about the companies Vendio has partnered with, such as DHL and Stamps.com.

Payment Services: Easy access to PayPal and VeriSign Referral Program. For six months Vendio will pay you 15 percent of the fees paid by new customers you refer to the company, either through word of mouth or through links or banner ads.

Vendio's site includes a searchable Knowledge Base should you have any questions once you become a subscriber (or even before when you're evaluating their services).

Of course, there's free e-mail support. And through its Personal Assistance plan you can use Live Chat or the telephone to reach Customer Service. There's a nominal monthly fee for this service.

■ **Pricing**   Vendio's Sales Manager services are available on a flat fee (fee plus per-listing charge) or variable rate (fee plus a final-value fee) basis. The monthly fees range from $14.95 to $39.95. There is also a pay-as-you-go plan and an Annual Listing Plan. Other services such as Vendio Gallery or Reports can be added to whatever service plan you go with, for an added fee for each service. For more information visit www.vendio.com.

ChannelAdvisor and Marketworks: A League of Their Own

A lot has changed in the three years or so since we first started researching auction management software. For example, companies offer much, much more space for hosting images, there's a lot more help available for sellers who want to move beyond eBay and sell on other channels, and some companies now offer services for sellers who take on consignments. One thing that hasn't changed though is that ChannelAdvisor and Marketworks remain the companies best able to handle the needs of eBay's biggest sellers.

PowerSellers are nearly unanimous on this point. "Anyone who is doing more than 100 auctions a week without Marketworks or ChannelAdvisor needs to have their head read," said Australian PowerSeller Phil Leahy. While Phil refers to CA and MW as "Coke and Pepsi," he'd be among the first to say it's important to choose the right one. Flash: As we went to press, ChannelAdvisor and Marketworks have merged.

›› ChannelAdvisor

ChannelAdvisor (CA) (along with Marketworks) are the 800-pound gorillas in the world of auction management. CA's purpose in life is to do a lot more than manage your eBay auctions for you. CA wants to manage *all* your e-commerce channels—your eBay auctions (or Overstock auctions, or Yahoo auctions, etc.), your Web site, your search optimization strategies, whatever. CA has a solution for it all.

Its Web site (see Figure 4-8) is noticeably sparse on details about its offerings. What it does is present a compelling case for the company as the industry leader, as the best of the best. We're

ChannelAdvisor

thinking details on specifics are sparse because CA would much prefer that you call and speak with one of their sales reps than decide based on what you've heard about them or learned from their site. That's fair enough. None of this is meant to disparage the company, whose services many PowerSellers use.

ChannelAdvisor provides both auction and "market management" software and services. Its clients range from mid-level and high-level PowerSellers all the way to Fortune 500 companies, including Sears, Nokia, and Motorola.

The company breaks down the services (solutions) it offers as follows:

- ■ **Marketplaces** ChannelAdvisor helps you build your brand across all e-commerce channels including eBay, Amazon, and Overstock.com.

FIGURE 4-8 ChannelAdvisor works with some of eBay's largest PowerSellers and can help you sell through many channels.

- **Search ChannelAdvisor** can help you learn how to sell more products and hit return on investment (ROI) targets through paid search marketing.

- **Comparison Shopping** can merchandise your products across more than 40 popular shopping destinations—including Google Base, Shopzilla, Nextag, Shopping.com, Smarter.com, and PriceGrabber.

- **E-Commerce with ChannelAdvisor** lets you create your own e-commerce Web site, which can deliver significant sales driven by search marketing and comparison shopping engine efforts.

- **Education and Events** ChannelAdvisor offers a variety of webinars that cover the most relevant and latest marketplace developments to maintain a successful business.

With regard to auctions, ChannelAdvisor enables you to do the following:

- List your products, track them, and maintain the optimal inventory levels.

- Maximize sales and margins.

- Complete your sales and then check them through a single report that covers all of your channels.

- Manage communications including feedback, unpaid items, and any other buyer notifications.

So, of course, CA will help you with the types of things any auction management company will. However, CA can also help you grow your business, not just manage it. Here's where it really distinguishes itself from the competition, helping you with:

- **Customer Acquisition** Migrate the customers you've gained through your auctions to your other sales venues, such as your own Web site.

- **Channel Diversification** Just as you know it's a good idea to diversify your financial assets, CA will help you diversify your business, too, when you're ready. Helping you add new channels and then folding in the servicing of those channels is one of its specialties.

Marketworks

■ **Managing your Consumer Base**   When you have customers flocking to your auctions, Web stores, and wherever else you're selling, tracking all those customers is a greater challenge than ever. CA not only helps you do that, but it also can help you build your brand awareness.

■ **Customer Support/Education**   ChannelAdvisor offers live chat support. You will also find a learning center, webinars, and forums on the site. Furthermore, you can submit specific cases for review and guidance. Classroom training is available in many major U.S. cities. For further information visit www.channeladvisor.com.

» Marketworks

Marketworks is a top provider of multichannel online sales automation and services for small- to mid-sized businesses. The company, whose home page is shown in Figure 4-9, began by providing auction management software to eBay sellers and is proud of the fact that they were the first eBay Certified Solution Provider (CSP). Today Marketworks states they have over 4,000 customers in 37 countries who depend on Marketworks to power their online businesses.

Marketworks targets the top-tier eBay sellers, but they also offer services to enterprise-level companies including Olympus cameras, Nautilus, and 3M, among others. Soon after Marketworks was founded, they gathered a group of 28 of the top 50 eBay sellers to create their Founders Club. They used this group to determine some of the most important features and functionality now found in their product. They turned to experienced eBayers to base their offerings on what these pros needed and wanted in auction management tools.

Marketplace management software, which includes a Marketworks hosted Web store, has the following features:

■ **Listing Capabilities**   Marketworks offers single- and bulk-item launching, scheduled launching, and customizable templates for creating listings. Thumbnail ad previews are available for bulk listings, and one-click relaunching of unsold items is possible.

FIGURE 4-9 Marketworks is another company catering to large eBay sellers, and it is especially strong in Web store design.

- **Image Hosting**   You may choose from 100MB to 1,000MB of image hosting space. You can do bulk image uploads of up to 15 images at a time. Services also include automatic image resizing and thumbnail views.

- **Inventory Management**   Marketworks includes database import utilities, bulk-inventory upload, customizable folder organization, an inventory monitor, and real-time sales activity.

- **E-mail Handling**   Automated customer notifications that include winning-bidder notifications, item shipped, payment received, and thank you notification messages are possible with Marketworks.

- **Postsale Features**   Included in Marketworks postsale features are Nonpaying Bidder notices, final value refund requests, and reciprocal feedback posting that automatically posts feedback once it's been left for you. Shipping label printing and automated invoicing with shipping and taxes calculated are also included.

- **Customer Service/Education**   Toll-free phone support, e-mail support, and online tutorials are available for helping you learn and navigate Marketworks.

- **Pricing**   You pay 2 percent of the closing price of each transaction that has a winning bidder. There's a $0.20 minimum for each successful transaction. Marketworks also has minimum monthly charges of $19.95 for up to 100MB of image hosting. If your total monthly transaction fees don't meet or exceed the monthly minimum service charge, you will be billed only the monthly fee and no per-listing fee. For further information visit www.Marketworks.com.

» Consider customized auction management software

Some PowerSellers have worked with software developers to create auction management software that is tailored to their own particular businesses. This ensures that the software they use can handle everything they need it to do. It also allows them to design the program so that it works intuitively with the structure of their own operation.

One advantage to doing this is that once you incur the initial expense of developing the software there are no ongoing expenses—you don't have to pay monthly fees to an outside company. You may, however, have additional costs down the road as you revise your software to keep it current and in synch with the changes eBay rolls out.

There are companies, such as Channel Velocity, that specialize in creating customized applications for eBay PowerSellers. They can do this by working with eBay's Application Program Interface (API). To learn more, try plugging these search terms into Google: eBay API custom "auction management." You may also consider hiring a recent college graduate for less than you'd have to pay an established company.

Consider customized auction management software

Finally, once you've got your customized auction management software up and running, you'll be able to decide if you want to sell it to other eBay sellers who are shopping for auction management software. You wouldn't be the first eBay PowerSeller to venture into the software market simply by having had the experience of developing an auction management program.

Meet
a
PowerSeller

Frank Tetro—Tessies-Toys

Frank Tetro named his eBay business for his beloved Great-Aunt Tessie. It seems she always encouraged Frank when he was young, and that encouragement helped him to have the faith he needed to start his own business. For years, before coming to eBay, Frank was in the computer business. Naturally, when he set up his eBay shop, he started with those products he knew well. He branched out into selling plasma TVs and did very well with them for a time. Today, Frank still sells Microsoft Windows software, but that isn't the main focus of his business. We'll explain the clever way Frank uses his Microsoft business before we end this profile; but, for now, let's focus on the rest of his eBay business.

Today, he sells used and refurbished electronics and cell phones. He especially likes selling niche products. "I don't like the product if it's too popular," he told us. "I like the niche products. With non-niche products, I have to beat competitors by price alone." Frank knows how difficult that can be. Niche products allow him to stand out by reputation. "If you search PowerSellers in electronics, Tessies-Toys has the finest reputation," says Frank. "The market for used electronics can be a very shady business. If you're honest, you'll stand out." Frank believes it's his personal touch that makes his business so successful. "I'm one man running a $4 million business out of my garage," he noted. "I'm sales, shipping, and customer service," chuckled Frank.

Consider customized auction management software

Frank has managed to create this successful business using eBay exclusively for his market research. Although he has tried selling on other venues, Frank still focuses his business on eBay. He considers eBay to be not only a monopoly market, but also a good business partner. He credits his own eBay PowerSeller representative with helping him get his Web site started. The same rep helped him include information about his Web site on his About Me page so that the information would be in keeping with eBay's rules. "He encouraged me not to put all my eggs in one basket," Frank told us.

Frank has built such a successful business that he no longer has to worry too much about locating sources of products or marketing his business. He still searches for new product sources, but he reports, "As you grow, they start seeking you out. They know you have the money to buy." As for marketing, Frank makes use of the SquareTrade warranty program. Because he sells refurbished electronics, many of his customers appreciate an extended warranty. He simply inserts the flyer about the SquareTrade warranty into his packaging. If the customer buys the warranty, he earns 30 percent of the fee. "I make many thousands of dollars using that flyer," says Frank. He also sometimes uses Vendio's mass mailing tool if he acquires a large inventory of products. "But, I try not to bother my customers too much," he said. "I wouldn't send a mailing out more than once a quarter, and I do get people who say, 'don't e-mail me.'"

His sales strategy no longer includes an eBay store. He claims his research has shown him that a Buy It Now and a 10-day listing are his most successful strategies. "If it's in the store, people are not compelled to actually make the purchase," he's observed. But with his 10-day listings on "day one and day two, I sell a few, but the last day, I can sell 30 phones." When we spoke, Frank was considering moving to 5-day and 7-day listings to increase the number of "last days" he could get into a month. It will be interesting to see if this change pays off for him.

Frank uses Vendio's auction management software, integrated with Endícia and automated e-mail. He uses QuickBooks for accounting. His preferred shipper is the USPS, which he uses almost exclusively. He especially likes the "beauty of the flat-rate 1-pound mailer. It's a great discovery," he remarked. "I can make my things fit into the mailer. Every month my USPS rep sends a truck with a shipment of supplies, and I have a truck come every day to pick up my orders." Those orders average 100 packages a day.

Now, about that Microsoft software. "I call it a loss-leader," Frank said. Because he's an authorized computer dealer, he can process his sales with credit cards. That lets him accumulate frequent-flyer miles at a rate of 100,000 a month! "I go first-class every time I fly!" When we spoke Frank and his family were just about ready to fly to Europe, first-class all the way. "I'm really happy with the way everything's progressed," he told us. "I once never thought I could make a living on eBay. My friends still don't believe it. I'm home every day with my kids, and I even take naps," Frank marveled.

Consider customized auction management software

Automate Your Auctions for Smooth Selling Checklist

✓ I've started researching auction management software. As I do, I'm keeping in mind: simplicity, learning curve, problem resolution, customer service, and software functionality.

✓ Auction Software Review is one of the sources I'm checking as I research.

✓ I'm starting my research with eBay's AM tools, and especially Blackthorne Pro and Selling Manager Pro.

✓ I've reviewed the capabilities of the third-party AM tools this chapter describes.

✓ I'll review ChannelAdvisor and Marketworks separately, and keep them in mind for the future.

✓ I'm considering whether or not customized AM software might be right for me.

Chapter 5

Get Your Auctions Going!

Congratulations, you're ready to start listing more auctions and earning some real money. You can be proud of yourself for all of the work that's brought you this far. You've researched your product line. You've got your "PowerShop" up and running. You've got enough inventory to get started, and you have some ideas now for where you can get more. Look at all you have accomplished. Now, let's make these auctions scream!

Chapter 5 will give you all of the ins and outs of listing your auctions. We know, you've created auction listings before, so you may be tempted to skip this chapter and move on to Chapter 6, where you'll learn to power-charge your eBay business. Please return to your seat and fasten your safety belt. You may have listed dozens of auctions already, but you haven't done it with PowerSellers' secrets in mind. We'll skip the basics, but you've still got a lot to learn about choosing the best keywords for your titles, timing your auctions, writing strong descriptions, and strategically pricing your items. We'll also cover how you can use some of eBay's community features to bolster your reputation and help keep your auctions in front of more people than you thought possible.

Before we start, here's a little word of warning. PowerSellers have very strong opinions. They didn't get to be successful without more than a little self-confidence. As you read this chapter, you'll see some conflicting tips. No, we haven't lost our minds by recommending one course of action in one tip and the opposite in the next. Different approaches work differently for PowerSellers, depending on such things as the items they handle and their personal preferences for how they operate their businesses. We decided to give you the best options suggested to us and let you decide which of those options makes the most sense for your particular business. We're not trying to confuse you, just show you the many different ways there are to be successful eBay sellers.

Your eBay Image

The eBay world is only going to know you through the image you present. Your auction listings speak volumes about your competence as a seller. Your member profile is your permanent record, and it's as precious as gold. That's even more true now that eBay has revised its feedback system so partners rate feedback variables on a scale of 1 to 5, going far beyond just positive, negative, or neutral ratings. Your customer service and shipping policies will be invaluable to keeping your eBay reputation sterling. But, there are still some other things you can do to create the kind of eBay image that will keep customers coming back and earn you a respected place in the eBay community. When all of your communication is via your computer, it's important to consider your image every time you send an e-mail or write an item description.

Your About Me Page

People tend to shop more regularly with merchants they know and trust. Your every action on eBay will contribute to your being a trustworthy business owner, but you can help your customers get to know you very easily by taking advantage of some of its community-building services such as the About Me page. You have the opportunity to use this page to create a "face" that you want the eBay world to see, so get this up and running right from the start. Once you create your About Me page a colorful (and clickable) me icon will appear next to your username wherever it appears on eBay. Members will know that by clicking on that icon they have another window into your shop and who you are as a trading partner.

If you already have an About Me page you'll want to consider changing it to include some of the tips PowerSellers have shared with us. Editing your About Me page is relatively simple. You can either edit the HTML code that's behind your current page, or you can create an entirely new one. We discussed HTML in Chapter 4, so you're already equipped to make this decision. It's a good idea to check back in from time to time just to keep everything looking fresh and current.

» Include pictures on your About Me page; show a little personality

Yes, your eBay business is serious, but here's a good place to let a little bit of the real you show. Remember, this is about image, and you want your customers to feel that they've learned a little bit about the person behind the auctions when they've read your About Me page. eBay says you can display up to two pictures on your page. So, put a picture of yourself on the page. Don't hesitate to also include one of your family members, pets, products, hobbies, or favorite possessions. Everyone loves pictures, and you become real to your customers through a visual image in a way that words simply can't match.

Have a little fun with the things you want customers to know about you. If you support a favorite cause, or if you have a special interest, tell the world about it. One seller included all of her pets as "employees" complete with descriptions of each one's job, personality, and special skills. The page was the subject of a discussion thread because it was so much fun to read. You don't have to go to quite this extreme, but reward your customers' curiosity by giving them something to smile about.

» Put your About Me page to work

Have some fun, but all play and no work isn't your goal. Make your About Me page earn its way. Use it to describe your business and products. Explain why you are the person your customers should trust. Toot your horn about your expertise and even give them some information that will prove you know what you're doing. Figure 5-1 shows you the About Me page for PowerSeller harleyglasses. You'll see how passionate Gary is about the sunglasses he sells and how well he pitches himself to his market.

Your About Me page is also the place to clearly state your policies and terms. Be sure your customers know how you handle payments, shipping, and returns. That's not to say you won't have to deal with customers who will still claim not to know your terms, but at least you'll know you're doing everything you can to minimize misunderstandings.

Include a link to your Web site in your About Me page. You'll learn even more about creating a Web site and why you'll want to do that in Chapter 6, but when you do, be sure to add a link to your site from your About Me page. eBay does not permit you to link any of your auction listings to outside Web sites, but you are allowed to include links to your favorite Web sites within your About Me page. Just make your own Web site one of your favorites. One PowerSeller, Chris of iCandy Clothing, even includes a Track Order link to his Web site so customers can check the status of their orders.

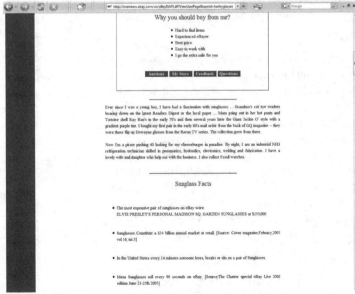

FIGURE 5-1 (a and b) PowerSeller harleyglasses uses its About Me page to provide interesting information and show a little personality too.

Use your My World page

Use your My World page

Every eBay member now gets a "My World" page. This can complement your About Me page. It provides another opportunity to show your buyers the face behind that member ID, so they can feel comfortable doing business with you. When you go to your My World page (myworld.ebay.com/<yourUserID>), which eBay has started for you if you're a registered member, you'll see that it looks a lot like a basic About Me page. For example, it will include your recent feedback. But you can customize this page with pictures and information about yourself and your business. You can include links to your auction and store listings. If you have an eBay store you can use the special store module with customizable promotion boxes. You can also briefly describe any Reviews & Guides you've written and showcase your blog. So your My World page can provide a much more textured portrait of who you are as a person and an eBay trading partner than an About Me page can. That's why you need both.

Set Your Rules

Of course, you'll need to establish rules for operating your business. Only you can decide what payment options you'll consider (Chapter 7 will help), what your refund policies will be, how much time passes between the end of your auctions and the time you expect to be paid, and how you'll handle shipping your products. All of these things are up to you, and you are well within your rights to make rules that your customers are expected to follow and then stick to the rules. You'd be foolish not to do this. You're here to make a profit, and you have reason to protect your business with good business practices and policies. Now we'll offer you some tips for striking a balance between letting your customers know the rules and sounding like a martinet.

Decide on your rules and make them clear

Once you have your rules established, you'll be able to include them in every listing, on your About Me page, and on your My World page too. Not every buyer will bother checking out your About Me, or My World pages, although we always do before we bid. You owe it to both yourself and your customers to be clear about how your business operates. For example, if you plan to hold shipment of an item for 10 business days while a personal check clears—and you should in some cases—say so in your listing. If you offer a discount on shipping for multiple purchases, be clear about it. Your goal in every listing is to sell the item with a minimum of e-mail exchanged between you and the buyer and a minimum of room for misunderstanding. Don't hesitate to make rules you expect your buyers to shop by.

» Don't threaten; don't scold; keep it friendly

With your rules in place, remember you set the tone for your business with words and pictures alone. No one can see the smile on your face as you share the rules with them. We've all had the experience of going into a shop owned by a crotchety character. You feel like that owner is just waiting for you to break something. Who wants to do business with someone who's just looking for an excuse to be ugly?

Words posted online can seem much harsher than you intend them to be. So here are some things you might want to keep in mind:

- Don't threaten. It sets a nasty tone. Don't say, "If you leave negative feedback for me, I'll leave negative feedback for you." That's too simplistic. You have a long way to go between a customer service problem and a negative feedback, so don't make the leap before there's even a problem.

- Don't scold. Don't say things like, "Nonpaying bidders will be reported." Of course, you'll file a nonpaying bidder report, but all of the people who plan to pay for their bids don't need to think of you as so eager to snap.

- Don't yell. Turn off the Caps Lock. Saying anything in all capital letters makes people online feel like you're yelling at them. If you want to say your item is FANTASTIC!, okay, use the capitals, but if you want to state a policy, set it off with a line space instead of yelling it at people.

- Don't use red type to state your policies. It sets the wrong tone. If your goal is to make them pop, change the font or box them.

» Make sure it's fun to shop with you

Don't underestimate eBay's appeal as a fun place to shop and browse. If it weren't fun to shop on eBay, more than 200 million people wouldn't be doing it. You want your customers to think that stopping by your auctions will be an enjoyable way to spend their time. If they don't, there are lots of other auctions they can explore instead. When you were a kid, didn't you love the shoe store that gave you a balloon with each purchase? Well, you don't have to give away a balloon, but you can set a friendly tone. And, if your customers return whenever they need the product you sell, so much the better. You can't actually smile at your customers as they walk through your door, but you can certainly make sure they think of you warmly. Wish them "Good Luck." Tell them "Happy Bidding." Thank them for stopping by your auction. Tell them you answer all e-mail inquiries. Make sure they know you're glad they're there.

You're One of the Crowd Now

Now that you've had some opportunity to think about and plan the face you'll show eBay, take it out for a test drive. We talked in Chapter 1 about becoming part of the eBay community, but it's hard to talk about your eBay image without revisiting the subject. You build your eBay image with every interaction you have on the service. Make yourself an active member of the community, and you'll reap benefits that far exceed the effort you will expend.

» Spend time on the Answer Center boards

eBay's Answer Center boards are fascinating places to explore. They are designed as a channel for members to communicate with other members, who have been there and done that. You will find boards for a wide variety of subjects from Auction Listings to Trust & Safety. You can get to the boards by clicking on the Community link at the top of most eBay pages. Answer Center will then be one of the hyperlinked options along the left.

The boards you'll find there are deeply educational, because people go there with every type of question and problem you can imagine and many you can't even begin to imagine. With

every question come answers that will lead you to ever more
...dge, facts, and understanding of eBay.
...is is a good first stop if you're having a particular
...m. For example, one day we were checking out auctions
...oup of PowerSellers we'd been working with. Every
...ne entered resulted in a response that said, "No auctions
...or this username." Now, since these are PowerSellers we
...oking for, that seemed a little unlikely. Stopping by the
... Center boards revealed that many users were having
...that day, both searching eBay and completing their
... It took only a few minutes to realize the problem was
...s, and it was a little bigger than our individual
...ion. That let us to redirect our energies to other, more
...tive pursuits, and sure enough, the next morning,
...ing was back to normal.
...u have other, even more self-serving reasons to make
...f known on the Answer Center boards. Every time you
...n answer—and trust us, you'll feel confident enough to
...very soon—you leave not only your username, but also a
...t allows others to view your auctions. It's a great way to
...fic to your auctions, and if you participate in a friendly,
...way, others are bound to be curious about what you do.
...stop by to take a look. If you have an About Me page the
...le "me" icon will be there as well. One PowerSeller who
...o remain anonymous says, "I try to spend at least three
...week on the Answer Center boards. It's time well

...w, here's a warning: it's very easy to lose yourself in the
...ion boards and forget to take care of the rest of your
...s. So, by all means, use the boards, but don't spend so
...me on them that you neglect your listings, your shipping,
...r e-mail correspondence. There's a wealth of knowledge
...le on the boards, it's true, but you'll also gain a wealth of
...dge by completing your day-to-day eBay tasks.

» Don't pick fights

As you explore eBay with the mindset of someone aiming for
PowerSeller status, you're likely to find other sellers who are
violating eBay rules. Some of these sellers might even compete
directly with you. If the violations are egregious, illegal, or
directly harmful to your business, you'll have to take the
problem to eBay. This is certainly the case for such serious

Don't pick fights

violations as shill-bidding (when you, or someone you know bids on one of your auctions to jack up the bidding price) or providing links to off-eBay Web sites within an auction. These actions potentially threaten the community at large, and as a good citizen of that community, you should act on them immediately. But, if the violations could possibly be accidental or simply based on a misunderstanding of eBay policy, don't be the first to go screaming to eBay about it. Whenever you report a violation against another seller to eBay, they not only explore the violation you're reporting, but they also take a look at all of your listings at the same time. That's only fair. After all, one competitor could make a claim against another just to cause trouble, so eBay is right to try to get a look at both sides of every story.

Take your concern to the Answer Center boards instead and ask other sellers for opinions about what you should do. Another solution in a case like this might be to contact the offending seller via e-mail and take care of it as one seller to another. Running to the teacher as a tattletale made us unpopular as kids, and it doesn't serve us well as eBayers either.

Your Listing Strategies

Your auction title, your description, and your photos combine to form each listing you will put on the eBay site. We'll explore each of these facets of your listing in just a bit, but first let's cover some strategic issues that will affect all the listings you create. We'll strategize about some best practices before we get to the more specific aspects of creating listings. You'll have a good, solid background then for dealing with the details.

How Much Is This Going to Cost?

You already know that eBay charges everyone who lists an item for sale on the site. When you were selling a few items here and there, these fees were negligible. When you become a PowerSeller, that's no longer true. "I paid more than $10,000 last month in eBay fees," reported a PowerSeller from the western United States. Now, that, like having to pay a lot in income tax, is the kind of problem most of us would be happy to have. eBay fees are a fact of life. It's simply the cost of doing business, and you must consider it equivalent to the overhead expenses you would pay if you opened a brick-and-mortar store. In view of this comparison, it's likely less expensive, but keeping track of your fees helps you set the price of your items and figure your profit margins when determining new products to introduce to your customers.

eBay's fees fall into two basic categories: Insertion Fees and Final Value Fees. The Insertion Fee is based on the opening value of the item you list. This fee is nonrefundable, and you pay it even if your item doesn't sell. The other fee is the Final Value Fee. This is a percentage of the final price your item brings when your auction ends. The Final Value Fee is based on a sliding scale, and here's how that works:

- If your item sells for $0.01 to $25, you pay 5.25 percent of the closing value.

- If your item sells for between $25.01 and $1,000, you pay 5.25 percent of the initial $25 (or $1.31) plus 3.25 percent of the remaining closing value balance ($25.01 to $1,000).

- If your item sells for over $1,000, you pay 5.25 percent of the initial $25 ($1.31), plus 3.25 percent of the amount between $25.01 and $1,000 ($31.69), plus 1.50 percent of the remaining value above $1,000.01. *Note*: if your item doesn't sell, there is no Final Value Fee to pay.

In addition to these two basic listing fees, eBay charges for listing upgrades and for extra photos you add to your listings. We'll discuss the optional listing extras in a bit, but the photos are a necessary expense, so we'll cover them here. The first photo you add to your listing is free. Each additional picture costs $0.15. The preview photo that appears at the top of your listing is free, but it will be the same shot you use in the main part of your listing. Other photo options and their prices follow. These options are available to you only if you host your pictures directly on eBay rather than on an image hosting service such as those discussed in Chapter 3. Remember, as we discussed in that chapter, image hosting is a great way to help you improve the quality of your images, and it will also help you cut your eBay fees too.

- You can supersize your images to up to 800×800 pixels for $0.75 each.

- You can choose the Picture Pack that allows you to add up to six pictures to your listing, supersize all the pictures, and display a photo in the gallery when your listing pops up in the search results screen for a single price of $1.00, as opposed to buying each of these features individually. (If you'd like to add up to 12 pictures the cost is $1.50.)

For a complete list of all of eBay's current fees, go to http://pages.ebay.com/help/sell/questions/seller-fees.html.

» Watch for eBay listing sales

eBay periodically offers listing sales. These sales may be for reduced rates for whole listings or for discounts on listing enhancements. Watch for the announcements of these special sales events. Reviewing eBay's Announcements area at http://www2.ebay.com/aw/marketing.shtml, discussed in Chapter 1, will allow you to stay abreast of these special listing days. eBay will also send you an automatic feed of these announcements via really simple syndication (RSS). For more on that free service go to http://www2.ebay.com/aw/rsshelp.shtml.

eBay doesn't usually give you much advance warning, which makes it all that much more important for you to know what's going on every day. Here's another good reason to subscribe to AuctionBytes and stay active on the discussion boards. Generally, the offers last for just a very short time, between one and three days. Be prepared to work overtime to take advantage of them. Also, be prepared for some technical challenges, because the volume of new listings on these days may make eBay quirky, and possibly slow the whole system down.

Appearance, Appearance, Appearance

It may be location in the world of brick-and-mortar stores, but on eBay, it's the appearance of your listings and how well your items are featured in those listings. You're working now to build a professional business image, so we're going to help you put the I'm-cleaning-out-the-closets-garage-sale approach behind you. It may work to slap up a card table in your driveway and dump the kids' outgrown snow boots on a neighborhood family with kids just a little younger. But you're not in the garage sale world anymore, so let's look at your listings the way you'd look at the display strategies of your favorite store in the brick-and-mortar world.

» Neatness counts

Your mother was right about this one. Neatness really matters to your listings. Here are some points that can make your listings speak well for you from the very beginning. You'll be doing all the work to create the listings anyway, so you might as well maximize their effectiveness by considering these PowerSeller proven bits of advice.

- Listings should be well organized so that all of the information is clear to see.
- They should be clean without a lot of extras that can distract your buyer.
- They should be complete so that all of the relevant information about size, color, material, condition, and use are easy to find.
- They should be professional so that your buyer can trust he's found a competent eBay seller. That means they should not have typos or misspelled words.
- They should include some distinctive branding such as a logo or characteristic style indigenous to your business to remind shoppers you're an established seller with long-term eBay goals.

You can see an example of a well-produced and professional-looking listing in Figure 5-2. Professional doesn't mean stuffy or stodgy. This listing is quite pleasant and appealing to the eye. It includes a clear picture of the bracelets being sold and then suggestions for building a collection of bracelets. How clever is that? The seller, beachcombers!, knows that buyers are concerned about how they would go about returning an item. Those details are clearly and prominently displayed.

As a buyer, you will view this listing and feel confident that you know all you need to know about this particular item. The seller has also made it clear what doing business together will be like. You can feel secure that you have little to risk here.

Neatness counts

FIGURE 5-2 (a and b) Here's a good example of a listing that sets just the right tone.

» Don't be too cute

Clever, yes; cute, no. You want to appear smart, clever, competent, and capable. But, you don't want to cross the line into cute, and please, we're begging you, guard yourself at all costs from cutesy! Suppose you decide to sell teddy bears. You get the sweet idea of adding background music to your listings; the "Teddy Bears' Picnic" seems a good choice. Now, I'll be the shopper who has a houseful of teddy bears and still can't get enough. I know every teddy bear seller on eBay, so I'm thrilled to see you sign on. The first time I stop in to look at your listings, I may very well think, oh how cute. This person knows the way around a computer. How clever to have added this little bit of music to the listing. The next time I stop in, I'll notice it, but not be surprised. The third time, it's going to start bugging me. It won't take me too long to decide that I just can't stand that stupid song one more time, so I'll go back to all the other people who sell teddy bears on eBay. We're not saying that adding music is never a good idea. But you should have a clear goal in mind for using it. And, you absolutely need to give people a quick way to opt out of hearing it. If you use a template that can accommodate audio, make sure it includes an easily accessible shutoff button.

Now, maybe you were never thinking of adding music to your listings anyway, but what about a little flashy character who runs back and forth across the screen? Or maybe a scrolling text line that does the same. Stop and reconsider. Your goal here is to get people to stop in to view your auctions frequently. You want them to not only check one auction out but be willing to browse your other auctions too. What seems cute to you on one listing can very quickly grate on the nerves of someone who wants to follow your auctions several times during the week and track your inventory regularly. Especially since this buyer is going to many auctions as part of her eBay shopping trip.

Aside from distracting and, worse, annoying your customers, these extras work against you in another way. Consider the eBay members who still use dial-up services rather than broadband. All of these extras slow down how quickly your auctions will load. Many online shoppers simply won't wait. They'll move on to the next listing instead. Don't give shoppers any reason to close out their screens on your auctions. Don't give them any reason to choose one of your competitors over you.

As we describe in our book *eBay PowerSeller Million Dollar Ideas*, adding audio or now even video to your listings can certainly enhance them in certain situations. One PowerSeller we know from Australia has that great accent, so audio in his listings may be fun. Another PowerSeller we've worked with sells expensive watches. He sometimes includes videos that show their elaborate movements. We just want you to be sure that the audio or video adds real value.

» Don't list more auctions than you can process

Sure, you want to list and list and list so that you can sell and sell and sell, but let's not get ahead of ourselves here. There's more to your eBay business than just listing items for sale. Every item that sells requires multiple e-mail interactions, payment issues, packaging, and shipping. You don't want to get so far ahead of yourself that you're not able to process your orders in a timely manner that will lead to positive feedback. (Remember, that goal is just as important at this early stage as earning money is.) Pace your listings so that you can manage the workflow.

When handling auctions manually, three to five auctions per day are manageable for a seller working alone. At seven, it starts to get stressful, and ten is stretching the capabilities of the average seller, recommends "Nick Sevino," a PowerSeller who writes for AuctionBytes under that pseudonym. Remember, it's not just the listing, it's also the order processing, the payment, the packing, the shipping, and all those e-mails. Before you get to the breaking point, you'll need to enlist help or move to an automated auction management system, as discussed in Chapter 4.

» Automate from the start

In Chapter 4 you learned all about auction automation software and why you must use it to become a PowerSeller. By now, we hope you've decided on a package that's right for you and are familiar with all of its features. Good. Now, work to automate absolutely everything you do from the very start of your business. Every keystroke you can enter once and use multiple times builds your business. Every template that you can design to get your information where it needs to be is money in the bank. It does not take anything away from the look of your listings to use automation. Take a look at Figure 5-3 to see a great example of an automated listing. This PowerSeller, Shoetime, had more than 3,200 items listed the day we took this screen shot. Notice the grid that gives all of the information you'd need to know before buying these sandals. That grid doesn't change from listing to listing, only the item-specific information that gets input for each pair of shoes changes.

Other types of information perfect for automating include payment options, shipping information, and customer service policies. Even if you're just using eBay's own Sell Your Item form, it's easy enough to store this basic material as templates

FIGURE 5-3 This is an excellent example of a listing created using an automated system.

that load into each listing you create. Not only does this save you time and keystrokes, but it makes it possible for you to control your spelling and grammar. You input it once, make sure it's perfect, and use it over and over again.

» eBay automates some listings for you

eBay's Prefilled Item Information option is an incredible timesaver, and therefore, a money maker too. You can use this feature to speed-list books, movies, music, video games, digital cameras, PDAs, and cell phones. Let's use a sample book listing for comparison. All you have to do is plug in some sort of unique identifier (the Sell Your Item Form will prompt you) and after that eBay automatically fills in all the details you could possibly want to provide, and then some. We use this form all the time when listing books and DVDs (see Figure 5-4). What a timesaver! We merely enter the DVD's title and eBay takes it from there adding a picture, content summary, and sometimes even reviews. What's added depends on the information that eBay has in its database for that item, but often it's all you need.

Just a reminder: The feature cannot fill in detailed product condition for you. With books, for example, you can select either New or Used from the pull-down menu. Those choices might be okay in some cases, but other times you'll want to provide more detail (e.g., used, but only read once, with a flawless dust jacket). Also, be sure to check the prefilled information, because on rare occasions details such as edition or publication date may be off.

But don't let these concerns keep you from using this feature. You're guaranteed to love it. And, if in using the prefilled form you find that for some reason your book, DVD, or other item is not in eBay's database, you can always list it "the old way." But you'll miss the speed of the new system big time.

Grading and Placing Your Items

You now have an understanding of some good practices in creating your listings, but there are two more details to consider before we study a listing. Grading and placing have as much to do with what you're selling as they do with how you list them. As we suggested when describing the prefilled listing option, you must grade your item to give your customers a clear idea of

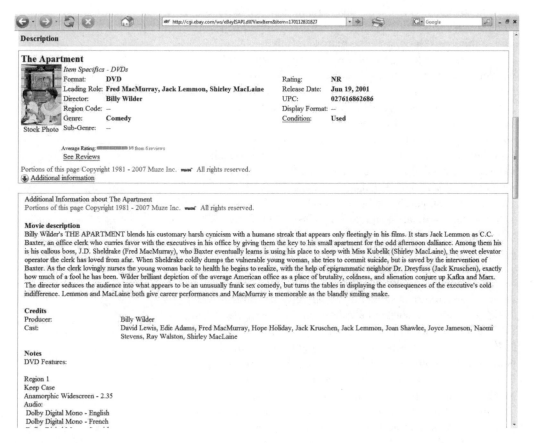

FIGURE 5-4 A listing created with eBay's Prefilled Item Information option shows how easy and effective that tool can be.

what condition it's in. That might be as easy as saying it's new, but in most cases that's not enough. You must also choose under which category your item will appear. That's a lot more complicated than you might first think, and making the right choice here definitely affects the success of your listing.

» Grade your item below what you think it's worth

Depending on the items you'll sell, grading an item can be very simple or simply impossible. If you're dealing in new merchandise, you have no worries. Everything you sell can be listed as new, in manufacturer's packaging, or new with tags.

Grade your item below what you think it's worth

Problem solved, skip to the next paragraph. If you, like many PowerSellers, sell a combination of new and used items, you'll need to think this through a little more carefully.

Grading items for sale is purely subjective. What looks like excellent condition to one may be very good condition to another. "Always err on the side of a lesser value," says Joe of Carrocel-restorations, a dealer and restorer of fine antique furniture. "Grade them lower than you think they really are," agreed Tony of Wegotthebeats, a CD seller. Both of these PowerSellers say it's better for your customer to get something and be delighted that it's better than they expected, than it is to get it and be disappointed. This may seem counterintuitive. It may seem you should be proud of your items and try to get the most you can for them. Won't you get a lesser bid if your excellent item is listed as very good? You'll soon see how to use photos and descriptions to make your customers want your items. Giving them the thrill of receiving something that's even better than they thought it was going to be, turns a one-time shopper into a return customer and, hopefully, a customer who thinks of you first whenever he's shopping for your type of item.

There is an exception to this grade-your-item-lesser-rule: that is, if your item has been objectively graded by a third party. Items like this might include fine jewelry and art. For example, if you deal in comic books, you know about a company that is well known and respected in the comic book industry, Comics Guaranty, LLC (CGC). For a fee, CGC will professionally grade your comic book and check to see if it's been restored.

They will then seal it between two slabs of hard plastic, adding the grade and other details (e.g., off-white pages) on its official label. As long as the seal is in place, that comic book is guaranteed to be accurately graded by the well-established grading system CGC uses. It's an industry standard and widely respected among comic book collectors and dealers. In selling rare comics, there can be a great price difference between a book rated "Good" and one rated "Fine." If your comic has been objectively graded as "Fine," there's no reason to list it as graded lesser than that.

Generally, without a guarantee from an objective third party, as long as you are the only one making the decision, you should stick with a lesser grade for your item. (We say "generally," because other areas such as coins, stamps, and trading cards have established grading standards commonly used by experienced collectors. If these are adhered to very closely, they can approach the legitimacy of a third-party grader.) That means, you'll never use "mint" condition, if the item has been opened even once. Mint would mean this product is now exactly as it was when it came from the manufacturer. Mint condition becomes "excellent" or even "excellent condition, never used." But, only if you're certain that it's never been used. If you can't vouch for that without a doubt, stick with excellent condition.

Choose Your Category

Choosing the right category for your item is like finding the right spot for it on a shelf in a brick-and-mortar store. eBay offers you hundreds of categories to choose from. When you consider all of the subcategories that fall within these main categories, you'll see how challenging this decision can be. It is an important decision too. Your goal in placing your item in the correct category is to increase the traffic to your auction and thereby increase the likelihood that your auction will receive bids.

Placing your item correctly can mean you'll get enough traffic to really start a bidding contest, and that can drastically affect your final price. On the other hand, if you misplace your item, you may miss some potential customers, and maybe not receive any bids at all. And intentionally putting your item in the wrong category to increase its exposure violates eBay rules. Fortunately, choosing the right category is a manageable task, with a little help from the PowerSellers, along with a lot of research.

» Know the categories

Your first job is to browse the categories so that you can become familiar with your choices. Along the left side of eBay's Home page you'll see the main categories. If you scroll to the bottom of this list, you'll see the choice All Categories. Click this link and you'll see a much more detailed list of the categories. But you can get even more specific. Go to the bottom of that page, and you'll find another link to All Categories. Click this link and the next screen (as shown in Figure 5-5) will show you all eBay's subcategories and the number of listings within each one. Now you will see which areas have the most listings. You can study the different subcategories and select the one that

Know the categories

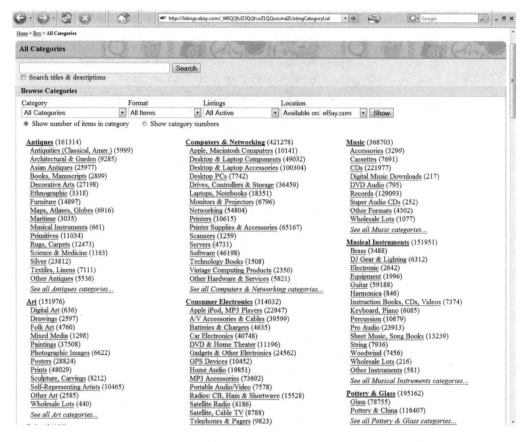

seems most suitable for your item. Base this selection on which subcategories get the most action. A PowerSeller, who is also an eBay educator, says this is the best strategy because it increases the likelihood that shoppers will see your auction. Any subcategory that has more than about 4,000 items is active. If you get above 10,000, you are in very popular territory.

Don't hesitate to place your items in very competitive categories. Those are the categories that are getting the most action, and the most shoppers. Place your item in an inactive category only if it's very specific and meant for a very targeted audience.

FIGURE 5-5 A partial glimpse of the All Categories screen lets you see some of eBay's categories and the number of items in each category.

 Now through eBay's Sell Your Item form, you can simply enter some keywords and the software will suggest categories for you to consider.

» Search for your item across categories

Once you're familiar with the different categories, determine which ones might be right for your item and then study which of those different categories seems to be the most profitable. Now you'll see exactly what your competition is. You will also see where other sellers have decided to place items similar to yours, and you'll have the opportunity to check out competitive listings. The best way to do this is to, once again, search completed listings for items similar to yours. Sort them by highest price, and check on the different categories other sellers used to place the items. Place your items in categories that brought the most money and had the most activity. Remember to focus in on the listings that actually resulted in a sale (the price will be green).

Listing Extras

Are listing upgrades, such as bolding, highlighting, and adding a subtitle worth it? Before we attempt to answer that question, let's review the available upgrades. As Figure 5-6 shows, you can upgrade your listing by spending anywhere from an extra $0.10 for using one of eBay's Listing Designer themes, to $79.95 for having two or more of your listings rotate on and off eBay's Home page. (They cycle on and off. They don't remain there as a banner ad would.)

eBay reports that the following upgrades will boost your sales, or increase your bids by the amount shown.

- **Bolding and Highlighting** When your item appears as part of a list within search results, you can make yours stand out by bolding it ($1.00), or highlighting it via a colored band ($5.00). On average this increases the final price by 21 percent for bolding and 25 percent for highlighting.

- **Gallery Picture** For $0.35, this adds a thumbnail photo (usually the first photo you upload as part of your listing) next to your item title as it appears in searches and listings. On average it boosts the final price by 12 percent.

- **eBay Giving Works** When you participate in eBay's Giving Works program, described fully in Chapter 6,

Search for your item across categories

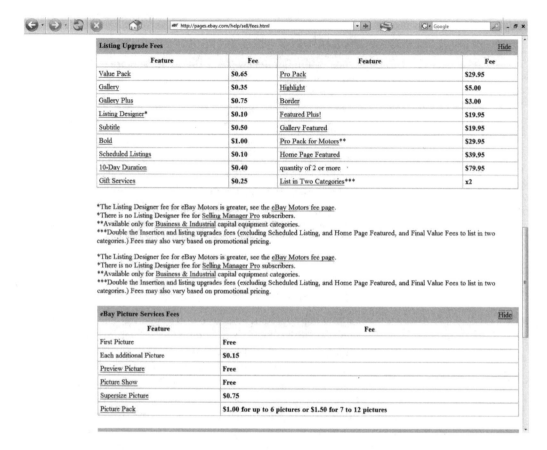

| | http://pages.ebay.com/help/sell/fees.html | | G▾ Google | |

Listing Upgrade Fees   Hide

Feature	Fee	Feature	Fee
Value Pack	$0.65	Pro Pack	$29.95
Gallery	$0.35	Highlight	$5.00
Gallery Plus	$0.75	Border	$3.00
Listing Designer*	$0.10	Featured Plus!	$19.95
Subtitle	$0.50	Gallery Featured	$19.95
Bold	$1.00	Pro Pack for Motors**	$29.95
Scheduled Listings	$0.10	Home Page Featured	$39.95
10-Day Duration	$0.40	quantity of 2 or more	$79.95
Gift Services	$0.25	List in Two Categories***	x2

*The Listing Designer fee for eBay Motors is greater, see the eBay Motors fee page.
*There is no Listing Designer fee for Selling Manager Pro subscribers.
**Available only for Business & Industrial capital equipment categories.
***Double the Insertion and listing upgrades fees (excluding Scheduled Listing, and Home Page Featured, and Final Value Fees to list in two categories.) Fees may also vary based on promotional pricing.

*The Listing Designer fee for eBay Motors is greater, see the eBay Motors fee page.
*There is no Listing Designer fee for Selling Manager Pro subscribers.
**Available only for Business & Industrial capital equipment categories.
***Double the Insertion and listing upgrades fees (excluding Scheduled Listing, and Home Page Featured, and Final Value Fees to list in two categories.) Fees may also vary based on promotional pricing.

eBay Picture Services Fees   Hide

Feature	Fee
First Picture	Free
Each additional Picture	$0.15
Preview Picture	Free
Picture Show	Free
Supersize Picture	$0.75
Picture Pack	$1.00 for up to 6 pictures or $1.50 for 7 to 12 pictures

you'll benefit from comarketing and promotional opportunities sponsored and supported by eBay, including a ribbon icon on your listing in search results.

■ **Featured Plus!** For $19.95, this places your listing in the top Featured area of search and listing results. This means when buyers search for a particular item, yours appears before all the regular (nonfeatured) items. On average this increases the final price by 76 percent.

■ **Home Page Featured** For $39.95 for one listing or $79.95 for two or more, this places your item in the Featured area of eBay's Home page, on a rotating basis. Statistics on how this may increase your final price were unavailable. There's no doubt though that it would increase your item's visibility and probably the number of bids received.

FIGURE 5-6 eBay's Listing Upgrade Fees screen gives you a quick glance at what your real costs will be when you add embellishments.

Search for your item across categories

Now we'll offer you the necessary caveats. The percentages eBay cites are based on only one month's sales (for most of the percentages just cited, that's January 2004). So, as the mutual fund companies would say, past performance is no guarantee of future results. eBay's own lawyers say it this way: No representation is made that a seller's final price, bids, and conversion rate on a specific item will increase by the average percentages noted above. What about the priciest upgrade of all, the Home Page Featured placement? eBay doesn't guarantee where your item will appear on its Home page, or even that it will appear for certain on its Home page. It may wind up on the main Browse page instead. Further, there is no guarantee when your item will rotate on and off the Home page. That could very well happen in the middle of the night when few people are there to view it.

Now, back to our original question. Are these upgrades worth the money? Knowing their costs and what eBay has to say about their results, start by looking at listings in a category that interests you. See if the bold ones, for example, really do catch your eye more. Try keeping track of some by bookmarking them, or adding them to the items you're watching through your My eBay page. Check to see if they really do have more bids or higher current prices, thereby justifying their cost. And once again, review Completed Listings for insights. The upgrades such as bolding and highlighting still appear for these auctions, so you can gauge their effectiveness.

PowerSellers who list hundreds, if not thousands, of items per month pay steep eBay fees to begin with. They are reluctant to add to their costs by upgrading their listings. That's understandable. Adding something as simple as bolding will add $1.00 to each listing. If your conversion rate is 40 percent, that means you'll pay, on average, $2.50 per sale for this feature. Multiply that by 100 or 1,000 and, well, you get the point. But if you list only a few items and you have starting prices of $50 or greater, try gallery view, bolding, or highlighting and test these yourself. Run similar listings at the same time without the features and see how they compare. "Adding bolding or highlighting does seem to increase the traffic to a listing, but I wouldn't use it if the item was worth less than $50," said one PowerSeller who asked not to be named. Finally, data analysis tools such as Terapeak's (www.terapeak.com) can be very helpful here. Terapeak provides ready access to archival data from eBay auctions. The data for the item you're researching

Search for your item across categories

(say a Thumbelina doll) will include the percentage of sellers with listings resulting in a sale *who used a given enhancement*. So if 75 percent of successful sellers of Thumbelina dolls used Gallery, you might want to spring for Gallery yourself.

Creating Your Listings

Now that we've explored the strategies behind creating your listings, you're ready to get on with the real work of combining your title, description, and photos to place among all of the other eBay sellers. We'll help you see how to make your listing stand out. Each of these three elements plays a vital role in selling your products. We'll help you understand the purpose of each part of the listing and suggest great ways to distinguish yourself and your products.

Titling Your Listings

People are not likely to ever see your auctions if you don't title them properly. All of the work you do to take your photos and describe your item will go for nothing, if shoppers don't find your listings. The most likely way for them to find you is through the eBay Search feature. Sure, in the previous section devoted to choosing a category, we focused on eBay's Browse features, but although browsing was a great way for you to learn about the different eBay categories, it is not the most popular way for users to find what they're looking for on eBay. It's just too time-consuming.

The great majority of eBay shoppers use the Search feature and look for specific items. The default for this search is a Titles Only search. It is possible for shoppers to specify the search to include title *and* description, but many won't do that if it's likely it would yield an unmanageable number of auctions to review. So, if you want your item to come up in the search results of your prospective customers, you have to carefully consider what words to use to create your most searchable titles.

eBay's search engine is really quite a simple one. You enter certain keywords and it shoots back the listings that include those keywords in their titles. Your results will reflect the keywords you specify. The secret to creating keywords that will pull up your auctions is to think like a buyer. What kinds of words would a buyer use to find the item you sell? When you can adequately answer this question, we can start working with the reality that you'll get only 55 characters to use in your title. We're going to set out to get you the proverbial bang-for-the-buck, and we've got some ideas that will make that happen.

---

eBay's Marketplace Research

As you saw in Chapter 3, tools, such as those from Hammertap, can help you uncover the most effective keywords. Now, eBay offers Marketplace Research to help you with the same task. Marketplace Research gives you valuable information about buying and selling trends on the site. You can analyze top searches, average starting prices, and average sold prices, among other choices. Marketplace Research is offered at two different levels of functionality.

Marketplace Research Basic gives you data from the past 60 days. At a cost of $9.99 per month, it allows you to view eBay's top searches and other metrics such as total number of items sold and average shipping costs. Through its Top Searches feature, you can see up to the top 20 keyword searches by category. You can also see the top keywords related to a keyword you specify. You can use this tool to check your keywords against the top keywords driving traffic toward products like yours.

Marketplace Research Pro, at $24.99 per month gives you access to 90 days of historical data, and gives you access to international data, too.

If you're not ready to commit to a monthly subscription, you can try Marketplace Research Fast Pass for $2.99. It allows you to access a trial version of the service for two days.

» Turn the key with your keywords

To determine which keywords to include in your title, put your buyer's cap on. Ask yourself, if I wanted this, how would I search for it? When you have a few ideas in mind, let's go back to the seller's side of the equation. (You can leave the buyer's cap on if you like it!) Do some searches with the words you've come up with and see what you get. How close to your item have you come with the words you first thought to try? How can you alter those words to get even closer?

Once you start getting results that look like the item you're selling, take some time to go back to those completed listing searches. Use the completed listings to see which items sold for the most and which auctions generated the most bids. (Or again, for a full picture, toggle back and forth between current and completed listings from any search.) Check the bottom of the listing pages to see if the seller included a counter. This is a great way to judge how many people stopped by to take a look. At this early stage, you aren't considering any of the other aspects of these listings. You are thinking of just the keywords. It won't take you long to determine which keywords were effective in getting people to stop by for a look.

» Don't confuse keywords with adjectives

It's very easy to think of snappy words that you'd like to include in your auction titles; fantastic, beautiful, one-of-a-kind, for example. But let's work on the distinction between a keyword and an adjective. A keyword might be a good adjective, but not all adjectives are good keywords. Some keywords have to be nouns. Where should you start? Let's start, as always, by exploring listings already up on eBay.

Let's begin with "shoes," a respectable keyword. If you enter a title search for shoes, you'll get so many responses that the search won't be useful to you. Our attempt brought more than 150,000 responses, far too many for us to deal with. So we'll add an adjective. Let's choose "women's." "Women's shoes" will still get you way too many hits, but we're down to just over 36,000 pairs of shoes, so it's getting a little better. Now, let's move to a more specific adjective and indicate size. The next title search will be for "women's shoes 7." Ahh, now we have only about 8,000 possible matches to our search. Let's think how else we can distinguish the pair we're looking for. Let's think clogs (hey, I'm co-authoring the book, and they're my favorites). Now, we'll search "women's shoes 7 clogs" for a result of 414 pairs. To distinguish this search even more, let's enter a particular brand of clogs, Born. Okay, now our search is for "women's shoes 7 clogs Born," and we get 40 matching results. Now we can look at each individual title and choose a pair. Oh sorry, back to work. Let's look at the words we chose to get us this far.

"Shoes" turned out to be an ineffective keyword. We can eliminate it by choosing to do our search in the category of Clothing, Shoes, and Accessories. So, let's eliminate it. If we searched for just "clogs," we'd get some cute little ones for kids, and some very large ones for men, so "women's" is an effective choice. The size kept us from wading through items that wouldn't fit, and specifying our favorite brand increased the chances we'd see something we like.

So, if you wanted to sell a pair of size 7 Born clogs, you can clearly see which words are worthy of your precious limited title space. By narrowing down the keywords to just a few, you have some room left for descriptive adjectives. Always choose your keywords first and then add the descriptors as space allows. No buyer is going to enter as a keyword "new" and hit the shoes category. When we did that, we got more than 60,000 items of every type. New is important information to a buyer, but only after that buyer has found the kind of product he or she is looking for. So, using our example, let's add some good descriptors.

Your basic title for this item would start "Women's Seven 7 clogs Born." (By including the number as a numeral and spelled out you can account for both methods of searching.) Someone shopping for a pair of clogs would get this result even without the word Born. But someone who was only shopping for Born clogs wouldn't miss it because you've included the manufacturer's name. The manufacturer's name is a very important descriptive keyword.

Think also of other words that your buyer may use to describe the item. For example, some shoppers might think of "clogs" as a type of "mule" or even a "slide." If room allows, include these keywords also, not because you think of the shoes that way, but because one of your customers might. In that respect, they are actually more important keywords than adjectives such as black or brown. This is the case even though, from your point of view, they aren't that descriptive of this particular pair of shoes.

Remember when titling, keywords are your hook. Adjectives and descriptors are nice, but only after your hooks are as sharp as you can make them.

» Don't let your titles L@@K like this!

Surprisingly, a search for L@@K brought more than 50,000 results. Most of those were for items in the clothing and collectibles categories, but more than a few were for expensive cars, real estate, and other fine items. Including L@@K is a ridiculous convention and uniformly scorned by PowerSellers. It looks cheesy, and it suggests that you couldn't think of anything more valuable to do with the precious 55 characters you had to work with. It reminds buyers of walking down the main row of carnival hawkers at the last carnival they attended. It might be fun for a warm summer evening, but it doesn't serve you well on your way to PowerSeller status. You've got other, better ways to attract attention to your auctions, mostly through careful planning, careful placement, and careful titling techniques. Please, we're begging you, as one of our readers, don't create even one auction that includes L@@K.

» Don't be redundant and repeat yourself

To help make every one of those 55 characters count, keep careful check on your redundancies. For example, don't use "antique" and "old." By definition, antique is old. If you're not really sure it's antique (generally considered to mean 100 years old), then just call it old. You'll use the description to make it clear just how old this item is. Old comes in handy when you're dealing with items that have been reproduced. For example, FiestaWare dishes are highly collectible from the 1930s through the 1950s. They were reissued in the 1990s and grew to be very popular again. If you have the older ones for sale, by all means, title them old to distinguish them from the reproductions that are now much more prevalent and less expensive.

Avoid "rare" as a descriptor. It wastes space, and it also can backfire against you. It may be rare in your neck of the woods, or it may seem rare because you haven't seen many. But eBay shoppers come from all over, and in some other areas, it may not be rare at all. If it's not rare and you say it is, you lose your credibility. If it is rare, your buyers will know about it. It's not worth any of your 55 characters.

"Vintage" is another one that you can skip. It means something different to just about everyone who uses it. It simply has no bang for the seven characters it takes away from your title.

» Ways to get around that 55 limit

It may seem like 55 characters is a lot. For our example of the Born clogs, it was perfectly adequate. But, what if you're selling books? Some titles take up almost that many characters and will leave you very little room for other types of information, such as condition, edition, dust jacket. As with everything else, titling your items will depend largely on what it is you're selling. Fortunately, eBay and its members have come up with some handy acronyms. They've created a shorthand language that lets you add valuable details to your titles without chewing up too much of your 55 character limit. The list that follows gives you just an example of some of the most common ones:

BIN	Buy it now
COA	Certificate of authenticity
COL	Collection
GBP	Great Britain Pounds
HTF	Hard to find
LTD	Limited edition
MIB	Mint in box
MIJ	Made in Japan
MOC	Mint on card
NBW	Never been worn
NIB	New in box
NM	Near mint
NOS	New old stock
NR	No reserve
NWOT	New without tags
NWT	New with tags
OEM	Original equipment manufacturer
OOAK	One of a kind
SH	Shipping and handling
VHTF	Very hard to find

This list, of course, is by no means complete. There are many acronyms unique or commonly used within particular categories. Book auctions, for example, may well include these additional acronyms:

1st	First edition
ANTH	Anthology
AUTO	Autographed
BOMC	Book of the Month Club edition
EXLIB	Ex library book
HB	Hardbound

Make your titles precise and perfect

HB/DJ	Hardbound book with dust jacket
HIST	Historical
NC	No cover
OOP	Out of print
PB	Paperback

For more information on acronyms commonly used on eBay, go to the Community Frequently Used Terms page at http://pages.ebay.com/help/basics/community-terms.html.

» Make your titles precise and perfect

Deb's dad was an air traffic controller. He was very serious about precision in language, because he said when directing air traffic, imprecise language could lead to tragedy. She learned as a small kid never to ask, "Do you know what time it is?" That would elicit a yes or no answer, depending on whether he was wearing a watch or standing near a clock. Then would come the lesson entitled, "Mean what you say and say what you mean." Dad could have had no way to know how relevant this advice is for titling eBay auctions.

As you know, the search engine on eBay's site does not, as of this writing, have any artificial intelligence capabilities, so it can't make any assumptions about what you mean. While it can address some common misspellings, for now you can only count on it to return search results matching your exact keywords. When creating your titles, don't allow any accidental misspellings, because if you do, you may be left out of all searches for the item you are selling. For example, if a typo lists your Gucci purse as a Guci purse, you are out of luck. Your only hope is that someone else will make the same typo and accidentally find your purse in a field of one. In that case, you won't have much competition, but more likely, your item will go unsold.

Writing Your Item Descriptions

After you've decided on your best title, it's time to work on the item description. This vital element of your eBay listing not only contributes directly to how well your item sells, but it also goes a long way to determining how smoothly your eBay business operates. Your goal with every description is to provide your customers with enough information about the product to make them decide they want to buy it. You want to be clear about all of the item's features and characteristics, and you want to give your customers all of the information they'll need to complete the transaction with you. Ideally, your customers will be able to read your listing and complete the transaction without any further communication. Cutting down on the time you need to respond to e-mail gives you more time to work on listing, processing your orders, and shipping. Realistically, you'll still get lots of e-mail questions from your customers. The number of people who don't actually read your entire listing, but then send you e-mail asking you for information you know you've included, may surprise you. You have no choice but to smile to yourself and answer politely, but making your listings complete can help reduce the number of these e-mails, even if it won't eliminate them.

» Use templates if you can

Just because you have to create item descriptions, that doesn't mean you have to write each one individually, starting fresh each time. If you are selling repeatable items, for example shoes, clothes, or CDs, create a template that will allow you to fill in the item fields for each listing. Figure 5-7 shows a listing from PowerSeller Bridewire. Because this PowerSeller sells scores of wedding dresses a week, she couldn't possibly write new copy for each listing. Instead, she has created a template that allows her to input specifics for each dress by using single-word descriptors. In addition, she has created paragraphs that relate specifically to this group of gowns, explaining where she purchased them and giving some background detail about the manufacturer.

Further down the listing, but not illustrated in Figure 5-7, is a sizing grid that will let the shopper estimate her correct size. This is also repeatable from listing to listing. As you can see, this PowerSeller provides great amounts of information without the need to keystroke hundreds of individual listings.

Your descriptions give you a chance to shine

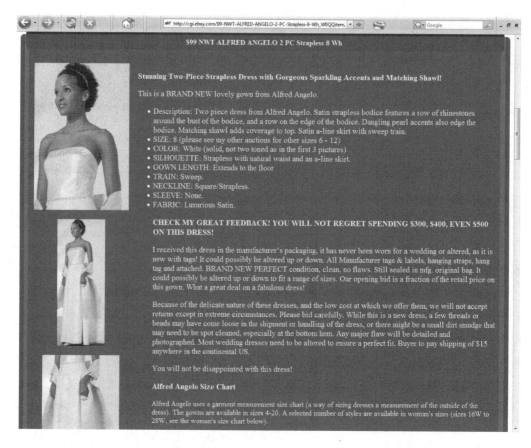

Stunning Two-Piece Strapless Dress with Gorgeous Sparkling Accents and Matching Shawl!

This is a BRAND NEW lovely gown from Alfred Angelo.

- Description: Two piece dress from Alfred Angelo. Satin strapless bodice features a row of rhinestones around the bust of the bodice, and a row on the edge of the bodice. Dangling pearl accents also edge the bodice. Matching shawl adds coverage to top. Satin a-line skirt with sweep train.
- SIZE: 8 (please see my other auctions for other sizes 6 - 12)
- COLOR: White (solid, not two toned as in the first 3 pictures)
- SILHOUETTE: Strapless with natural waist and an a-line skirt.
- GOWN LENGTH: Extends to the floor
- TRAIN: Sweep.
- NECKLINE: Square/Strapless.
- SLEEVE: None.
- FABRIC: Luxurious Satin.

CHECK MY GREAT FEEDBACK! YOU WILL NOT REGRET SPENDING $300, $400, EVEN $500 ON THIS DRESS!

I received this dress in the manufacturer's packaging, it has never been worn for a wedding or altered, as it is new with tags! It could possibly be altered up or down. All Manufacturer tags & labels, hanging straps, hang tag and attached. BRAND NEW PERFECT condition, clean, no flaws. Still sealed in mfg. original bag. It could possibly be altered up or down to fit a range of sizes. Our opening bid is a fraction of the retail price on this gown. What a great deal on a fabulous dress!

Because of the delicate nature of these dresses, and the low cost at which we offer them, we will not accept returns except in extreme circumstances. Please bid carefully. While this is a new dress, a few threads or beads may have come loose in the shipment or handling of the dress, or there might be a small dirt smudge that may need to be spot cleaned, especially at the bottom hem. Any major flaw will be detailed and photographed. Most wedding dresses need to be altered to ensure a perfect fit. Buyer to pay shipping of $15 anywhere in the continental US.

You will not be disappointed with this dress!

Alfred Angelo Size Chart

Alfred Angelo uses a garment measurement size chart (a way of sizing dresses a measurement of the outside of the dress). The gowns are available in sizes 4-20. A selected number of styles are available in woman's sizes (sizes 16W to 28W, see the woman's size chart below).

FIGURE 5-7 PowerSeller bridewire can list many auctions per week thanks to templates.

» Your descriptions give you a chance to shine

If you are selling items that require you to write each description, don't despair. Consider this your opportunity to shine and show off a little bit with some of the information you've gathered over all the years you've been pursuing your interests. Figure 5-8 shows you how this seller lists his lobby card (movie promotional advertisement). Notice, he gives all the information necessary to evaluate the item, but he also puts in some background on the type of lobby card offered for sale. Not only does this help his customers learn more about the item, but it also gives them confidence that he knows what he's talking about. If you've followed our advice from Chapter 1, it's

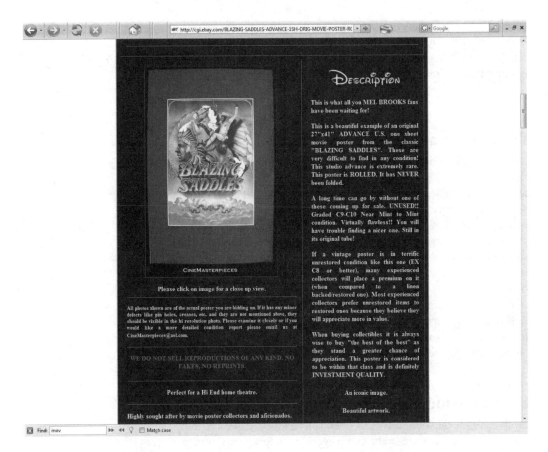

DESCRIPTION

This is what all you MEL BROOKS fans have been waiting for!

This is a beautiful example of an original 27"x41" ADVANCE U.S. one sheet movie poster from the classic "BLAZING SADDLES". These are very difficult to find in any condition! This studio advance is extremely rare. This poster is ROLLED. It has NEVER been folded.

A long time can go by without one of these coming up for sale. UNUSED!! Graded C9-C10 Near Mint to Mint condition. Virtually flawless!! You will have trouble finding a nicer one. Still in its original tube!

If a vintage poster is in terrific unrestored condition like this one (EX C8 or better), many experienced collectors will place a premium on it (when compared to a linen backed/restored one). Most experienced collectors prefer unrestored items to restored ones because they believe they will appreciate more in value.

When buying collectibles it is always wise to buy "the best of the best" as they stand a greater chance of appreciation. This poster is considered to be within that class and is definitely INVESTMENT QUALITY.

An iconic image.

Beautiful artwork.

FIGURE 5-8 This seller's listing includes background history on the item for sale.

likely that you're selling things you know and care about. Don't hesitate to let your customers know your areas of expertise.

» Don't just repeat your title

Your title was your hook to get people to open your auction listing. Now that they've done that, give them more than they expected. You don't need to repeat what you've said in your title, because you've already told them that. Tell them as much about the item as you can. Give them the color, dimensions, style, and manufacturer's information. If you've acquired this item through an estate sale, tell them something about the person whose estate was being sold. Give them a little history of the item and how it was used in the past. Add value to the

Be accurate and completely honest

description of the item by sharing information about it and its place in history. That way, even if the shopper doesn't make a bid, you'll leave a good impression. This particular item may not be what they're shopping for, but you could become a favorite seller who they'll stop back to visit for other auctions.

» Be accurate and completely honest

Your descriptions are your chance to shine, but not in the fiction-writing category. Tell your customers the exact truth about the item. Play up its positive features, of course, but don't suggest that it may be something it's not. If it has flaws, not only mention them, but highlight them. Make sure your customers know exactly what they're bidding on. Just because something may have a flaw, crack, or defect, that doesn't mean it won't find a buyer on eBay. Many collectors expect to have their items come to them with common forms of wear and signs of age. It's not necessarily a disadvantage, unless you're not honest about it. Then you not only risk having the item returned to you, but you also risk losing a customer for good and damaging your feedback rating.

» Be professional and positive

From the moment your customers open your listings, you want them to feel that they are in the company of a competent seller. Even before you attain PowerSeller status, you can make that happen through your listings. Remember that every communication you have with your customers gives them the opportunity to judge your professionalism, and don't waste a single chance to impress them.

As you describe your items, suggest alternative uses for what your customers are seeing. Show them your creativity by giving them some new ways to look at the item you're selling. If you've used the item before, give them some ideas of how you used it and what you liked about it. Help them to see themselves using what you're selling, and you'll make them want to have it or give it as a gift. Make yourself a consultant to your shoppers, not just a source of goods.

Don't allow a single negative to enter your listings. For example, never make statements that disparage yourself or your item. If you don't really know much about the particular thing you're selling, never say so. Hold on to it until you've educated yourself about it, and then list it when you can speak with authority. Even the flaws of the item can be called out without a negative. For example, in describing a collectible composite doll, you can say "the worn paint on her face reflects years of having been loved so well." You're making it clear that she's not perfect, but you're presenting her imperfections in a positive light. Compare that with "paint worn on face." The latter is shorter and required fewer keystrokes, but the former created a better impression of your doll.

)) Don't violate anyone's trademark

When you're writing your titles and your descriptions, be careful not to violate anyone's trademark or copyright. eBay's Verified Rights Owner (VeRO) program protects the owners of trademarks and copyrights from having their product names used inappropriately. For example, if a seller wants to list a purse that is very much in the style of one sold by Chanel, he or she cannot include "Chanel-like" or "Chanel look" or any other form of the trademark Chanel. (In fact, to include Chanel in the title merely to draw in hapless bidders would be considered title keyword spamming under eBay's rules.) More than 5,000 property rights owners are registered with eBay, and they will go after sellers using their product names or logos. All they have to do is file a Notice of Claimed Infringement (NOCI) form with eBay, and your auction will be removed. Repeat offenders will be suspended. To learn more about the VeRO program, do a search from the Help screen. You can also visit the About Me pages of hundreds of registered VeRO partners to see what the companies have to say about fair use of their names. Fooling around here is one of the quickest ways to get kicked off of eBay for good.

)) Make your descriptions neat and tidy

Once again, neatness counts. Your descriptions should be complete and descriptive, but they also must be neat and tidy. Spell-check and proofread every listing, recommends a Platinum PowerSeller from New York. You don't want to make small mistakes that detract from the overall feel of your listing. If writing isn't your favorite thing, develop some standard descriptive phrases and reuse them. Just make sure they are spelled correctly and don't contain any grammatical errors. Also, avoid using slang. You don't care if your customers think you're cool, just that they think you know what you're talking about. Nothing shakes a buyer's confidence faster than dealing with a seller who doesn't sound professional.

Here's an old proofreader's tip: Read your copy backward. By taking each word out of context, you see it only for itself, and you are more likely to catch the common typo or misspelling that way.

» Remember you're writing for an online audience

Writing text for a computer screen is different from writing for paper. People using computers process their information better if it comes to them in short bursts. So, keep your sentences short. Don't use long paragraphs. Put line spaces between your paragraphs. By creating more white space on the screen, you'll help your customers move their eyes across the screen, and your information will be easier to absorb. You'll also increase the likelihood that people will actually read all of your listing, and that's very important, since you'll pack so much useful information into your descriptions.

» Give them a little style

Just because your description has to be professional, complete, accurate, honest, and neat, that doesn't mean you can't have a little style and fun with it. Don't hesitate to use some small design elements to spice up your descriptions. For example, create a little icon that can represent your business—a stylized shoe, a little bunch of flowers, a train engine. Something that suggests your business will stick in your customers' minds and help build your image as a professional.

Backgrounds also add pleasant design touches to your listings. Most of the templates available through auction management companies discussed in Chapter 4 offer design element choices, but you can find others on the Web. Go to www.grsites.com/textures for nearly 6,000 different backgrounds you can add to your listings, and they're free.

Photos That Sell

When we asked PowerSellers for secrets about successful selling on eBay, the nearly unanimous advice offered was, "great photos." Nothing showcases your items like good, clear, detailed photos. In Chapter 3, we discussed the equipment you'll need to take great shots. You also learned why you should have a single area set up and dedicated to photographing your items. Here, you'll learn how to make the most of the equipment and photo setup you create. You'll also learn some great strategies for making the most of your pictures.

» Use great photos and lots of them

Even if you don't start out as a great photographer, practice can help you develop great techniques for showcasing your items. When capturing your images, make sure your photos are clear, big, and detailed. Focus your camera carefully so that the image is sharp. The first photo you show for each listing is free. Additional photos cost $0.15 each, but this is one case where paying extra is definitely worth the investment. One PowerSeller from Florida told us that the more photos you show, the more bids you'll receive. You want your shoppers to be able to view the item almost as closely as they would if they were viewing it in person. Figure 5-9 shows multiple images of a Roseville vase listed by a PowerSeller from New Jersey. Notice that the background contrasts somewhat with the item but doesn't interfere with the view. Also notice the multiple shots that show every angle of the vase, so prospective buyers can be certain they are seeing every important detail. So, use great photos and provide lots of them for each listing. Here are some tips to help you.

- Use multiple shots and capture the item from different angles. That way, your customers can see the entire item as though they were holding it in their hands and rotating it.

- Don't forget shots from above, and show the bottom of the item, too. Focus on details that make your item unique, such as signatures and manufacturers' markings.

- Capture the image from an angle to showcase the depth of the item and make best use of its shadows.

Use good lighting

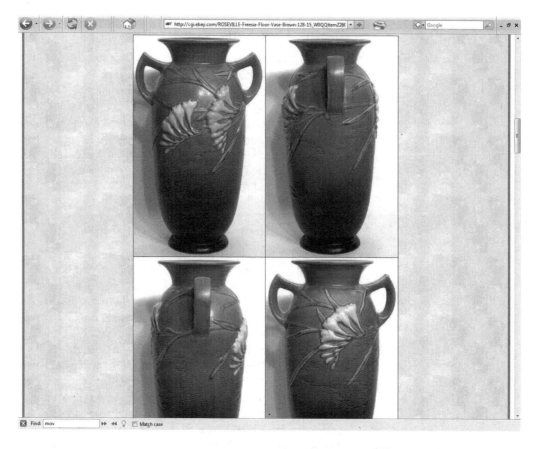

- Specifically photograph every flaw and make sure the flaws are visible in the photo. You don't want to cover anything up that will later reveal itself to be trouble for both you and the buyer.

- Use a tripod if your hand is shaky. You want every detail to count.

FIGURE 5-9 Here you can see every side and angle of this beautiful Roseville vase.

» Use good lighting

When capturing images, use good lighting to best show the details. The best light for photos is natural, so try to place your photo area near a window. If you want to shoot your pictures outside, do it out of the direct sun. Too much sunlight directly on your item will wash it out rather than highlight features. Direct light can also cause hot spots (glare and reflections).

When using artificial light, try to light the item from two directions at once to reduce shadows. Using light from two sources also reduces the glare from your flash. Some sellers swear by fluorescent lighting. They claim it gives a whiter light and truer color reproduction than the more yellow incandescent light from regular light bulbs.

» Make your item stand out

To make your item stand out, use a neutral but contrasting background. That means you'll need to have at least two backdrops, one light and one dark. Avoid patterns on the background because they can be busy distractions to the item itself. That doesn't mean you should feel stuck with using a white sheet or a black one. Rich color can add elegance to the photo, so consider using an eye-pleasing royal blue or deep violet for the dark background and a pale blue or pink for the light one.

Some of your items might benefit from being scaled for size. Consider placing a ruler next to the item. Another option is to photograph it next to something commonly recognized, such as a quarter or a penny. At a glance, your customers will know exactly what the size of your item is.

» Protect your photos

It may surprise you, but sellers have been known to swipe each other's photos for use in their own auctions. That may seem a little silly and petty, but it's serious to the seller who loses his photos. That's part of your intellectual property. It's time-consuming for you to produce your best images, and no one else should have the right to use your work without your permission. It's very difficult for eBay to police this type of seller-to-seller problem. Consider adding an identifier to your photos, such as your username. Even if another seller takes your image, it wouldn't do much good in someone else's auction. It will be apparent who owns the image, and having your username on your images will add a little advertising pop at the same time.

» It's not necessarily all up to you

Resourceful PowerSellers find other sources of photo images for their listings, besides capturing every image themselves.

Hire some help

If you're dealing in new merchandise, check with the manufacturer for stock images of the items you sell. That means all you do is upload the image that already exists, and you bypass the whole problem of taking photos.

If you sell books, CDs, DVDs, or videos, you can take advantage of eBay's automated listing service (discussed earlier) that includes a good many stock images of the items in these categories. When using stock photos, it's especially important to be up-front about your item's condition. Otherwise, some buyers may assume it's in the same condition as the one in the stock photo, and they'll be disappointed if it's not.

If you are selling paper goods such as postcards, sports cards, books, or comics, you can directly scan your items on a flatbed scanner. You'll still want to capture multiple shots, but you won't have to work with a camera to do it. Lighting and background won't be considerations, and you'll be able to address the size and features of each item in the description. Of course, you should still provide specific scans of any flaws or defects.

» Hire some help

If you are really intimidated by the thought of doing the photography, consider hiring someone to help you. Before too long, you'll be looking for help with your eBay business, anyway (see Chapter 6), so why not choose an employee who can also do photography? Most high schools and community colleges offer photography classes, and a young photo-bug, just starting out, would be delighted to gain some experience, build a portfolio, and get paid a little something at the same time.

Timing Your Auctions

Timing your auctions can seem a little like trying to time the stock market. No one can say for sure, and there are no guarantees. The glib response to the question "When should my auction end?" is when the bidding has reached its highest price. Fortunately, unlike the stock market, it's possible to apply a little common sense to the question of timing your auctions. You can't be guaranteed you'll hit the best time every time, but you can use some tips from the PowerSellers to increase the chance that you'll at least time them well.

Timing Tidbits

The first thing to remember when setting your auction ending times is that eBay operates on Pacific Time. If you're an early bird who lives back East, don't bother to get a jump on your listings and post them by 6 A.M. local time. You'll risk missing all of the potential customers out West who prefer to sleep at 3 A.M.

That's important to consider, because as with any auction, the real action happens within the last hours of your listing. "In a 7-day listing, the first 6 days and 23 hours is the viewing time. The real auction happens at the very end," says PowerSeller James of Jeralinc, and many others agreed. You want to try to end your auctions when most people are likely to be paying attention.

Keep in mind that your auction ends at the exact time of day that it started. Your auction begins when you complete your listing. No matter how long you choose to run your auction—and you'll learn more about that soon—the hour it starts is the same hour it ends. You can create your auctions, store them, and schedule them to start at a designated time. eBay offers this feature at an added cost, but your auction management software will do it for free.

» Consider your audience

Here is yet another example of how your research can pay off in real profits. Know who your audience is, and you'll have a better idea of when those people will be on eBay. "My audience is mostly women, ages 30 to 60," reported a PowerSeller from New Jersey. "When I first started, I was ending my auctions in the afternoon, because that was the most convenient time for me to list them. Soon, I realized that the people most likely to buy my products weren't even home in the middle of the afternoon, let alone on their computers. I switched my ending times to the evening and saw a big improvement almost immediately." If your audience is most likely to be made up of working people, follow this PowerSeller's advice. If, on the other hand, your audience is more likely to be stay-at-home moms, afternoon might work to coincide with naptime. Retirees may be more active in the morning than they are late at night. Experiment a bit, but do it with your audience in mind.

» Statistics favor certain times

Luckily for you, we have some statistics to turn to in determining the best day and time to end auctions. Your actual results may vary depending on many factors, including the products you sell, the time of the year, the weather conditions across the United States, and what's currently hot on TV, but statistics are a good place to start. For the past few years, AuctionBytes.com has completed a survey of eBay sellers to determine the best time to end an auction. Consistently Sunday evening has proven to be the most popular time to end your auctions. Overall, the evening hours, between 6 P.M. and Midnight (PST), have fared the best.

AuctionBytes.com was kind enough to allow us to include their research. Table 5-1 shows the best day to end an auction, with results going back to 1999 (the most recent survey results available are from February 2005). Table 5-2 shows the best time of day to end auctions. All times given are in PST.

2/05	2/04	3/03	1/02	2/01	12/99
Sun 56.8%	Sun 57.5%	Sun 64%	Sun 60%	Sun 54%	Sun 41%
Mon 11.5%	Mon 9.5%	Mon 11%	Thu 10%	Thu 18%	Mon 18%
Thu 7.3%	Sat 7%	Sat 8%	Sat 9%	Sat 11%	Mon 15%
Sat 6.2%	Thu 7%	Thu 7%	Mon 9%	Thu 8%	Fri 11%
Tue 4.4%	Tue 5%	Tue 4%	Wed 4%	Wed 5%	Tue 6%
Wed 3.8%	Wed 4%	Fri 3%	Tue 4%	Fri 3%	Thu 5%
Fri 2.6%	Fri 2%	Wed 3%	Fri 3%	Tue 1%	Wed 4%

TABLE 5-1   Best Day to End an Auction

Percentage of Respondents	Time of Day
52.6%	6 P.M. to 9 P.M.
23.4%	9 P.M. to Midnight
9.4%	3 P.M. to 6 P.M.
5.2%	Noon to 3 P.M.
2.6%	9 A.M. to Noon
2.6%	6 A.M. to 9 A.M.
1.1%	Midnight to 3 A.M.
2.9%	"Doesn't Matter"

TABLE 5-2   Best Time of Day to End an Auction

» It's clearly Sunday, except when it's not

Sunday has consistently been the favored time to end your auctions, but don't forget, there are exceptions to this rule. Super Bowl Sunday is clearly one of them. If the Sunday in question falls in the middle of a three-day weekend, you'll have less traffic. People travel and socialize more on holiday weekends than on regular weekends, and you'll feel their absence online. For long weekends, Monday evening may prove to be better.

Seasonal changes affect listing traffic, too. PowerSeller Aubrey of Jrgolfwarehouse had no listings posted at all one week late in March. When we spoke, he said the market for junior golf equipment would pick up in April when the weather improved and until then, he was concentrating on other parts of his business and holding back on his listings. Overall, PowerSellers remind newcomers that all businesses have seasonal ups and downs, and an eBay business is no exception. The important thing is to figure what your seasons are and prepare for them.

Seasons, like the weather, come and go. Some PowerSellers watch for changing weather across the greater part of the United States. When the forecast calls for snow, more people will be stuck at home and likely looking for diversion. That's potentially a good time to up your listings. Of course, the weather, like most predictions, is questionable. You don't want to choose a huge blizzard to list, because people who lose electricity are usually not online!

Armed with statistics, common sense, and the experience of PowerSellers, you can experiment with your products and customer base to find your best listing times. As with all other aspects of running an eBay business, be willing to stay flexible and try new things.

How Long Should Your Auctions Last?

Although you have fewer choices for the duration of your auctions than for when you should start and end them, the question of how long to run your auctions still brings varying answers from PowerSellers. You can choose to run your auctions on eBay for one, three, five, seven, or ten days. If you choose ten-day auctions, you'll have to pay $0.40 per listing for the extended time. The default listing is seven days, and certainly, this is a very popular choice among all sellers, including PowerSellers. Ten-day auctions are the next most popular choice, and three-day auctions have a special place in a PowerSeller's arsenal. Our discussion will focus on these three choices.

One-day listings are not generally useful to PowerSellers because they don't last long enough to generate strong competition, and they end so quickly that it's too difficult to keep up with processing them in large numbers. Five-day auctions don't share these drawbacks, but there's also not much point in ending the auction after five days when leaving it up for two more doesn't cost anything in extra fees. PowerSellers who use five-day auctions often tend to want to do it strategically to turn inventory over more quickly.

» A seven-day auction may be a week, but it's strong

Seven days seems to be the charmed length of most auctions. "I never, ever, run an auction for less than seven days. It costs me the same amount of money (listing fees) to run a seven-day auction as it does for me to run a three-day auction. I want all the exposure I can get for my money," says the PowerSeller known as Bargain Hunters Dream. Seven-day auctions will give shoppers ample time to watch the action and still check back in for bidding. They are also easy for PowerSellers to track. If you designate Sundays, Tuesdays, and Thursdays as your listing days, and you use seven-day auctions, you'll always know when your auctions are scheduled to end. This can simplify your workflow.

» Ten-day auctions; more time for more money

"If I believe an item will sell for more than $200, I run it for ten days in an attempt to get more exposure and, hopefully, a higher final bid amount," says Bargain Hunters Dream. PowerSellers of large-ticket items share this opinion. Lynn of Baronart deals in fine paintings and never runs auctions for less than ten days. She feels it takes this long for potential shoppers to find her items and decide on these big purchases. If you are dealing in very expensive merchandise, the extra listing fees for an extended auction won't matter.

Combining ten-day auctions with seven-day auctions is a popular technique for Tony of Wegotthebeats. He posts most of his auctions on Sunday evenings, but for some less-common CDs, he'll give them a ten-day run by starting them on Thursday. This way, all of his auctions still end on Sunday evenings, which is his preference.

» The one-two punch of the three-day sale

Most PowerSellers frown upon the three-day sale, but not all of them do. Adam of Acmeresale sprinkles his listings with some three-day auctions. According to this PowerSeller, the most active times in any auction are the first day, when the listing is new, and the last day, when the auction is about to end. If you run a three-day auction, you have good activity throughout almost the entire auction.

Adam also described a brilliant strategy for combining three-day auctions with five-day auctions. "If I have five pieces of the same item, I'll list three of them as five-day auctions, and two as three-day auctions. I know I'll sacrifice price on the three-day auctions, but all the bidders who miss out on those items and lose the auctions, automatically get e-mails from eBay directing them to my active five-day auctions. It actually generates much more traffic for the remaining auctions and higher final bids on the other items still for sale. It's worth sacrificing the lower-priced auction just for that."

» Do more research

We know, we sound like a broken record, but research is the key to your learning about your own niche on eBay, and deciding for yourself about the length of your auctions is yet another part of that learning. So, it's back to research once again.

As before, a good place to start is with completed auctions for competitive items. Look for the ones that sold for the highest price and see how long they lasted and when they ended. Then, experiment on your own. Try some of each of the different auction lengths to see which ones appeal to you the most. Your choice will be based on the price you can get for your sales, but it will also be based on how you feel about the flow of your work for each of the various auction lengths. You might find that sticking to a schedule is better for you, or you may prefer to mix it up so that auctions end throughout the week rather than on particular days only. As with everything else in your eBay business, you're the boss.

Pricing Strategies

There are basically two schools of thought about pricing. "Start it low and let it go," says Adam of Acmeresale. Many PowerSellers start all of their auctions at $0.99. They believe this is the best way to generate early interest in their items and build the pool of people looking at the auctions. Others say, list an item for the least amount of money you are willing to take for it, even if you don't sell it the first time and have to relist it. That way, you can't take a loss on something that doesn't recoup its acquisition costs. We'll explore both of these strategies more fully, but before we do, let's consider the different pricing options available to you through eBay.

Choose Your Format

eBay gives you choices in determining what pricing scheme you want to pursue. Most PowerSellers choose from among three variations: a standard auction format, an auction with a Buy It Now (BIN) feature, or a Fixed Price listing.

A standard auction is probably the type of sale you've already conducted on eBay. You choose the duration of the auction and the starting price. The rest is up to the customers you're able to attract, and the auction proceeds to its conclusion with the final price determined by whoever bids the most.

Adding a Buy It Now feature to your auction costs an additional $0.25 per listing. Your BIN price is just that, the price you would be satisfied receiving for your item if it were to sell immediately. When you list with a Buy It Now feature, your auction continues for the duration or until someone offers you the BIN price. As soon as someone does, the auction closes and your sale is complete. When someone bids on your item, your BIN figure disappears and the auction continues as any other auction would. So, a BIN price is not a guaranteed final price; it's just a way to end the auction early for a price that will satisfy you. PowerSellers use the BIN feature when they want to give customers the option of not having to wait for the auction to be completed. If you have a clear profit margin in mind, you can choose BIN for a price that will bring you the earnings you're looking for, and move along to other auctions.

The preceding discussion refers to a BIN auction without a reserve. You can also combine BIN with a reserve auction. In that case, the BIN remains until the reserve is met. The BIN price must be higher than the reserve (if only by a penny).

Fixed Price listings are a fairly new eBay listing format. In a relatively short time they've become so popular they represent a substantial percentage of eBay sales dollars. They are actually not auctions at all. When you create your listing, you establish a price and someone either pays that price or your item doesn't sell. Fixed Price listings can be for multiple items, so listing once you can specify that you have up to a quantity of ten identical items for sale. In the actual listing, the price will appear as a BIN, but the difference here is that the price will not disappear when someone makes a purchase. It will remain until the end of the auction, which is either when time runs out or when all of your items are sold. There is no additional fee for listing your merchandise as a Fixed Price sale. Very often, PowerSellers who use Fixed Price sales deal with new merchandise. They know what the item costs to acquire. They have a regular and repeatable source of inventory. They know the retail value of the item. They have a clear idea of their expected profit margin, and they establish a fixed price based on these factors. Operating your eBay business on a fixed-price basis is the option most similar to operating a brick-and-mortar store.

» Use "Best Offer"

One of the best parts about shopping at flea markets, garage sales, and the like is the chance to haggle with the seller. To say, "That's a bit out of my price range, would you accept . . . ?" It seems more often than not the seller accepts your offer. Then both parties win. The seller moves his inventory; you feel you got a bargain. Now you can do the same thing on eBay. When you're selling fixed-price items you can let buyers know you're open to reviewing other offers. You simply check the tab that says "Allow buyers to make best offers" when creating the listing. You can set a minimum offer you would accept. When a buyer makes a Best Offer it's still binding, like any other eBay bid would be. As the seller you have 48 hours to respond.

Should you use Best Offer? Based on our conversations with PowerSellers and others in the industry we feel you should give it a try. eBay doesn't charge you anything for announcing you're open to other offers. If you don't feel a buyer's offer is sufficient, you can direct him to other items in your inventory. Even a best offer that doesn't result in a sale is still a sales lead. A potential customer has started a dialogue with you, and that's always good.

---

eBay Express

eBay Express is a new eBay marketplace with its own separate address on the web (http://www.express.ebay.com/). It's designed for buyers looking to immediately buy new items, or certain categories of collectibles, from more experienced sellers only. As a seller, you must meet the following criteria to sell there:

- 100 or more feedbacks
- 98 percent positive feedback rating or above
- You accept PayPal (including payments from those with unconfirmed addresses)
- You're registered as a U.S. or Canadian seller

If you meet these criteria, and your item is listed in Fixed Price format, or an auction format with a BIN option, it will also appear in the eBay Express marketplace at no extra charge. For more details on eligibility, see http://pages.express.ebay.com/service/about/checklist.html.

---

eBay Express was meant to compete with Amazon and similar online retailers. Frankly none of the sellers with whom we spoke have had any real success yet on eBay Express. (You can track which of your sales are from eBay Express through your My eBay page.) While it's too soon to draw any conclusions from these early reports, it does mean we're unable to share any tips for success in this edition of the book! We just recommend making sure your items *are* in eBay Express if you are eligible. eBay is exploring increasing promotion, and it doesn't cost you anything to participate.

Now that you understand your pricing options, let's take a look at the two main strategies PowerSellers follow for pricing their items. We'll also consider the option of using a Reserve price, and we'll look at some strategies for bumping up your final prices.

» Start it low and let it go

Starting all of your auctions at the lowest price has some real strategic advantages. It is a sign of a veteran eBay seller who feels the thrill of starting an item at $0.99 and watching it climb to its final value. Aside from the thrill of the ride, starting your auctions low keeps your listing fees in line. Listing fees are linked to the starting price you set.

You may not think there's much difference between listing an item at $9.99 for $0.40 and listing that item closer to your expected final price of $25 for $1.20. For a single item, you're correct. But when you multiply a single item by the hundreds you'll be listing every month in order to become a PowerSeller, that $0.80 difference matters. If you sold 300 items this month, you'd pay $240 in additional fees for the sake of listing your item at $25. That's money coming directly out of your profits. Even if your final value for some of these items never reaches your target of $25, you'll still be ahead. Further, valuable items that begin at $0.99 almost always sell. Starting your items low has other strategic advantages. When you start low, your item comes to the top of the list of any search sorted by lowest price. Many shoppers sort their search results this way, and with low prices you're guaranteed a spot at the top, at least for a while until the price escalates. With your item at the top of the search list, you'll get a lot of attention early in the auction. This builds momentum. Once people bid on your auction, others tend to be more willing to place bids too. It's human nature for people to want what others have already shown they want too. Building momentum early in your auction actually increases the demand for your item and, therefore, your final value price.

» Find its worth and stick to it

As we mentioned, this approach is to establish the lowest price you'd be satisfied with and start your auction there. To control your fees, you may decide that price is going to be $24.99 or less. At this rate, you'll be adding a relatively modest increase in your listing fees, and this strategy may give you the peace of mind you need as you get started. Keep in mind, you may not get as many bids, and with decreased competition your final price may actually not be as high as it could be. But, you also won't be taking risks before you're ready.

If you find your item doesn't sell at all, you can relist it for another try. A simple click of a button allows the item to be automatically relisted. eBay will even credit you with the cost of relisting your auction if you meet the following criteria:

- You must relist the item within 90 days of the closing date of the original auction.

- Both the original listing and the relisting must be in the auction format or in the fixed-price format, so you can't use this with an eBay store.

- You may relist only single-quantity items.

- The starting price for the relisted item cannot be greater than the price in the original listing.

- You cannot add a reserve price to the relisting if one was not in the original listing.

- The relisting must end with a winning bid for you to qualify for a refund.

Clearly the choice is yours in terms of which pricing strategy feels right for you. Again, since you're the boss, why not try some auction listings in both strategies and see which ones bring you the best results?

Reservations about Reserves

Many new sellers seek comfort in adding reserve prices to their auctions. As you may know, a reserve is the absolute lowest price your auction must achieve before the item sells. You set your reserve price at the time you create your listing, and your listing shows that there is a reserve on the item. If the reserve price is never met, your item doesn't sell, and your auction just runs its course to the end, with no winning bidders. Believe us, we understand the security you have when you know your item has a rock-bottom price below which it simply can't be sacrificed. The fees for adding reserves to your auctions range from $1.00 for items priced $49.99 and below; $2.00 for items ranging between $50.00 and $199.99; and 1 percent of the reserve price (up to $50) for items priced at $200 or above. As a new seller, you may think this fee is well worth the security it buys. PowerSellers nearly unanimously disagree.

Most PowerSellers recommend that you never use a reserve.

The reason they state, again and again, is that it puts buyers off to your auctions. They report that some buyers won't even look at your listing if it has a reserve. With such strong buyer aversion to the reserve, it actually reduces the likelihood that your item will sell. The fees may not seem so steep, but when you factor in what a reserve does to your traffic, you find it actually costs you a great deal more than it seems to on the surface.

Is there ever a time when you'll use a reserve? Probably. You'll most likely want a reserve price if you're selling an item for someone else as a Trading Assistant. (Chapter 6 will tell you more.) In this case, you have not only your investment to consider, but someone else's too. You might also use a reserve if your item is in the category of rare or fine art. Lynn of Baronart uses reserves because her items sell for thousands of dollars each. She also has a much smaller, more specialized, target audience than other PowerSellers, and her customers are less likely to be put off by the reserve.

One last tip about reserves: PowerSellers agree, if you're going to use one, state what it is in the listing description. People generally don't, but that's really silly, in the long run. As one PowerSeller asked, "What's the big secret?" If you clearly state what your reserve is, you get the comfort and protection you seek, but your customers also get to see how much money they'd have to spend in order to get your item. It seems a reasonable compromise, doesn't it?

» Combine pricing and timing for smart selling

A combination of pricing and timing strategies can really boost your sales, and here are a few ideas to get you started. As we discussed in Chapter 2, building your inventory is a delicate balance between finding a popular item and overexposing your popular item in the marketplace. As a pricing strategy, don't flood your own market. You'll drive the price of your items down quickly. If you come upon a group of items, list them a few at a time across weeks so that you keep demand steady, but don't overdo the supply.

» Research and act fast

Here we go again. Go back for more research, but this time, don't just learn, move. Find competitive auctions that are doing very well and time yours to end right after them with a low starting price, recommends Adam of Acmeresale. Your auction will come up along with the successful one in any search that lists results by auction ending times. You'll catch the momentum of someone else's successful auction, and your low starting price will heat up your auction from the very beginning.

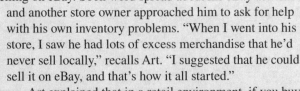

Arthur—Art Clem

For nearly 15 years, Art Clem operated brick-and-mortar hobby stores. By the time he sold his business in 1998, he had three of them. That's when he began casually selling on eBay. Soon word spread about his eBay activities, and another store owner approached him to ask for help with his own inventory problems. "When I went into his store, I saw he had lots of excess merchandise that he'd never sell locally," recalls Art. "I suggested that he could sell it on eBay, and that's how it all started."

Art explained that in a retail environment, if you buy 10 items to sell, you're really lucky to sell 9 of them. You'll always have that "remainder" problem with your merchandise. "I would have absolutely died to have this outlet (eBay) in the 15 years I was in a brick-and-mortar

business," Art exclaimed. Today, Art operates a successful eBay business selling nonelectronic games, such as Settlers of Catan and Axis and Allies. He has a catchy, friendly logo, and has branded his business well. To find new products, he travels to game-related trade shows. There he can branch out his product line and consider his next moves. He also studies the work of other online game sellers to identify his most successful competitors and watch what they're doing.

Art knows this research is vitally important to staying ahead of the curve. He also spends time on the discussion boards and groups. He uses the PowerSeller board a lot, and definitely recommends it to newer sellers. "The insight and knowledge I've gained from the discussion boards and groups like the Internet Merchants Association and the Professional eBay Sellers Alliance has proved to be rewarding both intellectually and financially," Art told us.

In addition to selling on eBay, Art also sells on Amazon, and he has his own Web store. He has been able to distinguish himself with a good solid reputation and name recognition among his customer base. He reported to us that he has an extremely high rate of repeat customers as compared to other eBay sellers. He attributes that to the niche in which he operates, great customer service, and fair shipping rates.

Art offers actual calculated shipping rates with each listing. When you view his listings, you'll see that your own ZIP code appears next to the shipping rate. "I know for a fact," said Art, "that we have customers who tend to purchase more, because they're not looking at exorbitant shipping charges." Another key element of Art's operation is that he has never gotten a negative feedback based on poor packaging. "You can eliminate that problem up front," he advises.

Art uses only fixed-priced listings. He said he realized some time ago, that 95 percent of his sales were being completed as Buy It Now transactions. That showed him that his customer base didn't want to deal with auction listings, but instead just wanted to buy his merchandise. Now he lists everything at a fixed price and moves the slower-moving merchandise into his eBay store.

When we asked him to advise new sellers, he recommended that whatever category you go into, scale your business and price your items so that you are going in with the intention of owning that category. "Scale your business for growth from the beginning," he said. "Our sales could double, and we probably would have to add nothing more than another employee." Currently, Art works with two full-time employees, and when we spoke, he was planning to add a part-time worker, too. He was also researching the field of educational games. He's never sold these before, but his research suggests that his customers would be interested in them. Art has built a successful eBay business by knowing what his customers want and providing it, at reasonable cost and with great customer service. No wonder he's an eBay success story!

Research and act fast

> **Get Your Auctions Going! Checklist**
>
> ✓ I've drafted or refined my About Me page, adding policies, pictures, and personality.
>
> ✓ I'm working on my My World page, to maximize its marketing punch by including links and fashioning a textured portrait of my eBay business.
>
> ✓ I've reviewed my policies as stated in my listings, and they're clear and comprehensive but friendly too.
>
> ✓ I'm keeping in mind how much time I can save by using eBay's Prefilled Item Information option when possible.
>
> ✓ When I describe the condition of the items I list I'm careful to be conservative.
>
> ✓ I consider listing extras when creating my listings, but I am aware of their cost and effectiveness.
>
> ✓ I wear my buyer's hat when writing titles for my listings, considering keywords, and space limitations.
>
> ✓ Templates can save me a lot of time so I'm always on the lookout for when I can use them.
>
> ✓ When I write my item descriptions I'm professional, positive, accurate, and honest. I'll show a little style too.
>
> ✓ It's smart to use photos liberally. I'm learning how to take the best photos I can.
>
> ✓ I know that timing my listings is important. I've considered the day and time my listings will end as well as what will work best for my given market.
>
> ✓ I have considered which format will work best for a listing, and I will give Best Offer a try.
>
> ✓ I've become familiar with eBay Express and will stay on top of its development.
>
> ✓ I'll experiment with pricing and remember factors that can affect it.

Chapter 6

Power-Charge Your eBay Business

Now that you've learned some of what PowerSellers know about creating great auction listings, it's time to start thinking of your whole eBay business from a PowerSeller's viewpoint. It's not enough to create great auction listings; you need to understand the many ways there are to make the most of these listings. Power-charging your auction sales will get you thinking of your eBay business in its totality. In the last chapter, you had to concentrate on each individual listing, but now it's time to put them all together and see what your eBay business looks like as a whole. Then you'll be ready to pump up your auctions, your sales, and your profits.

In power-charging your auctions, you'll consider your customers' needs, along with the effectiveness of your auction strategies, advertising options, and business practices. You are already moving from eBay hobbyist to potential PowerSeller, and the issues you'll explore in this chapter will take you even further along this journey. This journey will take you along a toll road, and the price you must pay is time in the form of trial and error. You'll have to stay flexible, use common sense, try what seems right to you, and be willing to move on if it doesn't work out. You will notice that many of the options we present to you here come with a price tag. We're not recommending that you spend your money by trying everything we offer. We're just showing you what's worked for PowerSellers and what the benefits of many different choices are. Which options you choose and how you allocate your resources will be up to you.

Your Business and Your Customers

Your business success depends on your success in attracting and retaining customers. That statement is incredibly simple, and yet at the same time it is terribly important. Without your customers, you can't succeed in business. Staging your business on eBay presents you with a set of challenges that you would not have to consider if you were operating a brick-and-mortar store. Not the least of these challenges is the fact that you most likely will never meet a single one of your customers in person. On the other hand, you'll have a pool of more than 200 million potential customers to draw from. But, you don't want to have to go back to that huge pool every time you make a sale. Your goal is to have a subset of those customers return regularly to shop with you. You want to build business relationships with your customers that will make them want to come back to you every time they need or want the products you sell. Let's take a look at some of the ways you can start building your customer base right now, keeping in mind that if you want to grow beyond eBay, your customer base and the knowledge you gain along the way are your two most prized possessions.

Court Your Customers

Every sale you make gives you the opportunity to make a customer for life. Think of your every interaction with a new customer as a chance to court a new friend. Your auction listings are already helping, because you're working to make them neat, accurate, and friendly. But there are still more things you can do to be sure your customers will remember who you are and think of you the next time they shop on eBay.

» Market through e-mail

"E-mail is probably the most ignored area of marketing," says Marketworks executive Paul Lundy. That's too bad because it's also one of the cheapest advertising methods.

Every e-mail you receive from a buyer becomes a point of contact with your customer. Once a customer sends you an e-mail to ask you a question about an item listed or gets in touch with you at the end of an auction, you are free to capture that customer's e-mail address and add it to your database. In the database, include details about the sale, including what the person bought, how much was spent, and any reactions you might have had to the sale. You can use this information if you need to contact the buyer again.

Now, you don't want to make a pest of yourself or get in trouble for spamming anyone, but you can put a link in your auctions to ask if your customers would like to receive e-mail about future products and auctions ("opt-in"). You should include a line that makes it clear you will not use the person's e-mail for any other purpose but to offer them more opportunities to shop, if they'd like. But many customers will be delighted to find another item up for auction and will be happy to take a look.

Writing in AuctionBytes, Brian Lawe of MyStoreCredit .com, advised sellers to view a relationship with a customer on his mailing list, as just that, a relationship. That customer should be courted with a "steady stream of e-mails." It's important to reward your customer for taking the time to read your e-mails (for example by offering them a discount if they make another purchase with you). Your goal should be to sell that customer something else within 30 days, Brian advised. You want them to return to you when they're in the market for a similar item, he counseled, instead of starting over with a search engine.

Done well this sort of marketing can be very effective. E-mail marketing is "a very powerful method to market to your past customers and soon-to-be customers (interested in your products)," says Chris of iCandyClothing.com.

» Try Constant Contact

Chris, like some other PowerSellers we've worked with, does his e-mail marketing through a company called Constant Contact. More than 100,000 small businesses use the service to create professional-looking e-mail campaigns.

Constant Contact enables you to:

- Create e-mails
- Create tracking reports
- Manage contact lists

Wizards and drag-and-drop features make creating e-mails simple (see Figure 6-1), and the company's templates are fully customizable so you can add your logo and colors, for example.

You can do more than fashion fancy e-mails with Constant Contact. You can find out who opened your e-mails and what they clicked on. This can help you determine when to send e-mails and which promotions are working for you. Finally, you can manage your list with features such as safe unsubscribe and a "join my mailing list box" you can add to your listings, About Me page, eBay store, or Web site. You can export existing mailing lists so you don't have to start building your list from scratch. Pricing starts at $15 per month, and a 60-day free trial is available. For more information visit www.constantcontact .com.

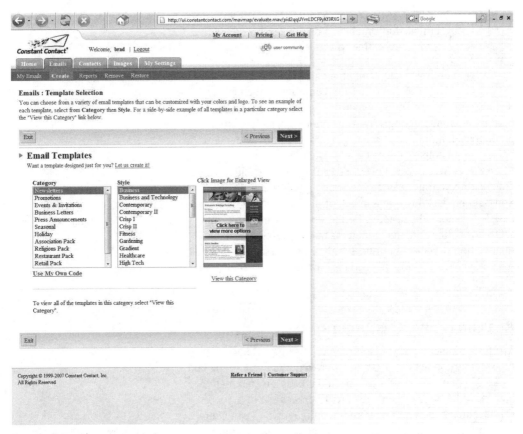

My Account | Pricing | Get Help

FIGURE 6-1 Constant Contact makes e-mail marketing simple (or simpler, anyway).

How about a Monthly E-Newsletter?

Because you're selling products you know about, you can provide valuable information and suggestions to your customers. Consider sending a monthly e-mail newsletter to your customers.

Here are some ways to gather names and e-mail addresses for your e-mail list:

- Use a third-party checkout process with an "opt-in" very prominently placed.

- Employ an e-mail footer saying "Join our preferred shopper club," etc., with a link.

- Offer a homepage promotion (on your Web site).

Try Constant Contact

- Use an About Me page promotion. To stay within eBay's rules, don't include a direct sign-up on that page, instead use a link to your homepage.

Every month you can send along a piece of news relevant to your products. You can offer advice for using the product or include a brief case study of a customer who is using the product in an interesting way. You can review a different product each month and perhaps include a brief review of a book your customers might be interested in.

A savvy West Coast PowerSeller offered these suggestions: "In creating your newsletter you want to be loose and friendly. Some sellers just throw in a bunch of their new items. A newsletter should be tasteful. Perhaps talk about the current season or holiday and include items that are related." Your imagination is your only limit. It only takes a couple of hours a month to create it, and it puts you in front of your best customers every few weeks.

Reassure Your Customers

Just for a moment, put yourself in your customer's place. Every time you buy something from an unproven eBay seller, you take a risk. No matter how well produced the listing is. No matter how clear the policy statements are. Even in view of a good, solid feedback rating, there comes a moment when you simply have to trust that the person selling what you want is going to live up to the promises made in the auction listing. That's one of the main reasons so many people stick with PowerSellers: they've proved themselves in this marketplace. Until you've achieved PowerSeller status of your own, you have a variety of programs available to you, both inside and outside of eBay, to give your customers some peace of mind in doing business with you. You certainly will not choose all of the programs we'll describe here, but some of them will seem right to you.

Of course, the first place to look for reassurance is eBay itself. eBay's Security & Resolution Center brings together many of eBay's services for researching and resolving transaction problems and fraud. You'll find it at http://pages .ebay.com/securitycenter/index.html.

Figure 6-2 shows the welcome screen for the Security & Resolution Center. You will find all of the community values and resources listed from here, and so will your customers. In

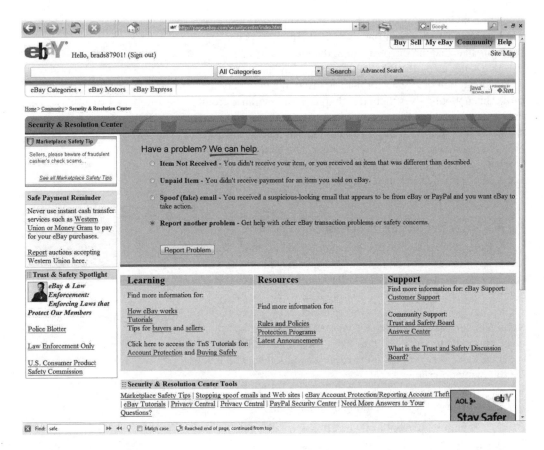

FIGURE 6-2 eBay's Security & Resolution Center should be the first stop for sellers when a transaction goes bad.

addition to this resource area, eBay also offers buyers some help in the event of seller fraud. If a buyer makes a purchase and the seller either never delivers the product or delivers something that is significantly different from the item description, the buyer can enlist eBay's help in getting the problem resolved. If the buyer paid with PayPal a buyer protection program is available that may include at least partial reimbursement.

» Use PayPal

We'll be spending a lot more time with PayPal in Chapter 7, when we discuss payment options for your sales, but PayPal is an excellent way to reassure your buyers that they have some protection in doing business with you. PayPal is owned by eBay and, as such, is part of the eBay dynasty. Settling disputes via PayPal is like keeping the problem in the family.

As a seller using PayPal, you offer your PayPal-member buyers the option of paying for their items with a major credit card. This not only gives them the charge-back assurance from their credit card companies, but it also provides them with two different types of PayPal buyer protection. The standard Buyer Protection program offers buyers monetary protection when purchasing a PayPal-backed item. The Buyer Complaint process is the other option available to PayPal buyers. Each is described in the sections that follow.

PayPal Buyer Protection Program

Buyer Protection offers buyers the chance to be refunded for losses up to either $200 or $2,000. Every item sold on eBay (except for vehicles and those sold through Live Auctions) is eligible for the $200 protection as long as it meets the criteria spelled out in PayPal's User Agreement (see www.pages.ebay .com/help/confidence/problems-support.html). Perhaps even more important to you as a future PowerSeller is the $2,000 in coverage available from the more experienced sellers who meet the following criteria:

- You have a feedback rating of at least 50.
- At least 98 percent of that feedback is positive.
- You have a Verified Premier or Verified Business Account (in good standing).
- The listing appeared on eligible eBay sites, such as eBay .com.
- The listing notes PayPal is an acceptable way to pay.
- You're from the United States, Canada, Germany, or one of a number of other countries (see that User Agreement).

Of course, if your item sells for more than $200, your prospective buyers will feel more comfortable about doing business with you if they're eligible to receive up to $2,000 rather than only a maximum of $200. eBay's item listing form includes a "buy safely" area (see Figure 6-3) where buyers can quickly see the level of protection that's available.

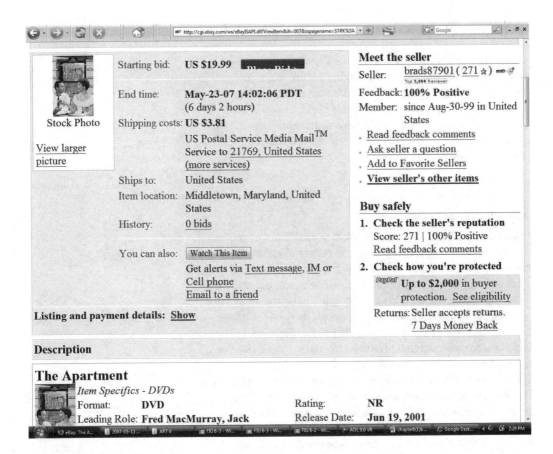

<figure> </figure>

FIGURE 6-3 Thanks to a redesign of eBay's item listing form, buyers can easily spot a seller's level of positive feedback and the amount of protection they offer through PayPal.

The Buyer Complaint Process

The Buyer Complaint process differs from the Buyer Protection program in that no refund is guaranteed in this case. PayPal agrees to investigate a complaint made through this process, but damages are subject to the successful recovery of funds that are owed to you.

We suggest you become familiar with the PayPal Resolution Center to learn more about these processes, both from a buyer's viewpoint and a seller's perspective. You can get to the Center from PayPal's homepage. Click the Security Center link at the bottom of the page and you'll see a link for it on the next page that appears.

As a seller you simply have to offer PayPal since the vast majority of your customers will want to pay via PayPal, and you can't even list on eBay Express unless you have a PayPal account.

While fraud is a concern that doesn't seem to be going away, you should prepare for it, but don't let the fear of it overwhelm you. Most disputes between buyers and sellers can be resolved long before they reach this point, as you'll see in Chapter 9. Plus, in Chapter 7 we have some other PowerSeller advice to protect you from buyers you may not want participating in your auctions.

» Try SquareTrade

SquareTrade is a privately held company that offers protection services to online buyers for eBay and other online merchant sites. You will find SquareTrade's Web site at www.squaretrade .com. When you sign up for the SquareTrade Seal program, the company verifies your address and contact information and does a check of your feedback rating and past history of settling customer service disputes on eBay. If you qualify, you will become a registered SquareTrade member, and you will have the SquareTrade Seal added to all your auction listings as verification that you are an approved seller. The seal tells buyers that you've met the verification standards and that you agree to participate in SquareTrade's Online Dispute Resolution service should the buyer need to resolve a problem purchase. Figure 6-4 shows the profile that appears when a buyer clicks on the SquareTrade Seal that automatically appears in all your listings once you become a member. SquareTrade Seal membership costs $9.50 per month, with the first month free as a trial, or you can sign up for a full year at a discounted rate of $95.

In addition to the SquareTrade verification process, SquareTrade also offers both an online mediation service and warranties for consumer electronics. Mediation is a valuable service when buyers and sellers get into a dispute they cannot resolve directly and need a third party to step in and help. SquareTrade can offer the chance for buyers and sellers to "calm down" and see a compromise. SquareTrade maintains a network of over 250 mediators who will step in to resolve an issue between the buyer and the seller. The person who files the case agrees to pay a fee of $29.95. (A $10 discount for PowerSellers who enroll in an expedited resolution service is also available.) Both seller and buyer must enter all relevant

FIGURE 6-4 SquareTrade's
buyer protection coverage
statement for a particular
listing, ensuring customers
that this seller is trustworthy.

information into a secure case page that is also accessed by the professional mediator.

SquareTrade does not guarantee the problem will be resolved through mediation, but the company does estimate an 80 percent success rate in cases where both parties participate, and those cases number more than 150,000 per year. Chapter 9 includes a profile of a SquareTrade mediator.

SquareTrade's mediation service also enables sellers to withdraw feedback left by buyers who "disappear" or who don't bother to respond to the mediation process. In order to qualify for this service, the claim must be filed within 30 days of purchase. This helps sellers address a tarnished feedback score when the buyer won't cooperate.

Yet another feedback service from SquareTrade is an expedited filing process for sales that result in a negative feedback. If a seller receives negative feedback, SquareTrade will notify the seller immediately and offer to mediate a settlement with the buyer and a possible withdrawal of the negative statement. This process carries a discounted mediation fee of $19.95, but no guarantee that the negative can be removed.

PowerSellers are not terribly supportive of this program. One PowerSeller noted that this seems to hit a person at his most vulnerable moment. When the negative feedback is fresh,

Try SquareTrade

the seller is often so angry that he will agree to pay the $20 fee just out of an emotional reflex. In view of eBay's Mutual Feedback Withdrawal program, discussed in detail in Chapter 9, some PowerSellers view this service as obsolete. Some even suggest that keeping this program going is SquareTrade's attempt to capitalize on a seller's devotion to a spotless feedback rating.

Much like PayPal, SquareTrade's protection services are heavily weighted toward the buyer. The benefit that sellers gain from participating with SquareTrade is the affirmation with their buyers that they have met SquareTrade's standards and have agreed to abide by SquareTrade's programs. This is not negligible. SquareTrade does not offer a perfect set of tools for sellers, but it does offer a level of assurance to buyers that sellers are not able to offer on their own. So, go ahead and sign up for SquareTrade. You'll find it a valuable tool as you build buyer confidence in your services.

SquareTrade Guarantees It

For PowerSellers of consumer electronics, SquareTrade offers a unique warranty service directly to buyers called CarePlus. SquareTrade With CarePlus electronics sellers can easily offer warranties to their buyers for most new, refurbished, and used electronics sold on and off eBay. Not only does the offer of a warranty attract buyers to bid, but sellers also earn a commission on each warranty sold. "SquareTrade inserts a warranty button in all my listings. I put a flyer in all my packages advertising the warranty," says PowerSeller Frank of Tessies-toys. "I earn many thousands of dollars each year in commissions, and the beauty of the program is that customers love the warranty." Frank sells used and refurbished cell phones and electronics.

A SquareTrade warranty extends the manufacturer's warranty on an item by two or three years. This gives buyers the peace of mind that they are covered if an item breaks down under normal use. If a buyer has a problem, the buyer calls SquareTrade or files a claim online, and SquareTrade will either have the item repaired or refund the item's full purchase price to the buyer. Buyers who chose a SquareTrade warranty will have a convenient online interface to buy, see, and manage all their SquareTrade warranties in one spot. The program covers unique items that can be hard to purchase warranties for such as the gray market, refurbished, and used goods often sold on eBay.

SquareTrade's warranties are simple to use and are generally more than 30 to 50 percent less expensive than those offered by big retailers. SquareTrade charges consumers only 10 to 15 percent of the item price on eBay (based on condition of the item) and only 10 percent for new items sold elsewhere.

» Have your ID verified

eBay's ID Verify program proves your identity to your potential customers. For a $5 fee, eBay will use your personal information to verify that you can prove you are who you say you are. You submit personal information such as your home address, phone number, date of birth, and certain installment and credit accounts with their associated monthly payments. This information is not a credit check, and the credit account information is used only for verification purposes and is never stored permanently on eBay. Only your contact information and date of birth are kept on file. Once you pass the verification process, the fee will be added to your eBay bill, and you will remain ID verified until your name, home address, or telephone number changes. You will then receive an ID Verified icon that will appear in all of your auctions. ID Verify helps you prove yourself to potential customers and helps assure them that you are a valid eBay seller.

Unlike other buyer assurance programs, ID Verify also offers real advantages to the seller. Once you are verified, you can list in Multiple Item or Fixed Price formats, you're eligible to use the Buy It Now or Best Offer features on any eBay listing, you may bid in an amount above $15,000, and you can sell in eBay's Mature Audiences category. Currently, ID Verify is only available to residents of the United States and U.S. territories (Puerto Rico, U.S. Virgin Islands, and Guam). Keep in mind that once you request ID verification, you will not be able to alter your contact information for 30 days, but with this in mind, the program is definitely worth the small investment it requires. To learn more about this program go to http://pages.ebay.com/help/confidence/identity-idverify.html.

» Consider a warranty

As you saw through the SquareTrade warranty program, you can go a long way toward reassuring your customers by offering some form of warranty. As PowerSellers described their policies to us, they ranged from "100 percent satisfaction guaranteed, no questions asked" to "refunds offered for merchandise that is significantly different from the listing description, please ask questions before bidding." Many PowerSellers offer a limited-time return policy, but almost all PowerSellers offer their

Consider a warranty

customers some means of finding satisfaction in the face of disappointment. The last thing you want is for a customer to close a deal with you and feel that he or she didn't get what was due. We'll cover these issues in much greater detail in Chapter 9, but for now, no discussion of customer assurance can be complete without at least a brief mention of warranty offers.

eBay offers a Service Plan that buyers can add to their computer and electronics purchases. The plans are offered by a third-party company, N.E.W. Customer Service Companies, Inc., a leading provider of extended service plans. Your buyer can choose either a Standard Service Plan or an Extended Service Plan. The standard plan is for products that don't come with a manufacturer's warranty. The coverage on these products begins 30 days after the end date of the auction or beyond the Buy It Now date of the transaction. The extended service plan allows your buyer to extend a 90-day, 6-month, or 1-year manufacturer's warranty. New, used, and refurbished items are eligible for coverage, but if a product is used, it must be less than five years old. All products must be fully functional at the time of the sale. These plans are not available to customers living in Maine, Alaska, Guam, or Puerto Rico, because of local statutes against the sale or purchase of extended service plans in those areas. In other areas, the service plans are available for computers and computer peripherals, cameras and photography equipment, video games and consoles, and musical instruments.

For the seller, there is very little risk in offering a buyer an extended service plan. For further information on these programs, go to http://pages.ebay.com/help/warranty/seller_overview.html. You will find links to the HTML code that you can copy directly into your item descriptions. You can choose to use a graphic and text or text-only link. You are obligated to use the HTML in both your listing and your e-mail to the customer who purchases the item, but that's where your obligation ends. If the customer decides on the service plan and clicks that link in your listing or e-mail your customer jumps directly to N.E.W., to complete the service plan purchase. That's when you earn a little kickback for every service plan your customer purchases. For every plan you sell, eBay will pay you a cash bonus of 25 or 50 percent of your eBay Final Value Fee for that item. The bonus is 25 percent if the product is below $200; 50 percent for products $200 and above.

Now, we personally never buy the extended warranty, but then we enjoy living life on the edge. Even if you only sell one warranty every few months, any little savings on your eBay fees goes toward improving your profit margins. With no investment and no risk to you, why not add a warranty option?

» Consider buySAFE

In 2006 one of eBay's largest companies, GlacierBayDVD, shut down, leaving hundreds of its customers without the products they ordered and paid for. Fortunately, GlacierBay was bonded so all of its customers eventually either received their products or were reimbursed. The company behind this bailout was buySAFE, Inc.

In conjunction with financial institutions such as Liberty Mutual Group and Travelers, buySAFE offers bonding services for people who sell through online auctions or their own e-commerce sites. Sellers bonded by buySAFE go through a qualification process that validates them as dependable, reliable sellers of good reputation. Bonded sellers receive a buySAFE logo to include in their auction listings. This seal not only proves that the seller has met the necessary requirements of the bonding process, but it also offers the buyer financial protection against fraud and default. In exchange for the program's vouching for your decency as a seller, you pay buySAFE 1 percent of your final transaction price. If your item doesn't sell, you pay nothing.

To qualify for bonding through buySAFE, you must be based in the United States and have $1,000 in average monthly eBay sales and 100 eBay feedbacks.

Certification by buySAFE assures your customers that you will ship the item when you've said you will and that you'll be willing to work with buyers to resolve any disputes. Your buySAFE bonding includes protection of up to $25,000 per transaction. Whether or not it's worth it for you to become buySAFE certified is something you'll need to find out for yourself. Frankly, many of the PowerSellers we've spoken with don't feel it's necessary. If you're already a PowerSeller, you've proved yourself to be a reliable, dependable seller. The question becomes then why do you need to pay a percentage of your final transaction fee to a company that will verify you are a reliable, dependable seller? But others feel that the 1 percent fee is money well spent. Coin and bullion dealer Jim Orcholski, for example, thinks buySAFE "is a wonderful thing," and that people are glad to see their logo on his listings. Our technical editor, David Yaskulka has also used buySAFE and notes it separates you from the pack in two important ways:

1. You've gone through an extensive vetting process, which has allowed you to be bonded.

2. You can offer your buyers iron-clad protection.

What's more, in 2006, buySAFE reported the results of a study showing that merchants using buySAFE increased their revenues by 6.8 percent.

Reward Your Customers

You will reward your customers by providing them with quality products and great customer service. In addition to those two necessary elements, you can also reward them with little bonuses and treats. Every time you please a customer, you increase the likelihood that your customer will return for more shopping. PowerSellers have come up with ways to reward their customers, and some of these ways may seem just right for you, too.

» Offer a coupon

Most of us love getting a little bit off the price of a purchase, and a coupon is a great way to do this. When you ship your item, include a coupon for dollars off the customer's next purchase. Or, you can offer a percentage off, if that seems a better choice to you. Spend a little time creating a coupon that says, thanks for shopping, and here's a little incentive to come back and shop again. "When shipping my product, I randomly include a coupon for $10 off," says a PowerSeller with more than 33,000 positive feedbacks. That customer is bound to feel like a winner and return to use the cash-back offer. Figure out your price point and your profit margin, and then decide what type of offer makes the most sense to you, but consider offering an incentive to stop by again.

» How about a little thank-you gift?

PowerSellers have devised lots of creative ways to send a little love out to their buyers. A coupon is only one way to look at this. You may keep it as simple as printing little thank-you business cards that get popped into every package. Of course, these include your username and some graphic representation of your business. You may include a favorite recipe with every shipment. Try to choose something that will make a connection between the bonus and your business. One DVD-selling PowerSeller includes a bag of microwave popcorn with every shipment. Until you can afford that added expense, there are many creative ideas you can use. Just remember that you can't advertise your bonus gift in your listings without violating eBay's rules, but you can certainly slip it into your shipping boxes as an added surprise. Maximize the value of your little gift by making sure it includes your Web site address and your eBay username on every piece. Here are just a few of the creative ideas PowerSellers shared: magnets, pens, key chains, candles, calendars, flower seeds, cell phone antenna boosters, gift boxes, and Infrared transceivers for wireless transfer of data from a notebook to a desktop computer!

Your Business and Your Auctions

Let's turn away from your customers now and take a look at your auctions to see how you can maximize them to your best advantage. PowerSellers have advice for linking your auctions, advertising your business, and making the most of your space on eBay. Once you've read about the different ways PowerSellers manage their listings, you'll have many ideas for how you can get your auctions power-charged too.

›› Keep the traffic flowing

"I constantly run 10 to 12 fixed-price listings of my most popular items, all linked to my other auction listings," says a Florida-based PowerSeller. He knows these listings will sell, and his constant presence on eBay not only keeps him available to his return customers but also drives traffic to his other listings, allowing him to expand his product offerings and try new markets.

›› Relist your unsold items

When you have an item that doesn't sell the first time you list it, go ahead and relist it to try again. Just do it within 90 days of the closing of your first auction. If it sells during that second

Relist your unsold items

listing, eBay will refund the second listing fee, so your cost will not be greater than if it had sold the first time. To qualify for this refund, you must relist the item at the same original price or less. You also may not add a reserve if the first listing did not have one, and if it did, you can't increase the reserve. Before you relist, consider changing the title, improving the photo, or reworking the item description. See if you can come up with something to freshen the listing for its second time around. Relisting an item is a simple process. From the My eBay page, click the relist link from the Action drop-down menu next to the item to get the sale going again.

Unfortunately, if the item doesn't sell the second time, you'll be charged for the second listing fee as well as the first, so do your best to make it move when you relist it. Now's the time you may want to move it over to your eBay store, where it will remain active for 30 days. We'll explore your eBay store options in much greater detail in Chapter 11.

Give Your Bidders a Second Chance

You will certainly have an opportunity to offer your bidders a second chance to purchase something you've listed. If your winning bidder does not pay for the item, you are free to get in touch with the next highest bidder and offer that bidder the chance to buy it. You can also contact the highest bidder in an auction that does not meet your reserve price if you decide that you are willing to sell the item for that price after all. Finally, if you have multiple items, but you only list a single one in an auction, you are free to contact the other bidders and offer those items for sale. None of these actions will violate eBay policy, and they all make good business sense. It's just a matter of turning a nibble into a good catch! Here's what you'll do to create a second-chance offer:

- Go to your My eBay page. Under the All Selling link along the left-hand margin, click the Sold or Unsold link.
- Are Second Chance offers enabled for an item? If so, you can get to the Second Chance link through the pull-down menu in the Action column.
- Just click the Second Chance Offers link, then click continue.

■ Choose the bidders you'd like to receive offers, along with the offer duration. Write a personal note to the bidder.

Note that some auction management services can automate this process so it's much simpler.

When sending Second Chance offers follow eBay procedures closely. Unfortunately, due to the frequency with which fraudulent Second Chance offers are sent, some members will be suspicious of these offers. eBay's Safeguarding Member IDs program, launched in 2007, should help stem the tide of fraudulent Second Chance offers and ease buyers' fears of fraud. Under this initiative, User IDs are not shown on listings where bids reach $200 or greater; instead aliases are used to identify members (e.g., Bidder 1, Bidder 2). Sellers though can still access bidder details through the bid history pages as well as through their My eBay pages.

Advertising Your Business

Advertising is a business expense that any business owner must consider. Your eBay business will draw upon different forms of advertising, but it's wise for you to plan to spend some time and money promoting your new business. We've already given you some PowerSeller advice in recommending that you send out little reminders and gifts to the people who buy from you. That's sharply targeted advertising directed to people you already know are interested. You've also seen that keeping a steady stream of auctions listed at all times helps direct a flow of traffic to all of your listings. But there are still some additional advertising investments that you'll want to try. As you might expect, most of your advertising will happen right on eBay, but you'll also see some ways you can branch out to the rest of the Internet to entice new customers.

» Do well while you do good with eBay Giving Works

eBay Giving Works is the charitable program beloved to many of eBay's most successful sellers. The Giving Works program is administered on eBay by MissionFish, a nonprofit organization dedicated to charitable fundraising through e-commerce. When

Do well while you do good with eBay Giving Works

you create your listings through the Giving Works program, a portion of your proceeds goes to a charity you choose (from over 10,000 choices). That nonprofit's logo and mission statement will automatically be included in your listing, along with an official guarantee from MissionFish. Your business steps into a spotlight of charitable contributors on the eBay Web site, and your listing gets a special ribbon icon that appears in search results.

Participating in the Giving Works program puts you in a terrific strategic position on eBay. Shoppers can designate their searches to include only those merchants who participate, so you will automatically stand out from your competition within that group of shoppers. The fact that you are willing to put your efforts toward more than just profit also makes a strong impression on your potential customers and speaks well for the values you hold as a member of the eBay community. But, let's not discount the boost you're likely to get for your own business through your charitable work.

A survey from Opinion Research Corporation found that 68 percent of consumers said they are likely to look at a company's reputation for supporting causes when deciding which company to buy from. Plus, MissionFish makes the giving simple. When you sign up, you process your sale just as you would any other sale. MissionFish will collect your donation, send it on to the nonprofit you've selected, and issue you a receipt for tax purposes. This program allows you to partner with large, well-known nonprofit brands.

Happily, eBay also wants to make it easier for you. Not only will they give you marketing benefits, but eBay now has a fee credit policy giving you refunds on your eBay fees (listing and final value fee on successful listings) pro rata with your donation percentage. So donate 10 percent and save 10 percent on your eBay fees!

Finally, it was a certain independence and self-motivation that brought you to your eBay dream. That dream is all the more gratifying when you can use your business efforts to do the charitable work closest to your heart. Strategic philanthropy is good for the business, good for the business owner, and good for the society that makes the business possible. For more information about the Giving Works program, go to http:// givingworks.ebay.com.

Benefit from Prominent Charity-Related Auctions

A great way to drive traffic to your own eBay Giving Works auctions is to piggyback off the tremendous traffic that auctions from companies such as Kompolt (www.kompolt.com) generate. Kompolt is an agency that creates auctions for high-profile clients (think Jay Leno and Elton John), who want to auction off items for their favorite charities. Their auctions often attract tens of thousands or even hundreds of thousands of visitors because they're so prominently promoted by Kompolt, in the media, and even on eBay's Home page.

Kompolt auctions include a link to "buy other items" within eBay Giving Works (eGW) auctions that benefit the same cause (see the eGW box in Figure 6-5). Every eBay seller can create eGW listings for the same cause and appear on the page buyers see when they click that buy other items link. And the more related items you have for sale, the higher up you appear on that page. What a fantastic way to drive the kind of traffic to your auctions that you could otherwise only dream of!

FIGURE 6-5 eBay sellers who create listings for causes can piggyback off the mass exposure Kompolt auctions receive. See the Buy Other Items link in the eBay box at the bottom of the figure.

» "Guide" buyers to your listings: write Reviews & Guides

As an eBay member you can share your opinions and expertise with millions of other eBay members as well as the Internet community at large. Just post a review—or better yet a guide—to eBay's Reviews & Guides area. If you've been on Amazon or Epinions you can imagine what eBay's reviews are like. You can critique and then rate books, DVDs, cameras, monitors, and other specific products you're familiar with. It's the guides though that you should pay particular attention to, as someone with products (and yourself) to sell.

You can write a guide (sort of a primer) on anything in which you have expertise. Brad has written guides about

FIGURE 6-6 Writing reviews and guides is a great way to share your expertise with the eBay community and promote yourself.

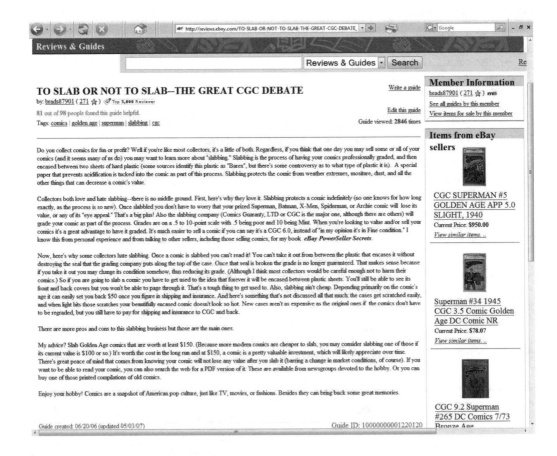

telecommuting, grading vintage comic books, and eBay powerselling. They can take some time to write, but the payoff is there. Search engines such as Google index these guides as they crawl the Web. So anyone searching for information on your topic may come across your guide. Better yet, when you write a guide eBay puts some of your current listings right next to it. As one prolific guide writer explained to us "this is invaluable free advertising aimed at your exact audience."

But can they really help you sell items? Are they worth the investment in time? "Certainly," says PowerSeller Hugh Vaughn-Williams, one of eBay's Top 100 reviewers. One of Hugh's most popular guides is *Writing Antique Listings That Sell*. "They increase my eBay store sales (buyers often mention my guides)," he says. So head over to eBay's Reviews & Guides area, http://reviews.ebay.com/, and share the wealth! Figure 6-6 shows a guide that Brad wrote about protecting valuable comic books.

» Blogs can bring bucks

Blogs (a contraction for Web log) are informal newsletters, collections of postings, or articles that anyone can create. Blogs have done more to democratize the publishing process than anything since the printing press. Why write a blog? As with guides they're a way for you to demonstrate your expertise. They're another way for you to advertise your eBay listings too, since they're indexed by search engines. Your blog is what you decide it is, so you can include links to your listings within it. Kelvin Cook, an eBay seller specializing in Navy-themed collectibles writes several blogs related to the items he sells. He knows they drive traffic to his listings because of the messages users have posted. Tools like the free, simple-to-use blogger (www.blogger.com/start) can help get you started as a blogger.

» Explore Google AdWords

Surely you're all-too familiar with those little text ads that appear to the right of Google search results. Advertisers have paid for those ads, which appear when Web users search using the keywords they have specified. They set up their advertising through Google's AdWords service.

Many of eBay's top sellers participate in these kinds of programs, and we recommend you explore them also. For example, when video game PowerSeller Steve Grossberg buys keywords through AdWords, they're usually game titles such as "Eternal Darkness." When someone searches Google for that game, his ad will come up. You'll need to experiment to see which keywords give you the best bang for your bucks. While AdWords campaigns can help drive Web surfers to your listings, they're especially important if you have a Web site to advertise (see Chapter 11). Finally, although PowerSellers seem much more likely to use the Google service, Yahoo has a similar program called Yahoo Search Marketing.

» Use your own Web site

As you saw in Chapter 3, having a business on eBay makes it very important for you also to have your own Web site. Fortunately, now you know how to go about getting one. Using that Web site to advertise your eBay business couldn't be easier. You already own a domain name, and since you followed our advice, you chose one that reflects your eBay business. Now, every time someone does an Internet search relevant to your products or business, it's possible that your domain name will pop up in the search results.

You'll simply include a link to your eBay store and auctions from your Web site, and all the visitors who stop by there can easily see what you have to offer for sale on eBay. "I don't even let my customers get into the main part of eBay. I link all my advertising directly to my eBay store, that way I bypass all the competition," said a PowerSeller with a 99.99 percent positive feedback rating.

» Join eBay's Affiliate Program

Join eBay's Affiliate Program (see Figure 6-7) and you can start earning money without even selling anything! Once you're a member, every time you send someone to eBay, say through a promotional link on your Web site, you'll earn a considerable commission. There are two ways you can earn a commission. One is by sending people to eBay who then become active eBay members. eBay will pay you from $25 and $35 (depending on your monthly total of new members) for each new active member you generate for the company that way. The second way occurs when someone who came from your site wins an

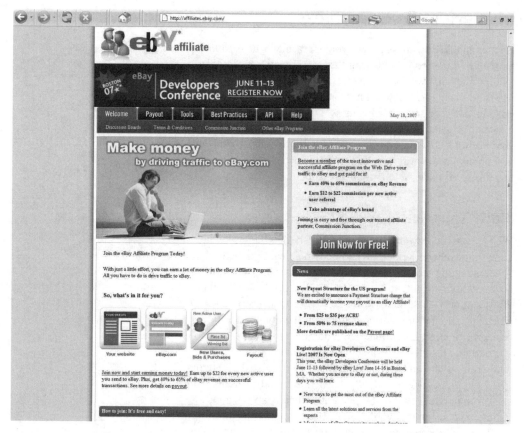

FIGURE 6-7 Some sellers make thousands of dollars (or more) through their participation in eBay's Affiliate Program.

auction or buys something through BIN. You earn this commission whether the customer buys something from another seller or from you. When that happens, affiliates earn from 50 to 75 percent (percentage varies with the total monthly revenue generated) of eBay's revenue (the total percentage of fees it receives for the listing). eBay recently changed the rules for its Affiliate Program so you can now earn commissions on your own sales that you referred from your Web site, newsletter, etc. Note that eBay will not pay a commission on traffic emanating from paid search (e.g., Google) campaigns.

Being an affiliate can really pay off. eBay says some of its partners earn their livings through the program, with its top 50 affiliates averaging over $1 million a year in commissions. For more information go to http://affiliates.ebay.com/.

Taking Care of Your Business

Having an eBay business allows you to learn as you go, and you must keep doing both right from the start. Learn your lessons, incorporate what works, move on from what doesn't, and don't be afraid to cut your losses. There is no magic formula for your eBay business or any other business. Operating on eBay makes it easier for you to be flexible. You should use that flexibility to your advantage. Never miss an opportunity to learn something new about a better way to take care of your business. Here are a few tips from PowerSellers that should help.

Study Your Sell-Through

When we asked PowerSeller Steve Grossberg what lesson he knows now that he wished he had known a year ago, he said, "understanding sell-through ratio." In Chapter 2, you learned about identifying potential sources of good products to sell on eBay, and now it's time for you to test your theories. Use a practical formula for determining your sell-through rate. For a period of time, let's say one month, take the number of auctions you had that resulted in a sale and divide that number by the total number of auctions you ran. Suppose you listed 100 items in the month of June. As of July 1, you have sold 60 items. Your sell-through rate would be 60 percent, which is a very good number and a sign that you're on to some good products.

Your sell-through rate is important because it reflects what your actual cost is to do business. If your sell-through rate is below 50 percent or so, you are actually paying more than the going rate in listing fees because you're paying for all of the auctions that don't result in sales as well as the auctions that do. That adds to your listing fees for the successful auctions. So, you want to keep a careful eye on your sell-through rate. By studying your sell-through carefully, you'll be able to identify the most profitable parts of your business, and you'll see new business opportunities. At the same time, you'll see what isn't selling well, and you'll learn what not to pursue any further.

Use Your Auction Management Software

As you learned in Chapter 4, most PowerSellers use auction management software, and you should be using it too. Most auction management programs can help you analyze your data and get a feel for what your sell-through is. You can print monthly reports that show all of your listings and all of your items that sold. These will help you calculate what percentage of your listings is actually selling. You will also find these monthly reports invaluable to your record keeping when we get to Chapter 10.

» Use your counters creatively

You learned in Chapter 3 about why you should be using a counter on your auction listings. Now, it's time for you to use those counters to study the results of your efforts. Here are some good ways to do that:

- Run listings in different categories. Double-check your category choices by running listings for similar items in more than one category. Then, watch your counters carefully to see the results. This will allow you to keep refining your category choices for increased traffic.

- Run listings with different titles. By using different titles for similar items, you can check on your keyword choices. This will help you see which keywords are generating the most hits and the greatest traffic to your listings.

- Use counters to refine your auction timing. Watch your counters carefully to see when your auctions are getting the most traffic. Then you can change your auction ending strategies to take advantage of your greatest number of visitors.

- See what other eBayers are saying about you. One little tip to remember is that if your auction is getting a lot of traffic, but no bids, people are talking about you on the discussion boards! It may seem like a huge universe, but it's not that enormous that gossip doesn't travel. Just consider the listing featured in Figure 6-8. Not only did he have more than 15 million viewers before his auction ended, he made it onto eBay radio and national television!

Use your counters creatively

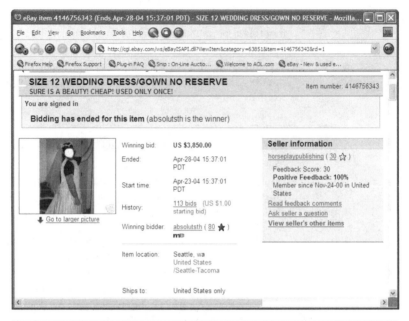

FIGURE 6-8 These two views show an unusual eBay listing and the counter recording of how many people viewed this auction, even after the item was sold!

» Consider Sellathon ViewTracker

As your business grows, you may find you want more exact data than you can gather from either your auction management software or your counters alone. That's when you may be ready to turn to Sellathon and their ViewTracker product. ViewTracker not only keeps track of all your auction visitors, but it also tells you how they found your auction, if they saved your auction to their My eBay pages, how many times they've checked in, and much more too. For more information see www.sellathon.com.

Here's how it works. When you are a Sellathon user, every time you create an auction listing, you add a little code to the bottom of your auction. Once this code is added, two things happen. First, you get a little Sellathon banner that appears in your listing. Second, every time that banner loads on your auction page, it sends a huge amount of data from the viewer's computer to Sellathon's computers. When you check on your Sellathon listing pages, you'll find the following information for each visitor:

- The sequential number of that visitor, whether he or she was the fifteenth or the fiftieth to view your listing

- The date and time the visitor arrived

- The visitor's IP address, the numbers that are unique to each computer

- The visitor's geographical region

- If the item already had a bid

- If the visitor is watching the auction in My eBay

- Whether the visitor browsed a category, searched a category, searched all of eBay, used eBay's Product Finder utility, came to the auction through your See Seller's Other Items link, or found your item in some other way

- The category this visitor was either browsing or searching in when your auction was found

- The search terms the visitor used if he was searching

- Whether the search was for "Titles Only" or "Titles and Descriptions"

- Did your visitor choose to view Auctions Only, Buy It Now, or both?

- Which search preferences and options your visitor

Consider Sellathon ViewTracker

chose. For example, show/hide pictures, sellers that accept PayPal, etc.

■ The visitor's method for sorting results. For example, high price, low price, auctions ending first

Sellathon users can also view their own auctions for information about the traffic they receive. That information includes the following:

■ The most active time of day for each auction

■ The most popular ways visitors are finding the auction

■ The most popular search terms used

■ The type of search, Titles only or Title and Description

■ The preferred sorting method used to view the auction

■ The total number of visitors to the auction

■ The busiest day

■ The most frequent IP address for this auction

■ The page number visitors are finding your auction on most frequently

■ The current high bid for the auction

At this point, you probably don't need as much information as Sellathon provides. You've got too many other things to concentrate on now before you'll be ready to use this much information. When you've built a solid business, you might want to invest some money and give this program a try as you fine tune your business. You'll be able to check your keywords, timing strategies, and category placements on the basis of solid data. Sellathon ViewTracker is not inexpensive, but it does provide a lot of value for the money. You can buy the licensing rights for one year for $49. That allows you to track 25 simultaneous auctions. If you list more than 25 auctions, you'll receive an e-mail offering you an upgrade to the next licensing level for a fee of $89 per year, which will allow you to track up to 250 auctions. You don't have to upgrade, but then only the first 25 auctions will be tracked. The highest level of licensing will cost $199, which will allow you to track a limitless number of auctions. Auctiva, one of the auction management companies we covered in Chapter 4, recently acquired Sellathon, so keep your eyes open for changes.

» Use Medved's eBay Auction Counts

Since 1999 Medved Auction Counts has been monitoring eBay auctions 24 hours a day, 7 days a week. By checking their site you can see the number of listings in various categories, as well as the sell-through rates for those categories. What's more Medved breaks out BIN auctions so you can compare results from BIN auctions to those in other formats.

Medved's Web site provides users with graphs of daily, weekly, monthly, and yearly data. You can also see the sum total of all the data they've collected in a single graph. To view the graphs, go to www.medved.net/cgi-bin/cal.exe?EIND. Let's take a look at just a couple of these graphs so that you can see how valuable they are to you in gathering information about your business.

The weekly chart shown in Figure 6-9 shows that listings were highest on Sunday. That's not surprising, given what we know about the popularity of Sunday evening auctions. Listings bottomed out on Tuesday morning and then, for this week, steadily increased toward the next weekend.

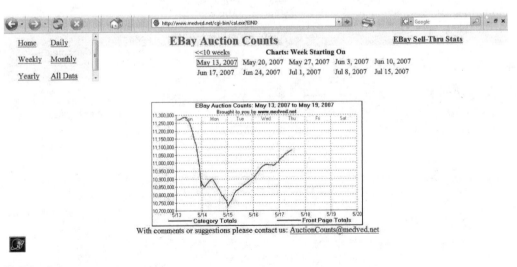

FIGURE 6-9 The weekly chart from Medved shows a typical weekly flow of traffic on eBay.

Use Medved's eBay Auction Counts

By checking other weeks in comparison, you'll see that the standard advice of Sunday nights and Thursday nights for ending auctions, while generally reliable, is not cut in stone. Take a look at this chart for just a few weeks earlier, shown in Figure 6-10, and you'll see quite a different pattern. Sunday listings were just average, while listings on several other days that week were considerably higher. Turns out that Sunday was Easter, a time when many people were doing other things, which points out how important it is to pay attention to the calendar when planning your auctions!

Carefully studying the weekly charts can help you determine the best times for you to list and end your auctions. The monthly charts Medved provides are also useful. You can use these to track slow and busy seasons for you and other eBay sellers. You can determine if your slow month corresponds with months that are just slow for you or slow for other eBay sellers too. This might help you determine if you'll need to broaden your product offerings to get you through those slow months by targeting things that might sell better in the months that are slow for your standard product line. Just as PowerSeller Aubrey of Jrgolfwarehouse, mentioned in Chapter 5, knew to plan for a slow month in March, you'll be able to plan for your particular slow months too. If you find your slow months are also slow for most other sellers, you may decide those are the months you'll use to plan your vacation.

FIGURE 6-10 This weekly Medved chart shows just how unpredictable eBay traffic can be.

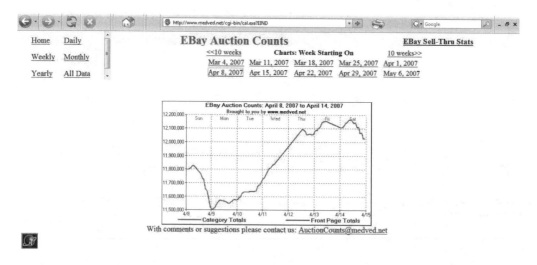

Manage Your Business

You're the boss now, so it all comes down to you. Here are a few suggestions for you to keep in mind as you go about your business. PowerSellers learned most of these things the hard way. Aren't you glad you don't have to?

» Turn over your inventory

Your goal is to move inventory into your business and out of your business. That's where the profits lie. But, suppose you buy a load of items and in studying your sell-through, you can see they really aren't going to earn what you hoped they would. Get them going. Even if it means you only make your costs or even if you occasionally have to take a loss, it's more important to get some money out of that inventory so that you can put it in more profitable items. "Rapid turnover and reinvesting your money for more products is one of the keys to long-term success on eBay," a PowerSeller from New York told us. "Turning over your inventory is the key to high profits," agrees a Florida-based PowerSeller. No one likes to settle for no profit, but sometimes it's the best alternative you have.

» Automate everything

"Work constantly to automate and streamline your process. Listing, e-mail, shipping, everything that can be automated makes your sell-through better, and gives you time for building your inventory. It's not as easy as you'd think," said a PowerSeller who specializes in coins and collectibles and maintains a 99.9 percent positive feedback rating. "I wish I'd started earlier trying to integrate all aspects of my auction business, to make everything seamless. I'm constantly trying to make the 'flow' a little smoother," he added. He had to retrofit his operation, but thanks to his willingness to share his experiences, you don't. You can build these systems into your operation as you go, giving you an advantage from the very start.

You need to think and work like a PowerSeller. Use every tool you have, from your auction management software, to your Web-hosted photos, to your automatic feedback procedures, to replace your day-to-day tasks with an automated process that you can manage.

» Hire help

"Hire help early on. Look at the end result of what you want. If you want high volume, you have to have help," advises PowerSeller David of Cultureandthrills. This is a difficult thing for new sellers to do. First there is the money to consider. Then you have to be willing to trust something you're just starting to build to someone else's work habits. It's difficult to give up control and allow someone else to do what you're just getting used to doing yourself. Do it anyway.

Look at it from a different perspective. By bringing someone in to help you early on, you'll be able to have that person train along with you. You'll be perfecting your systems while you're teaching them to your employee. This will give you, not only your own perspective, but someone else's too. You'll be learning the process with two brains instead of just one.

"My energies must go to acquiring inventory and properly cataloging what I have. I can't possibly be successful if I have to do all the listing and shipping myself too," added our PowerSeller. Know what you must do as the boss, and find parts of your business you can turn over to a trusted employee.

Remember you don't need to hire full-time help. You certainly are not ready for that. You don't have the volume, you don't have the money, and you don't have the need. Instead hire part-time helpers. Perhaps start with someone who comes in two afternoons a week for a couple of hours to do all your shipping. Maybe you'll then move on to train that person in listing auctions, leaving you to do all of the e-mail responses along with the inventory management. You'll find your own way to make use of help once you have it.

Now, where will you find a trusted employee? There are many places to look. The local high school is full of reliable, worthy, and capable students. Get in touch with the principal for some recommendations. You will most likely find a pool of potential helpers who would so much rather work for you than flip burgers for spending money. Plus, these people are very likely to be completely at home in front of a computer. They can probably teach you a thing or two about HTML also! The next step would be the local community college. You're bound to find students here who need some extra cash, and they'll be even more likely to come to you with computer skills you'll find useful.

For many of your tasks, don't overlook the stay-at-home mom. By the time moms have kids in school, many are looking for a little diversion during the day that can also help supplement the family income. You can provide them with a little work on a flexible schedule that could easily integrate with the demands of their families. Plus, you could be helping them to learn a business they'll then want to pursue for themselves. Or, consider a retiree. They can be the most reliable employees of all.

Don't look at the expense of hiring help as a draw against your bottom line. Look at it instead as a way to maximize your effort. "When my helper comes in for the afternoon, and I'm free to do listings and plan inventory, I'm always so surprised at the end of the day to see how many things I also have packed and ready to be shipped," crowed a PowerSeller from New Jersey. You don't have to offer a huge salary for these part-time workers either. If you stick with minimum wage, and you pay for four to six hours of work per week, your employee wages will be no more than many people spend per week on babysitting fees. Chapter 10 will tell you more about the record-keeping issues and concerns for hiring help. The return on your expense will be well worth the investment.

Become a Trading Assistant

Once you've gained some experience and feel confident with your ability to list and sell on eBay, you may want to leverage this confidence into another branch of your business. Trading Assistants (TAs) sell products on eBay for people who don't want to do it themselves. Often these are people who are intimidated by computers or who don't feel confident in their abilities to successfully navigate in eBay's waters. Their intimidation can translate into profits for you. We spoke with many PowerSellers who are also Trading Assistants, and it's a good match. As you build your business, you will already be putting all of your systems in place. You'll have all of the equipment and expertise necessary to create excellent auctions, so you might just find that you enjoy offering this expertise to others.

» Get listed in eBay's Trading Assistant Directory

Becoming a Trading Assistant on eBay couldn't be easier. You must meet some basic requirements, but these are not difficult to achieve. You must have sold at least four items in the last 30 days. You must have a feedback rating of at least 100, with a positive rating of at least 97 percent. And your eBay account should be in good standing. Once you've met these requirements, registering with eBay as a TA is easy. You can use the Site Map to go directly to the Trading Assistant Program overview as shown in Figure 6-11. From there you can learn more about becoming a TA or sign up to become one. Click on

FIGURE 6-11 Think you may want to become an eBay Trading Assistant? Visit the program overview page shown here to start your research.

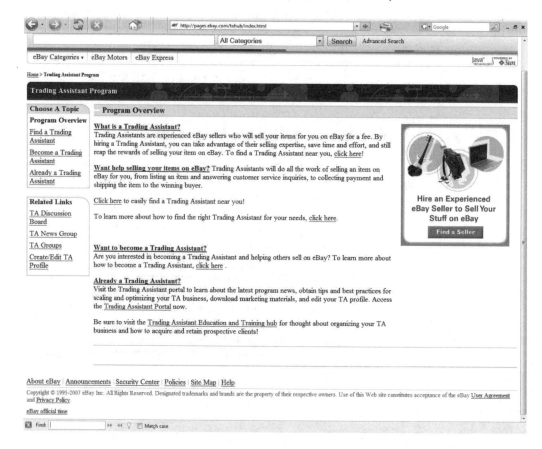

the Find a Trading Assistant hyperlink along the top left of the screen to get to the Trading Assistant directory. You can search this to find other TAs in your area. By default, Trading Assistants are listed according to how far they are from the location specified. But you can also sort the results by number of feedbacks. Once you become a Trading Assistant you can register in the directory at no charge and start marketing your services worldwide.

» Decide on your policies up front

In order to decide on your policies, you have to complete the only part of becoming a Trading Assistant that is complicated. That is deciding how you will charge your customers and what your policies for operating your Trading Assistant business will be. As the Trading Assistant, you will be billed for all eBay listing fees whether or not you sell the item you list. That's a point of negotiation between you and your customer. Will you cover these fees as an expense of doing business, or will you charge a base fee that will include that charge no matter what the outcome of the auction is? Will you charge a base fee for picking up the item? Will you earn nothing at all if the item doesn't sell, or will you charge a fee for your services in processing the auction? Will you establish a base value below which you will not take an item on consignment? There's not much profit to be made on selling something for $50, when you only get a commission from the sale. You must decide for yourself before you complete your directory listing so that you can clearly state your policies to prospective consigners.

» Know your competition

Using the Trading Assistant directory, search by your ZIP code to see who your competition is. Then by reviewing their listings you can see if your competitors specialize in particular categories, and you can see what their areas of expertise are. Now, you can tailor your own marketing efforts to areas they may be missing. You'll be able to distinguish yourself from the crowd in your own niche.

» Market yourself as a Trading Assistant

eBay encourages you as a registered Trading Assistant to promote your services in your auction listings, your About Me page, and your local hometown. You can include a link to your Trading Assistant directory listing from all of your auctions, your eBay store, and your About Me page. eBay also has some materials you are free to download to use as advertisements you can post in the local grocery store or other local bulletin boards. Go to http://pages.ebay.com/tradingassistants/collateral/index .html for examples.

Search for Possible Consignments

Marketing yourself as a Trading Assistant will help drum up business for you, but there are some other things you can also do to get the consignments coming your way. Talk to everyone you know about your new venture. Make yourself the local eBay guru. Here are just a few suggestions to help get you started:

- You'll find that many older people who may be considering a downsizing move might be more than happy to let you take some unwanted items for them.

- Go to successful small brick-and-mortar businesses and offer them your services. They have very little to lose in allowing you to open up a whole new market for them.

- If you go to yard sales, ask if there are any items the sellers might not have included in the sale but might want to sell in a more profitable venue.

- Approach your religious community to see if there are any items just stored away in the building that could be turned into needed cash. Forging partnerships with local nonprofits may mean you can manage their entire in-kind donation program.

» Prepare a standard contract

When you enter into an agreement with a prospective client, be prepared with a standard contract that clearly states your services, fees, and responsibilities. You can get some ideas for how you may word your contract by reviewing the Terms and

Conditions sections of existing directory listings. Make sure you include all possible charges, including listing enhancements the client might want. It is a good idea to include a chart of eBay's listing options so that your client can see very clearly how the fees add up. Make sure your client also understands that in addition to the listing fees, he'll have to pay the Final Value Fees from his proceeds as well.

Make your standard contract as comprehensive and clear as possible to prevent any misunderstandings that might arise in dealing with someone who is not experienced on eBay. You are well within your rights, for example, to charge a flat fee for listing the item whether it sells or not. If this fee is modest, your client shouldn't complain about it. After all, it will take you time to research the item and prepare it for the listing, and you deserve to be paid for that time. Just make sure your client understands that this fee will be assessed whether or not the item sells. And, of course, reassure him with your excellent eBay reputation that you are likely to get his item sold because you are a proven, successful eBay seller.

Include some basic eBay operating rules in your contract. For example, make sure your client knows that he can't go onto eBay and bid on his own item in order to bump up the price. Make sure he understands that once the item is listed, he cannot easily back out of the agreement. Be sure he knows the item will sell to the highest bidder even if he thinks it hasn't earned quite enough money. A reserve is not a bad idea when you're working with an inexperienced client, because it offers a level of reassurance that a newcomer might need.

» Trading Assistants pricing advice

Most Trading Assistants agree that a sliding scale is the best way to charge your customers. With a sliding scale, you'll begin with a significant percentage of the sale price as a fee and move to a smaller percentage as the price of the sale item increases. For example, you may charge a rate of 30 percent for an item that sells for $100. That rate will steadily decrease as the price of the item increases. You may even go as far as only 2 percent of an item that sells for $25,000 or more.

Most Trading Assistant/PowerSellers we spoke with agreed that in order for the percentages to work out favorably, you should not accept items for consignment that bring less than $100 as a final value. Of course, as you're just starting out, you may be willing to work at a slightly lesser profit margin, adjusting your needs as your business grows and you attain PowerSeller status.

» You're a professional, so make a professional impression

Part of the joy of having your own eBay business is that you are free to operate it in your own style. If you want to work all day in your pajamas, who's to stop you? But, this is no longer true if you're trying to branch out as a Trading Assistant. Now, you'll need to exude competence and professionalism. Always make sure you look professional when you meet a prospective client. Remember how important image is on eBay? Well, it's just as important when you're courting prospective Trading Assistant clients too. Why should people entrust you with something they consider valuable if you don't make them feel that you know just what you're doing?

So, dress the part. Have nice business cards printed so that you can leave one behind for further contact. Send all correspondence to prospective clients on your own letterhead. When you present your contract, make sure it's printed neatly and is clear and easily understood. Putting some money into these tools will pay back in a professional image for your Trading Assistant business. For further advice and ideas see the Trading Assistant Discussion Board at http://forums.ebay.com/db1/forum.jspa?forumID=106.

Meet a PowerSeller

Chris Santos—Icandy-clothing

Chris is a young PowerSeller with a thriving eBay business in Urban and Hip-Hop clothing. Although his eBay store was less than two years old when we spoke, he's already learned a great deal about operating a successful eBay business. For example, he's very good at identifying and reaching his target audience.

Chris uses software and services from a company called Constant Contact to create his e-mail marketing campaigns. "E-mail marketing is a very powerful method to market to your past customers and to customers interested in your products," Chris noted. He's also addressing his customer base in another new and fascinating way. He's working toward creating an online community. His will be built around a particular Hip-Hop dance known as "C-Walking." As it happens, Chris's brother is the force behind a tremendously popular Web site about C-Walking. (Go to www.Cwalk-Movement.com for an amazing example.)

You're a professional, so make a professional impression

 Because Chris's customers are likely to be interested in this dance, he's coupling his advertising efforts with the blogs and videos on his brother's site. "It is a perfect partnership," says Chris. "If you look at any of the great successful businesses in the world," Chris noted, "they are involved with their local community and giving back." It just so happens that in this case, "local" means anyone in the world with Internet access!

It's no surprise that a young eBay PowerSeller would turn to the Web and social networking to build his business. He knows who his customers are, what's likely to appeal to them, and how to find them. That's a great way to turn an interest into an interested customer. To cinch the deal, Chris offers free two- to three-day shipping on all of his purchases, and a generous money-back guarantee to ensure that people who shop with him will be happy.

Chris has used PayPal's Online Merchants Network to answer some of his questions about e-commerce. "It is definitely a place to learn," he said. "I wanted people to view my site and give me ideas how to improve, because in any business, there's always room for improvement." Chris has taught himself most of what he now knows about running a business. "I learned mostly by trial and error," he remembers. When he found eBay, he researched other big sellers, found articles and forums online to learn about selling on eBay, read some great books, and got started. He taught himself accounting and bookkeeping, how to do his own taxes, and even enough computer programming to integrate online payments. Now he has private investors backing his business, he's able to buy directly from the manufacturer, and none of his profits go to a middleman. Chris has accomplished all this in less than two years. He has left his full-time job and is now running his business instead. His advice for those just starting out? "Keep pushing and trying, even when you fail. Fail faster so you know what *not* to do. Once you have done everything wrong, you'll know what's right to do." It's tough advice, but it's worked for this young and talented PowerSeller.

Power-Charge Your eBay Business Checklist

✓ I'm researching how to use e-mail marketing to regularly reach my customer base. I've considered Constant Contact.

✓ I offer PayPal, and I am familiar with the PayPal dispute process.

✓ I've signed up for a free month of SquareTrade, and I'm thinking about offering SquareTrade warranties.

✓ I've reviewed the warranties available through eBay.

You're a professional, so make a professional impression

✓ I'm considering BuySafe bonding for my eBay business.

✓ I'm trying some different ways to reward my customers such as thank-you gifts and coupons.

✓ When I run Fixed-Priced listings, I include links to my other listings.

✓ Before I relist unsold items I consider how to improve my listing.

✓ I know a lot about (fill in the blank, and don't be modest)! I'll write a guide for eBay's Reviews & Guides area.

✓ Would a blog help my business?

✓ I'm researching how Google's AdWords program may increase traffic to my listings.

✓ I've joined eBay's Affiliate Program and plan to start counting the commissions soon!

✓ I know my sell-through rate.

✓ My bookmarks now include Medved's Auction Counts Web site.

✓ I mark down my items when I must to keep inventory turning.

✓ Am I thinking of hiring someone to help me?

✓ I'm deciding if I'm ready to become an eBay Trading Assistant. I'm thinking about competition, policies, and marketing.

Chapter 7

Close the Auction and Collect the Cash

Here's the moment we've all been waiting for. You have a winning bidder and you're ready to get paid. It feels wonderful, don't you agree? This is the reason you started all this to begin with. Before we get too carried away with joy, let's not get ahead of ourselves. The celebration will have to wait until the details have been worked out, and there are plenty of those. There is no part of the relationship between buyer and seller that requires more careful handling than the payment part. When it goes well, it's no issue at all, almost seamless. When it goes badly, it can lead to misunderstanding, hard feelings, negative feedback, and mediation. You can go a long way to prevent a bad outcome by understanding payment options and how to make them work most effectively. You can also ensure a smooth experience by remembering that on eBay, communication is king.

When you created your auction listings, you carefully outlined your payment options to prospective customers. That, of course, does not mean that the winning bidder will have paid any attention to what you stated so carefully. When the auction ends, eBay will automatically send an "end of auction" e-mail to the winner. Your payment options will be again detailed there. You'll have the winner's complete attention for the moment, and now's the time to take advantage of that. Because so much trouble can be averted by clear communication between seller and buyer, you mustn't miss this opportunity.

That's not to say you should anticipate trouble from each transaction. Most of them will go through without a hitch. PowerSellers wouldn't be able to process hundreds or even thousands of transactions a month if this weren't true. Most people on eBay, both buyers and sellers, are there to do business and are honest, trustworthy, decent people. Except for those who aren't. Just as in any other community, there is a small subset of people on eBay who are there for fraud, cheating, lying, and stealing. We'll show you some ways to protect yourself from them.

eBay payment options fall into two major camps: PayPal and everything else. PayPal is eBay's preferred method of payment, and that's easy to understand, because eBay owns PayPal. When you sell something on eBay through PayPal, you'll pay your eBay fees, and then you'll likely also pay PayPal fees. That's a great way for eBay to get paid twice for the same transaction. In return, you and your buyers will both gain benefits from using PayPal. Your buyers will have all of the buyer protection services outlined in Chapter 6. They will also have the choice of using any one of PayPal's multiple payment options, including credit or debit cards, PayPal balances on their account, e-checks, and transfers from bank accounts. The flexibility of choice makes your auctions more attractive to your prospective customers. You will also enjoy the ease of using PayPal and the security it offers your buyers in knowing that they are backed by protection services. Also, eBay claims listings offering PayPal as a payment method are 6 percent more likely to sell and show an average 5 percent boost in the final price. Add to that the fact that eBay Express sellers *must* accept PayPal as a payment option, and you have a compelling case for accepting it yourself! Much of this chapter will be devoted to discussing the ins and outs of PayPal, but first, let's take a look at everything else.

Payment Options That Are Not PayPal

You have a variety of options available for receiving funds from your buyers. Variety is the way for you to go. The more choices you give your buyers, the more likely they are to find one they like. You also establish yourself as a professional seller if you are able to offer your buyers a choice of payment methods. Remember, you are trying to get your customers to find it fun, easy, and secure to shop with you, so be flexible in choosing your payment options.

Just as with most other subjects, PowerSellers have a wide variety of opinions about what methods of payment they prefer. Much of this has to do with their personal experiences. Some sellers, once burned, will forever swear off a particular payment method. Other, more fortunate sellers may stay open to that same payment method and never have a problem. Don't be so afraid of being cheated that you close yourself off. Sometimes the risk is worth taking, and among the most successful PowerSellers, you'll find the widest variety of payment options.

Very few people pay with cash on eBay, but it does occasionally happen. The risk in sending cash for payment is largely on the buyer. There is no paper trail to trace transactions, and we've all seen the statement on payment envelopes from bills that warns, "Don't send cash through the mail." Cash payments are a bad idea for the buyer, but some buyers will send them anyway. From the seller's viewpoint, cash can still be a problem. First of all, if you don't receive U.S. currency, you'll have the exchange rates to deal with, which will most likely cut into your profits. But your real problem with cash is if it gets "lost" in the mail. You've never received payment, and the buyer can't prove that he's paid, but he's out the money and the item, which you surely won't ship without payment. It's bound to cause bad feelings, and negative feedback is a possible result.

It's against eBay policy for a seller to solicit cash payments, and those who do may find their listings shut down. You can always state in your auctions and end-of-auction e-mails that you don't accept cash payments. In the end, it won't happen often, but you may still get cash through the mail, and you'll have to deal with it on a case-by-case basis.

» Accept personal checks

PowerSellers have mixed feelings about personal checks. Some won't accept them as payment, but most do. The problem is, even if you say you won't accept personal checks, buyers are going to send them anyway. They require a little more effort on your part. You have to deposit them to your account and hold the item for 10 business days to make sure the check clears the buyer's bank. The check may clear in fewer than 10 days, but that's the default recommended by most banks. If the check doesn't clear, you have to do the paperwork necessary to return the check, and there are some bank hassles and possible bank fees to consider. But overall, most checks go through without a hitch. The real benefit to accepting checks is that there's a subset of buyers who prefer them. They are easy. They don't build credit card debt. And they provide the buyer with a good, solid receipt. It's easier for buyers to protect themselves from a fraudulent seller if they have a canceled check to prove they've paid.

» Don't always insist on holding the check

Your payment policy statement should make it clear that you will hold the item for 10 business days while the check clears. That's your right, and it's a way to protect yourself from bad check writers. No one can fault you for it. Once you've been clear about your policy, take it on a case-by-case basis. For the vast majority of checks you receive, make your buyers wait. But

Don't always insist on holding the check

if you receive a check for a smaller purchase (you decide the amount, but less than $25 is a good sum for discussion purposes), check out the buyer's feedback. If this is a person with a high feedback number and a very clean feedback rating, don't make the buyer wait for the check to clear. This buyer is not a risk. Show some respect for the fine reputation he or she has built on eBay and go ahead and ship the item. The buyer has earned your confidence, and your consideration will go a long way toward encouraging that person to come back and shop with you again. The same is true for your repeat buyers. Everyone likes to feel appreciated, and you will likely be rewarded with positive feedback.

Money Orders and Cashier's Checks: No Longer Risk-Free Options

We wish we could say that there's no risk at all in accepting money orders or cashier's checks. When they're genuine, they're guaranteed funds. They can't bounce, and they are just as good as cash. You can cash them easily.

The problem is that nowadays there are counterfeit money orders and cashier's checks out there. So you will need to know how to handle money orders or cashier's checks that seem suspicious to you.

Money orders are available from many places, of course, from the post office to the MiniMart down the street. You can rest assured that money orders from the United States Postal Service are genuine. Those that come from other sources though require closer inspection. If a money order seems suspicious to you (and some fake ones are actually from someone's printer), you have every right to hold the item until you can be assured that it's genuine (your bank or even the police can help there).

For cashier's checks our advice is the same. You can't be 100 percent sure that they're genuine any more so you should verify the authenticity of any check that seems suspicious to you. One evil scheme involves buyers who send cashier's checks for much more than the item's amount. In those cases, the buyer may ask for reimbursement of the extra amount. The problem is the check they've sent is a fake. eBay's advice here is quite clear: "You should never accept overpayments from buyers for items where the buyer is asking to be reimbursed for overpayment."

» (Almost) never use wire transfers

Generally, if your trading partner *insists* on using a wire transfer, you should walk away from the transaction and send a report to eBay. Any buyer or seller who wants to transfer funds should be happy to go through PayPal to do it. That's the secure route for transferring money between accounts. If someone is *insisting* that you do a wire transfer outside of PayPal, the chance you'll be entering into a fraudulent transaction is high. Wire transfers are one of the main sources of fraud in online auctions, and there's simply no reason to leave yourself open to risk here. Be very clear, it's either PayPal or nothing for transferring funds from one bank account to another. There are two exceptions to this rule. First, if you have done business with the buyer before, then you can consider accepting a wire transfer. However, be sure to confirm with your bank that the funds have cleared before shipping the item. The second exception, surprising enough, involves transactions for expensive items, say a car. In those cases, some legitimate buyers may prefer to pay with a wire transfer. As long as you go through an escrow service (discussed soon) you should be fine.

PayPal and Why It Really Is Your Friend

Among PowerSellers, you will hear a certain amount of grumbling about PayPal. Yes, it is an eBay-owned company, which means sellers pay fees twice, once to eBay and once to PayPal, also eBay. It's true PayPal's protection services are weighted in favor of the buyer. PowerSellers have legitimate complaints on these issues, but with that said, you must still consider PayPal your friend.

If you are already a PayPal user, you know how fast and easy it is to pay for something this way. While the auction is running, you'll see the PayPal logo. When you've won the auction, that logo becomes a Pay Now button and you simply click it to process your PayPal payment.

Buyers like PayPal because it is so simple, and they also like the protection services PayPal offers. You must offer your buyers PayPal if you are going for any kind of volume at all. It's all part of making it as easy as possible for people to shop with you. If you don't do this, your customers will have no trouble finding other sellers on eBay to buy from. Consider that as we write this there are more than 143 million PayPal accounts worldwide. Remember that although the greater advantage to the service is for the buyer, you also have the advantage of having a registered and confirmed customer base when you use PayPal. Don't concern yourself, just yet, with whatever grumbling you might find on the discussion boards about PayPal. Far more common than these grumblings are the many successful PayPal transactions that you never hear about.

PayPal Account Types

If you have spent most of your time buying on eBay, you most likely have a Personal PayPal account. This account is free of charges. It allows you to send money through funds kept on your PayPal account or through a registered credit card. The only time you will be charged a fee for using your Personal account is if you ask for an exchange of foreign funds. You can also receive funds as payment for sales on eBay, but you cannot receive payments funded by credit or debit cards. You'll have to have funds sent by the buyer directly from his PayPal account.

The two other levels of PayPal accounts are the Premier and Business accounts. Both of these account types allow you to receive funds from a buyer's credit or debit card. It is still free for you to pay for items from your own PayPal account, but now you will pay a fee every time you receive funds from a buyer. Figure 7-1 shows the PayPal fees screen that can be found as of this writing at https://www.paypal.com/us/cgi-bin/webscr?cmd= _display-fees-outside.

Premier accounts are for sellers running small businesses, and that's the one you will be most likely to use. The Business account is for operations that are bigger than individual sellers. It offers services that allow businesses not only to use PayPal but also to have multiple logins, so that employees at a variety of levels can access the accounts. That way, a business owner can allow an employee who does shipping to have access to the portion of the account that includes shipping information, but still deny that employee access to the financial parts of the account history.

PayPal Fees

PayPal's "Standard" rate to receive payments is 2.9 percent (of the item's price) plus $0.30 for each transaction, and that

(Almost) never use wire transfers

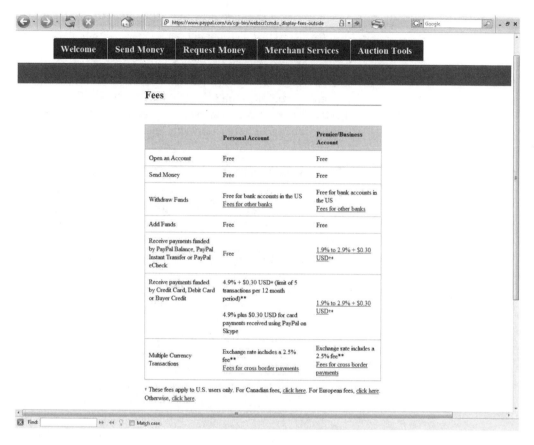

FIGURE 7-1 PayPal's fees for receiving funds vary with the type of account you have.

applies to both the Business and Premier accounts. This fee is for U.S. sellers only; there are different fee schedules for Canadian and European customers. These rates also assume you are accepting a PayPal payment from a U.S.-based customer. Otherwise the rate is 3.9 percent (again, plus $0.30). This higher rate includes a cross-border fee of 1 percent of the sale for U.S. dollar (USD) payments and 0.5 percent of the sale for all other PayPal-supported currencies.

Keep in mind, it is a violation of PayPal's user agreement as well as most credit card companies, for you to try to charge the buyer extra to cover any of these fees. You're stuck with them, but we do have some advice from PowerSellers about how to keep them as low as possible. Read on.

» Sign up for a Merchant rate as soon as possible

Once your monthly volume exceeds US$3,000 you should apply for Merchant rate pricing. The Merchant rate begins at 2.5 percent (plus that $0.30 fee per transaction) on sales over the $3,000 level. If your monthly sales exceed $10,000 it drops to 2.2 percent (plus $0.30). If they exceed $100,000 you're eligible for the lowest rate—1.9 percent (again plus $0.30).

As with the rates for Business and Premier accounts, Merchant rates are boosted by 1 percent of the sale price for U.S. dollar payments, and 0.5 percent for all other PayPal-supported currencies. Keep in mind that you must maintain this level of earnings. If your monthly volume drops below $3,000 you'll be bumped back to the Standard rate. Of course, you're not likely to let that happen.

It might surprise you to learn that some PowerSellers don't realize they are paying higher PayPal fees than they have to. That's understandable. When you first sign up for a Premier account, you can't have the Merchant rate. In the drive to build your business, it's easy to overlook a little detail like this, but this little detail can save you big money. So set your sights on achieving the volume you need to qualify, and then make the switch just as soon as you can.

» Get a PayPal ATM/debit card

PayPal offers its qualified users a PayPal MasterCard ATM/debit card, which allows you to make cash withdrawals and which earns 1 percent cash-back rewards on purchases. The card is free from PayPal, and you can use it as an ATM card to withdraw funds from your PayPal account or from the bank account linked to your PayPal account.

To qualify for the cash-back rewards, you must use the card to make purchases that do not require a PIN number for processing. That includes most stores, restaurants, and other online and brick-and-mortar merchants. Just select the credit option with the merchant (rather than the debit option), and it will be processed for the cash-back rewards. Remember, funds will be immediately deducted from your account, because it is actually a debit card, but you must specify it as a credit transaction to get the rewards. "I save thousands of dollars

Get a PayPal ATM/debit card

a year by using this debit card as much as I do. I even pay my eBay fees with it," says one savvy PowerSeller from New York.

To qualify for the rewards program, PayPal users must meet eligibility requirements. First, the plan is offered only to U.S. PayPal users. As of this writing, these are the eligibility requirements:

- You must have been a PayPal member for at least 60 days.

- You must have registered a credit card with a monthly statement that is sent to a physical address, not a P.O. box. PayPal will only mail the debit card to that address, and all statements and transaction information will be available only on the PayPal Web site.

- You must have linked a bank account to your PayPal account and verified that you control that account.

- You must hold a Premier or Business account.

- You must be approved through PayPal's Account Review department as being an active PayPal member in good standing.

To apply for a card, log in to your account. Then click the ATM/Debit card link at the bottom of any account-related page. If your application is accepted, it will take about two to four weeks for your account to be processed and your card mailed. Once you receive your card you must activate it by logging into www.paypal.com and following the instructions on the Activate Debit Card link of the Account Overview page. At this point, you will select your PIN and be ready to start earning your rewards.

To keep your rewards coming, you will have to list PayPal in all of your auctions as the only online payment option you accept.

PayPal Auction Management Tools

After reading Chapter 4, you're an expert in the field of auction management software. To make things simple for people who don't have all of your advantages, PayPal offers its users a set of auction management tools directly from their PayPal accounts. Through PayPal, you can get help from the time your auction begins to when you need to manage your PayPal fees.

PayPal History

You can view your PayPal statements for the past month or for any period you specify. These statements include all the details you'll need to track your closed auctions. Information available includes:

- The Item number and title
- The end date and time
- The price you earned
- The quantity you sold
- The buyer's complete contact information
- Whether or not the buyer has paid
- If you need to send an invoice
- Your shipping status and costs

Now you can use one single display page to see all of the details for all of your PayPal auctions.

Shipping Center

PayPal, in partnership with the USPS and UPS, has integrated some shipping services to make shipping your items easier. You can use PayPal to calculate your shipping costs and track your shipments online. You can also purchase and print your own shipping labels with this tool.

Reporting Tools

The PayPal reporting tools can help you measure your sales by analyzing your revenue sources, automating some bookkeeping tasks, and reconciling your transactions. As noted, monthly account statements give you a summary of the credits and debits to your account balance. Merchant sales reports track your weekly sales. A customizable history log can give you an online view of all your payments sent and received.

» Sign up for PayPal's Virtual Terminal

Believe it or not, some people still aren't giving credit card information over the Internet, and with Virtual Terminal they don't have to. That means more money in your pocket. With PayPal's Virtual Terminal you can accept credit card payments

Sign up for PayPal's Virtual Terminal

in person, over the phone, by mail, or by fax. Your buyer doesn't even need to have a PayPal account. PowerSeller Andy of Debnroo is a big fan of Virtual Terminal, and says that before he offered it he was losing sales because some customers weren't comfortable giving credit card details online. You can add Virtual Terminal as an additional payment option for $20 per month. It's also a part of PayPal's Website Payments Pro, a service for those with their own e-commerce sites.

Protect Yourself with PayPal's Seller Protection Policy

While it may seem that most of the protection from PayPal goes to the buyer, there is *some* protection in place for sellers.

One of the things you can do is review the history of the person you are trading with before you accept a PayPal payment. From the My Account tab, choose the payment in question and select the status link in the status column, for example, Pending. Now you will be on the payment details page. You'll see the sender's name and verification status. In order to be verified on PayPal, you have to confirm a bank account with the service. Verification is not the same as vouching for the honesty of the buyer, but it does prove that this buyer did provide PayPal with enough banking information to suggest that she or he isn't attempting to defraud anyone. You should also have your account verified to reassure your buyers that you are also a legitimate trading partner.

PayPal's seller protection centers on protecting a seller from charge backs. It's not difficult for buyers to charge back items with PayPal. PayPal's seller protection is primarily meant to protect sellers from out-and-out fraud. You won't find much help if you just meet up with a buyer who wants to be difficult. The protection you're eligible for is limited to $5,000 in coverage per year (and this is for U.S. sellers; different limits apply to those outside of the U.S.). That may sound like a lot but if you're dealing in expensive items and you have a high-volume business it's not much at all.

How do you protect yourself? It's actually not easy, and you won't get much help from PayPal if the buyer claims that the item never arrived. Your only hope in getting protection through PayPal is to follow all of their seller's protection guidelines exactly, and doing that can sometimes conflict with your selling goals. Here's what you have to do to get any protection through PayPal:

- Have your account verified.

- Ship only to the address displayed on the Transaction Details page, and make sure that's a confirmed address.

- Ship within seven days of payment.

- Keep all proof-of-shipment records that can be tracked online.

- Insist on delivery confirmation of items above $250. Remember, protection applies only to tangible goods. Accept only complete payments from a single PayPal account.

- Do not surcharge the buyer for your PayPal fees, except in the UK, where this is allowed.

- Respond to PayPal's requests for information within the time period they specify.

- Accept international payments from only approved countries.

Let's focus on a particularly problematic requirement on this list and see what PowerSellers have to say. One of the problems in shipping only to the address displayed on the Transaction Details page has to do with an issue of fairness. PayPal will not back you up if you ship your item to an unconfirmed address. (Note that to sell on eBay Express you must "ensure your PayPal account settings are set to ship to unconfirmed addresses, or make sale-by-sale decisions.") At the same time, they will allow buyers to submit unconfirmed addresses. Why should that be allowed? This is a question PowerSellers ask on their discussion boards but are never completely able to answer. Just because a buyer lists an address, don't assume it's confirmed. Get the buyer's information page from PayPal and double-check. But when you're trying to build volume in your business, this is time you could be spending on more productive pursuits. You may consider stating in your listings that you will ship only to confirmed addresses. This may encourage your buyers to contact you if they wish to have the item shipped to an address that is not confirmed.

The issue of unconfirmed addresses is a big problem for international sales. The reality is that no address outside of the

Sign up for PayPal's Virtual Terminal

United States can be confirmed. Every time you ship something through PayPal to an international customer, outside of Canada or the UK, you are automatically giving up any right to the seller protection policy.

Protecting Yourself on eBay

In eBay's early days, it was often compared to the Wild West. Our image of that time in American history is of a freewheeling, lawless society where the smart, the quick, and the rugged survived. Figure 7-2 reminds us of just how rugged that time could be. Now that eBay has matured, much of that Wild West bravado has faded. After all, the West never came complete with a Live Help feature! Still, when it comes to protecting yourself from fraud and loss, you should consider yourself to be your own best line of defense. As a company, eBay prides itself on providing a level playing field for all its participants. That's one of its great strengths and part of the

FIGURE 7-2 The Wild West, before eBay.

reason so many people are able to come to eBay and operate their own businesses.

At the same time, that philosophy has made it difficult for eBay to police itself too closely. Yes, you will get support from eBay on issues of fraud and illegal activity, and the company is instituting new policies to discourage fraud. But for the day-to-day operation of your business, it's best to depend on yourself.

The first thing you'll have to decide is how much risk you are willing to take. Each seller has to determine that individually. For example, you will find many PowerSellers who refuse to accept personal checks. They don't want to be bothered holding items for 10 days, and they don't want to leave themselves open to the hassle of having to deal with returned checks. You'll find other sellers who won't even consider international sales. They consider them too risky and don't want to be hassled with the extra paperwork necessary for customs. On the other hand, you'll find other sellers who welcome personal checks. They may find that they rarely, if ever, have a returned check problem, and holding the item for 10 days isn't such a big deal. Other sellers actually welcome international sales, figuring that the billions of people in the world who don't happen to live in the United States offer them a customer base that's worth an extra bit of trouble. All of these decisions are made individually, and we'll give you enough information here so that you can start considering them for yourself.

You'll have to decide for yourself what feels right once you find the balance between risk and security that will make you comfortable. Remember, any business has to contend with fraud. Any brick-and-mortar business has to contend with shoplifting, for example. You may want to follow Drew of whitemountaintrading's lead and set aside a fraud fund to cover such events.

International Sales

Some PowerSellers still debate whether or not to offer international sales. It's easy enough to see why some people shy away from them. They do require more effort. Each sale must be declared through customs, which requires extra forms and paperwork. It is difficult to track shipping across international borders. Dealing with foreign currency exchanges can be expensive and bothersome, and dealing with insurance claims for lost items is nothing but a hassle. Still, more and more

Sign up for PayPal's Virtual Terminal

PowerSellers welcome international sales, and they have compelling reasons to do so.

Husband and wife eBayers Andy and Deb of Debnroo agree with Tony of Wegotthebeats, even though they ship a great variety of items in many different shapes and sizes (see the following sidebar). "Yes, we are the most enthusiastic people we know about international sales, but it may be tantamount to masochism. It really can be a form of torture, in terms of shipping and customs forms, but in particular insurance claims. You can't even start an international claim with the USPS until 60 days after the shipment. And shipping times have suddenly jumped to about twice the normal on a fairly regular basis."

Selling Internationally

PowerSeller Tony of Wegotthebeats sells CDs and has very strong feelings about offering international sales. "There are sellers, like me, who make decisions based on 'what's good for the business' and what is the professional, customer service–oriented solution to a particular problem. We do not waiver from them even though we know that a small percentage of customers will exploit them to their advantage," he told us. "One basic issue with shipping overseas is simply fear of the unknown. 'Do I have to fill out lots of forms?' 'What if I can't speak German?' 'I've heard that people in Canada cause lots of problems and expect lower shipping rates.' 'What if they pay me in Euros?' The list goes on. Once you've shipped a few, it becomes old hat.

"There is a little bit more work involved, especially if you are selling many different-sized products, as many sellers do. I am fortunate that my merchandise is basically all one size, so I can clearly state up front and with total accuracy what the shipping rates will be for the United States and any other country in the world. Other sellers will have to either figure out the different shipping rates ahead of time and post them in their auction listing, or wait for e-mails from interested customers asking them to figure out what the exact shipping rate will be for their particular country.

"Fifty percent of my business is shipped overseas. I'd say 80 percent of that is paid for with PayPal. Every single one of those could file a claim of 'non-receipt' and PayPal would give them all instant refunds. It's never happened once. That said, I'm well aware of the possibility and am doing what I can to reduce the risk, namely encouraging payments using money orders through Auctionpayments.com or other methods of payment.

"For me, this is a calculated risk. Statistically, I have many more problems with domestic buyers than overseas. With so much of my business going overseas, the risk is clearly worth it. For others, it may not be worth it. Generally, I think it is important to leave

---

yourself open to as many bids as possible. Sometimes the international bidders won't win, but they'll boost your final price while trying to win.

"Payment, on the other hand, has actually not been much of an issue. We get a significant number of international money orders sent through the postal system from Canada, and, to a small degree, the UK. The vast majority of international payments are now coming from PayPal. We find that Auctionpayments.com works as a good backup to PayPal.

"In our opinion, those who are not servicing international markets are more than welcome to continue their policies. It is making it far easier for those of us who want to get a leg up on our competition. Once USPS, UPS, and other international carriers adapt to the modern needs of international retailers, those of us with experience with this more difficult system will have a much easier time adapting than those who have turned a nose up to the other 5.8 billion people on the planet all this time. We are confident that existing shipping and payment barriers will continue to crumble and that the future for servicing the international markets just gets brighter."

You'll have to decide for yourself how risk-averse you are to the idea of international sales. That will be based largely on the products you sell, and your personal philosophy and hopes for your business. It may be too much to ask of yourself when you're just getting used to selling in volume, and you may decide to wait on international sales until you become more confident in yourself as an eBay seller. Overall, as you've heard before, it's best to keep your customer base as broad as possible when selling on eBay. Offering your items to all the citizens of the world is a way to do that.

» Stay up to date on international scams

That said, there are some countries that have developed a reputation for having a high potential for credit card fraud. You're better able to offer international sales to the vast majority of people who want to honestly trade with you if you are armed with the information you'll need to protect yourself from the pockets known to be unreliable. We suggest you make it a habit of visiting eBay's International Trading Discussion Board to stay abreast of current trouble spots and scams. You can reach that by clicking the Community link, then Discussion Boards. You should also regularly review PayPal's new Online Merchant Network, shown in Figure 7-3 and located at http://www.onlinemerchantnetwork.com/.

Consider the language barrier

FIGURE 7-3 The Online Merchant Network is a newer discussion board where PayPal users can get advice and exchange tips.

» Consider the language barrier

PowerSellers who do accept international bidders have some advice for sellers when dealing with the language barrier between buyer and seller. One PowerSeller from south Florida recommends keeping your e-mails short and simple. "When you receive an e-mail from someone who is using broken English, keep your replies as simply written as possible. Do not use complex conjugations of verbs or unusual words," he advised. In dealing with people who are not fluent, it's very important to keep your communication simple.

Remember the cultural differences in communication too. For example, in the U.S., we generally sign our e-mails with

© 2006 Overture Services, Inc.

FIGURE 7-4 With easy-to-use online translation services language barriers can come crashing down.

"sincerely" or "best wishes." From England and Europe you are more likely to receive a "regards," a term that can sound a little snooty and off-putting to Americans. Don't take it the wrong way; it's nothing more than a different version of "sincerely," and the person writing it thinks no more of it than that. Be sure in your responses that you don't use slang. Think carefully about the things you take for granted because they are so familiar to your culture; your buyer may have no idea what you're talking about.

Technology is starting to make translation much simpler. Through eBay's Global Trade area (click on the Site Map link and then the Sell Internationally link), you can reach the Babel Fish translation service (see Figure 7-4). From there you can enter a block of text written in a dozen or so languages (for example, Dutch, Italian, German, and Japanese) to have it translated into English or whatever your native language happens to be. So what may be a barrier to your business now is becoming a road to new opportunities. Because eBay itself owes its very existence to technological advancement, there's reason to stay optimistic about the ways these advancements will continue to bring us new opportunities.

Consider the language barrier

Using Escrow Services

Buyers and sellers can agree to process their payments through an escrow service, which can eliminate some stress for both partners. If sellers agree to this process, their auction listing will include escrow as a means of payment. Buyers may then elect to send their payment directly to the escrow service. That service will hold payment and notify the seller that the buyer has paid. The seller then ships the item to the buyer for inspection. If the buyer agrees that the item is just as the seller stated, the buyer notifies the escrow service that he or she accepts the item, and the escrow service sends payment on to the seller. Escrow only makes sense for big-ticket items (eBay suggests those selling for $500 or more), because the escrow service will charge fees that cut even deeper into your profit margin. If you are selling cars or luxury items such as jewelry, your buyers may insist on escrow.

To use escrow, both parties must agree to the escrow service. Before any funds get transferred, both parties should also agree about who will pay the transaction fees, although it is customary for the buyer to pay the escrow fees. Other details of the escrow transaction to consider include:

1. Who will pay shipping?
2. What will the shipping method be?
3. What is the length of the inspection period?
4. Will the shipping fees be refundable, and if so, under what circumstances?
5. What are the terms under which the item can be returned?

All transactions between seller and buyer should include good, clear communications, but this is even more important with an escrow transaction. Don't assume the buyer and you agree on even the slightest detail. Make sure of it. Get everything worked out in writing, and be sure to save all of your e-mails related to the transfer.

The only online escrow service that eBay endorses for domestic escrow transactions is Escrow.com. If you are going to offer escrow services, do it through this company. Don't agree to go with any other, and if a buyer (or seller) insists on another, walk away from the deal and report that person to eBay. Escrow services, particularly online services, are fertile ground for fraud, and you can easily be taken in by offers from disreputable companies. Note that for international transactions eBay recommends the following escrow services (depending on the seller's location):

- Escrow Europa
- Iloxx Safe Trade
- Triple Deal

One of the main sources of escrow fraud is e-mail. Never respond to e-mail from an escrow service other than Escrow .com or one of the others listed here. Also, don't click any links in e-mails you may get, even if they look like they've come from Escrow.com. Any time you need to conduct business with the escrow service or check on information, log on to the Web site by typing in the complete URL. Don't use an auto-type feature from your browser; it's too easy to be diverted to a fraudulent site that way.

Protect Yourself from Spoof and Phish E-Mails

Spoof and phish e-mails are phony e-mails designed to tempt eBay and PayPal users into revealing personal information. Now, you may think, "I would never fall for such an e-mail." But the fact is, the fraudsters have gotten to be so good that you may get an e-mail that looks exactly like one generated by eBay or PayPal, unfortunately the two biggest targets for fraud. If you're not careful, you can get caught. So be vigilant and don't respond to any e-mail that requests you to click a link so you can give information about your accounts. Many of these e-mails will claim that your account is in danger, and you'll be shut out of the service, but don't fall for it.

If you get an e-mail that purportedly is from eBay, you can always verify its authenticity through your My Messages box on your My eBay page. A copy of that e-mail should be there. If it's not, it was a spoof.

Be particularly careful with e-mails that include attachments. These are never legitimate, because eBay doesn't send e-mails with attachments.

Consider the language barrier

Also, when you are logging in to eBay, make sure you are actually on an eBay page. All eBay pages have "ebay.com" before the first forward slash (/). If there are extra characters before the final forward slash, such as an @, it's definitely not from eBay. For a complete list of true eBay domestic and international sites, go to http://pages.ebay.com/help/confidence/ isgw-account-theft-spoof.html.

As mentioned, PayPal users are a favorite target for fraud. Be especially vigilant with your PayPal account, since it is likely to be a holding place for a significant amount of funds, and it is linked to your bank account and credit card information. One new eBay user reported that she received an e-mail from PayPal that requested her personal information. She went through with clicking the link. It took her to a site that looked exactly like PayPal, and she wasn't suspicious, because she recognized all the buttons and features of a PayPal page. Well, she completed the form and submitted the requested information, only then becoming suspicious when she didn't receive a "thank you" or a confirmation from PayPal. After calling PayPal and learning the sad truth, she got in touch with her bank and had to freeze her accounts. Ten days later, she had a new bank account and had to switch all of her passwords on all of her accounts all over the Internet. Fortunately, she didn't also lose money, but you don't want to spend your eBay time this way. You want to be building your business, and as anyone who has ever been a victim of identity theft will tell you, fixing it is simply a nightmare.

PayPal will never ask you for any of the following information via e-mail:

- Credit card numbers
- Banking account numbers
- Social Security numbers
- Driver's license numbers

If you get an email that's supposedly from PayPal open a new browser, type https://www.paypal.com, then log into your PayPal account. PayPal advises you not to click on any link in an e-mail asking for personal information. If you receive a suspicious e-mail, forward it in its entirety to eBay and/or PayPal.

Both sites are working hard to cut into the fraud perpetrated by spoof and phish e-mails, and they need the help of the users

FIGURE 7-5 PayPal is constantly working to improve the security of transactions for both buyers and sellers.

who are the targets of these schemes. Be sure to forward the entire e-mail, including the header, so that the companies will have all of the information to help them track down the culprits. Send it to spoof@ebay.com or spoof@paypal.com. For updates on PayPal security issues specifically, visit PayPal's Security Center (shown in Figure 7-5). Just click the Security Center link that appears at the top of PayPal pages.

Unpaid Items

Nothing gets the juices flowing among PowerSellers quite like unpaid items, also known as nonpaying bidders (NPBs). What are the reasons someone would bid on an item and then not

Consider the language barrier

pay for it? Well, there are actually quite a few reasons this happens:

- People often get caught up in the bidding and bid more than they actually want to spend on an item.

- Some inexperienced users may not have read eBay's terms of service closely enough to understand that a bid enters them into a binding contract, and they may then back out of their offer.

- Some people may actually bid on an item to ruin the auction for the seller. If the highest bidder refuses to pay, the seller gets stuck. The best sellers can hope for is to make a successful second-chance offer to the next highest bidder, but they may well be stuck with the listing fees and the aggravation of filing for a Final Value Fee refund. Plus they'll have to relist the item and do the auction all over again, hoping to get a price high enough to compensate for the extra time and trouble.

- There are some people who bid on items just for sport. They never actually intend to complete the sale; they just want to be part of the bidding action.

- Plain old buyer's remorse.

Nonpaying bidders are a fact of life for PowerSellers. You have to decide if you're going to take them in your stride or fight them at every turn. The PowerSellers' discussion boards are filled with angry exchanges about NPBs, but most of the PowerSellers we spoke with said their energies were better directed toward getting the refund of their Final Value Fee (FVF) and moving on with relisting the item for auction. Since there's really no way to avoid them, they noted, what's the point of expending too much energy being angry about them?

eBay has established the following procedure for dealing with unpaid items:

1. Sellers may file an "Unpaid Item reminder" seven days from the listing's close. This initiates a dialog between eBay and the buyer, whereby eBay reminds the buyer of his or her obligations, provides instructions on how to pay for the item, and offers a structured way for the buyer and seller to communicate.

2. Sellers may immediately file a "Mutual Agreement Not to Proceed." If this is done, the buyer must confirm the understanding. After the buyer does so, eBay will issue a Final Value Fee credit to the seller. Sellers will also receive a Final Value Fee credit should the buyer not respond within seven days. You can file an Unpaid Item Dispute by clicking on the Dispute Console link on your My eBay page, and then the Unpaid Items link.

Generally, you must file an Unpaid Item Dispute from 7 to 45 days after the transaction date. But there are two circumstances in which you can file immediately: (1) The buyer is no longer a registered eBay member. (2) You and the buyer agree to mutually withdraw from the transaction. Finally, some auction management programs (such as ChannelAdvisor's) can take some of the sting out of this by automatically sending out e-mails at key times during a transaction, to prod your buyer into action. Failing that, the software can go through the whole NPB process for you, eventually filing for your FVF refund after the number of days you specify have passed.

» Always file for your Final Value Fee refunds

There is nothing you can do about your listing fees when you have an NPB, but hope that the item sells with your first relisting so that you can be reimbursed for them. As for your Final Value Fees, that's another story. Don't allow yourself to get so caught up in running your business that you neglect to file for these refunds. Once you file an Unpaid Item Dispute, the buyer has seven days to respond to eBay's attempts to convince that person to pay. If after that seven-day period has passed, the buyer has not responded, you can file for your Final Value Fee credit (or have your software do that for you).

» Use Immediate Payment for time-sensitive listings

As troublesome as NPBs are for your regular auctions, they can be even more disastrous when you're selling time-sensitive items such as concert tickets. Just ask PowerSellers Harvey Levine and Marcia Cooper. Kids would sometimes bid on their concert tickets thinking mom and dad would cough up the cash.

Learn to avoid problem bidders

When they didn't, Harvey and Marcia were stuck. It was too late to relist the item—the event had passed.

Harvey and Marcia now safeguard themselves against this by requiring Immediate Payment. The first step in doing this is to set a Buy It Now price when creating your listing. If you've listed PayPal as a payment option, you can then specify that the item requires Immediate Payment. In that case, until the buyer actually pays for the item it remains available to other buyers. All shipping and handling fees must be included in the listing so that bidders will know exactly how much they have to spend to purchase the item. You can specify immediate payment for any listing format, as long as the item has a Buy It Now price.

» Learn to avoid problem bidders

Honestly speaking, you will encounter troublesome bidders and NPBs. All big sellers on eBay do, and if you generate the volume you'll need to become a PowerSeller, you will too. There simply isn't a way to protect yourself from every single possible bidder who is out to do harm to a seller. You could check on the feedback rating of every bidder, but then you wouldn't have the time you need to do everything else your eBay business requires. Plus, the cost-benefit equation simply doesn't support such paranoia, since most eBay transactions don't generate headaches and trouble.

You can get a feel for your trading partners through the e-mail communication you have with them, and if you spot a red flag, you certainly should do some checking. But what constitutes a red flag? Some sellers stay away from new eBayers, who have little or no feedback. But weren't you once also a new eBayer? What's to be gained by shunning someone just because she or he has some learning to do? If you get a bid from a new user, send that person an e-mail. Introduce yourself, welcome the newcomer, and offer any help or guidance the bidder may need. At the same time, reiterate your payment choices, and your shipping and customer service policies. You'll seem like a friendly neighbor. Not only will you reduce the chance that this bidder will make a new user's mistake, but you may just offer a port in the storm of eBay that helps this person feel secure and creates a regular customer for you.

You will learn a lot about problem bidders from spending time on the discussion boards. Sellers are happy to share the usernames of people who have caused them troubles, and you can be forewarned about them by learning from the bad experiences of others. Remember that eBay buyers have feedback ratings, too, and you can learn a lot about your bidders by checking on theirs. While it may not be feasible to check out every bidder when you're selling modestly priced items, it's a good idea to randomly check from time to time to see who is shopping with you. If you see negative feedbacks for a bidder, again be proactive. Send that bidder an e-mail to see if the person has any questions or needs any support in making the offer. Initiate contact with the bidder before there is a problem, and keep all of the e-mails you exchange just in case.

With all of these warnings, keep in mind once burned, twice shy. When you do encounter a problem bidder, you can block that person from ever bidding in one of your auctions again. Simply go to http://offer.ebay.com/ws2/eBayISAPI.dll ?BidderBlockLogin and enter the User ID for the eBay member you wish to block. Now this person is blocked from all of your listings until you decide to let this buyer back in. If you do ultimately resolve your issues, you can go back to this page to delete the User ID. But until you do, you are free of the problems the bidder may have caused you.

Canceling a Bid

You won't have many reasons to cancel a bid and that's good, because canceling a bid isn't so easy. You may cancel a bid if a bidder contacts you with a reason to back out. You don't have to let the bidder off the hook, but be reasonable. Bidders are human, and they sometimes have emergencies or other reasons why they can't follow through on a bid they've made. If you get a request to cancel a bid, consider it on an individual basis. Check out the bidder's feedback rating. Has this person done the same to other sellers? Are there negative comments that make you think this is more a habit than a single occurrence? If the bidder has a good, solid feedback rating and seems sincere in the request, why not go ahead and be understanding? Especially, if there's still plenty of time left in your auction and you have other bidders interested. On the other hand, if you suspect that the bidder is a deadbeat or you're out of time, go ahead and hold onto the bid. You'll most likely have to file an NPB report and pursue your Final Value Fee refund, but you will also bring the bidder to eBay's attention. Making bids and not honoring them

Learn to avoid problem bidders

violates eBay's terms of service and will ultimately lead to a bidder's suspension. So, add yourself to the list of sellers who noticed that this person doesn't operate in good faith. The number of retracted bids that have occurred over the previous six months becomes part of a member's profile.

You are free to cancel a bid if it comes from a person whose identity you cannot verify. If you've tried to find this person on eBay, and you've requested contact information only to come up with a phone number that isn't connected, you don't have to take the risk. Just remember that once you've canceled a bid, it cannot be reinstated, so be sure you mean it when you do. The only other reason for canceling a bid is that you no longer have the item available for sale. In the rare event that something happens to the item between the time you list it and the time the auction ends—for example, a couple of kids, a game of catch in the house, and a vase—you must cancel all of the bids before you close the auction. Send an e-mail to each of the bidders explaining the unfortunate turn of events, and you shouldn't have any further trouble from the incident.

Some Famous (or Infamous) Buyer's Scams

Once you spend some time on the discussion boards, you'll learn all about the many ways unscrupulous people have come up with to cheat sellers out of their earnings or goods. It can be astonishing to the noncriminal mind to discover how ingenious some of the schemes and scams are. Because sellers are so careful to guard their feedback ratings, they can sometimes be held hostage to a negative feedback. The feedback system actually makes sellers vulnerable. We are slightly less innocent than we were before we started researching this book, but we still have to agree, we never would have thought of most of these things. Thanks to PowerSeller Jeffrey of Hessfine for providing us with some of the nastier things there are to know about eBay buyers. Read on.

"I really like it, but . . ."

Sometimes an unsavory buyer will receive the item and then contact the seller with a line that says, "I really like the item, but it's got, this, this, or this wrong with it. I don't want to send it back, but I'd like you to cut the price and refund some of my money." In this case, you can decide to take the hit and send a refund, or you can insist that the buyer send the item back to you, and you will refund the entire amount once you receive it and verify that it is still in the same condition it was when you sent it. Of course, as PowerSeller David Yaskulka says, "If a buyer writes to say 'It looks like a hammer hit it,' and you make them send it back, then you can be sure it will look like a hammer hit it." David feels the real trick is to avoid patterns of abuse rather than isolated cases.

"I'll file an insurance claim"

In this variation, the buyer claims that the item has been damaged in shipping, but he still wants to keep it. He wants some of his money back because of the damage, but he'll take care of the insurance claim himself. Suggest that he send the item back to you, and you'll take the insurance issue on for yourself or take the loss.

Contacting Your Winning Bidder

Sometimes you'll find that your winning bidder gets an e-mail from someone who claims to have exactly the same item. The e-mailer will offer to sell that item to your bidder for less money, and your winning bidder will be lured away to make the purchase elsewhere. Whether or not that bidder ever gets the item, you'll still have to deal with this as an NPB and relist the item for auction.

Contacting Your Underbidders

As we've stated elsewhere, phony Second Chance offers have been a problem in the past. eBay has recently done much to thwart would-be scammers by hiding the identities of bidders where the high bid reaches a price of $200 or greater. But in the case of less expensive items, where bidders' identities are known, some experienced scammers will contact your underbidders and offer to sell them your item for less money off of eBay. They may even corrupt your e-mail address so that it seems you are contacting your own bidders. Often these e-mail addresses end in @juno or @hotmail, because addresses on these services are a little harder to trace. The unsuspecting underbidders may see the similar e-mail address and assume they are doing business with you. They'll send their payments on according to the directions in the e-mail, but of course, there is no item to be sold. Then they'll come back to you angry that you've not fulfilled your part of the "bargain." The best you can do here is to try to help them report the fraud and soothe their suffering.

Your Item Is a Fake

If you are selling something unique and of value, you may find someone is sending e-mails to your bidders warning them that the item is a fake. This person may also offer to sell your bidders the same authentic item off the eBay site. Jeffrey of Hessfine told us of a German dagger he listed with no reserve. The auction reached $2,800 when people started to back out of their bids. He learned they were receiving e-mails from someone claiming that the dagger was fake. He got one of the e-mails and saw it had one of the suspicious endings we just mentioned. He pulled the auction listing and had the dagger appraised by three separate and independent appraisers. He then relisted the item with a guarantee of authenticity. It ultimately sold for $5,300, but he still had to cope with all of the aggravation it took to make this sale.

Finally, you shouldn't shrug off *all* claims that an item you've sold is a fake. It's not unheard of for perfectly respectable sellers to mistakenly sell fake items. In fact, some sellers have gone months or even years without realizing this was happening. So if more than a couple of eBay members are writing you about this, do some homework!

Credit Card Fraud

Some buyers may contact you and ask you to split the cost of the item between two credit cards. Then they'll go ahead and charge back on one of these charges and purchase your item for only a fraction of the closing auction price. The credit card company will automatically refund the sale, and you'll have a headache trying to prove that the charge was legitimate.

College Students and Bank Accounts

Perhaps this is the most chilling scam of all. People from outside of the country have contacted college students to appeal to their naiveté and their overall willingness to help. Such a criminal will contact a college student in a chat room and start up a friendship. Then he'll mention that he wants to sell things on eBay, but he can't get a U.S. bank account from his foreign location. He'll ask to have the money wired to the student's account, and he'll offer to pay the student 30 percent of what he earns as a reward for the help. Then, he'll go to your bidders and offer to sell them the identical item you are listing at a reduced price. He'll have them wire the money to the student's account, where he'll be free to access it. Of course, there is no item to sell, but the bidder doesn't know that and neither does the poor student who was only too willing to help. This is another example of why you should be skeptical of a wire transfer outside of PayPal, and why you should continue to worry when your kids go off to college.

These are just a few of the many ingenious ways people have devised to cheat, lie, and steal in the electronic world. Consider them our contribution to the many you'll discover for yourself as you become a PowerSeller.

Meet
a
PowerSeller

Chris Chapman—Snowsportdeals

Chris Chapman found his niche first and then moved his business to eBay. He has operated a wholesale ski business for years, and here's how it works. He buys used skis and sells them to ski resorts for rental purposes. That requires him to buy his skis in large lots. With every lot, he found tall racing skis that were actually quite valuable, but of no use to the resort communities that made up his customers. It was these tall racing skis that first brought him to eBay.

Today, he has branched out into selling both used skis and new ski accessories such as goggles and boots. "You have to keep changing in any business," notes Chris, "but on the Internet, you have to be prepared to revamp every six months." To complicate this model even further, Chris's business is highly seasonal. From October through March, he has no time for anything but selling and order fulfillment. Any changes to his business plan or operation have to wait until his off-season when ski customers aren't shopping. Then he can analyze his growth, address his business from an operational viewpoint, and plan for the next season. To make life even more challenging, Chris has to do this without the help of employees. "We're strictly a family business," he says. It's not practical for Chris to hire and train someone who will only work for a few months during his busy season. The time required to complete the training makes it impractical, and it's difficult to find reliable employees who are willing to work like crazy for only a few months of the year!

Learn to avoid problem bidders

Every year Chris attends the most important ski equipment shows. He goes, knowing that he won't buy any inventory for his business from the current year's crop of offerings. But, this year's innovation is next year's inventory for Chris. He gathers all the product catalogues, and keeps them for reference materials to be used next year when he starts sourcing his used skis. He has a long-standing library of ski catalogues that help him stay educated about his product line.

Chris has worked hard to overcome an inherent challenge to his business plan. Because he sells used equipment, his customers are likely to be a little let down when their "new" skis arrive. Used skis are guaranteed to be scratched. Chris says he was the first in his category to wax and clean the skis before they're shipped, but no matter what, the skis are still used. "We make the bottoms look good, but they're still used," he told us. "To compensate for that, we offer great customer service and liberal returns." How used are they? Getting that information to the customer accurately is a big part of Chris's job. "Because we're a family business," Chris said, "we try to treat the customers the way we'd want our family to be treated."

Chris makes his business stand out with each package he ships. Not only are his skis cleaned and waxed, but he uses only custom-made boxes for his skis. He calls them his "three-way boxes." "We can ship it there, ship it back to us, and ship it once again to the customer," he said. He makes sure every box arrives with the product tight in the box, and nothing poking through the cardboard. "Skis are tough, it wouldn't really hurt them," Chris told us, "but the perception would be terrible." His boxes cost more, but he finds them to be worth the extra expense.

Chris also inserts little extras in his shipments. If customers are buying ski boots, he includes a guide to properly fitting the new boots. Ski boots are tighter fitting than customers might expect. "We guide them about how to put the boots on," Chris said. "The whole idea is to make people feel comfortable." Chris often includes coupons good for purchases made from his Web site, and he offers special discounts for shipping multiple orders.

Although the bulk of Chris's business is still on eBay, he has begun to diversify within the last few years. He currently sells on his own Web site, and also on Amazon.com. He has found ChannelAdvisor to be a good partner as he branches out away from eBay. He still operates an eBay store, mostly for the slower-moving ski boots in his inventory. "I'm never going to sell a size 4 ladies ski boot on the core site," he noted. "But I can keep it in my store until it sells."

When we spoke with Chris, it was at the end of a warm winter ski season. He was looking forward to his off-season projects that would allow him to further analyze his next business moves. Among that research, he planned to work on "branding" his online presence, fine-tuning his auction strategies, and developing his customer database. We look forward to seeing what happens next with this innovative and creative PowerSeller!

Close the Auction and Collect the Cash Checklist

✓ I am accepting personal checks, and I am selective about when I hold them.

✓ Since I know counterfeits are out there, I am careful with money orders and cashier's checks.

✓ I refuse wire transfers except for large purchases that go through escrow services.

✓ I'm watching my monthly sales figures so that I can sign up for PayPal's Merchant rate as soon as my monthly sales top US $3,000.

✓ My PayPal ATM/debit card is now giving easy access to my PayPal funds and is earning cash-back rewards.

✓ I am using PayPal's tools to track my PayPal transactions, analyze my sales, and help with my shipping.

✓ I'm researching PayPal's Virtual Terminal Service and considering signing up for it.

✓ I'm planning to start selling internationally, if I'm not already doing it!

✓ I am aware of spoof and phish e-mail schemes. I know how to authenticate messages purportedly from eBay or PayPal members.

✓ I always file for my Final Value Fee refunds when I qualify.

✓ I now require Immediate Payment when I sell time-sensitive items like concert tickets.

✓ I block problem bidders.

✓ I'm always on the lookout for current buyer scams.

Chapter 8

You Sold It, Now Ship It

Continue to buy things on eBay

The ultimate test of your life as an eBay seller comes the moment your customer opens the package to get to the merchandise you sold. It is the most concrete way for customers to know how you value their business, and it is the one thing your customers will remember about you long after they've forgotten everything else about their transactions. Your customers form a clear expectation about the product they're getting from your photos and item description, but the packages they receive remain a great unknown until the very end. Be sure your shipping procedures make your customers eager to shop with you again. Please them in this area, and you'll see them return to buy more.

Proper packaging and shipping is not just a matter of being nice to your customers. It's also a matter of protecting your business and keeping it moving smoothly. When you ship correctly, you eliminate customer complaints, damaged goods, and negative feedback remarks. Take a look at a PowerSeller's feedback history, and you'll see comments such as "fast shipping" and "great packaging," again and again. Trust us on this. It matters.

This has always been true, but now, how you pack your items and how quickly you ship them is more important than ever. As you know, eBay's feedback system allows for seller ratings that are much more detailed. Buyers may now rate a transaction on two shipping-related criteria: shipping time and shipping and handling charges. If you don't perform well in these areas your feedback profile will suffer for it.

When you're planning your shipping operations, you'll need to develop procedures for packing your items, including sources for all the materials necessary to make a professional-looking finished package. You'll need to consider a fair and reasonable price to charge your customers for shipping and handling, and you'll need to choose your favorite shipping methods. All of these decisions combine to create your own particular shipping policies and procedures. There's also some psychology involved in setting your shipping and handling charges that can have a definite impact on the effectiveness of your overall marketing efforts. Fortunately, PowerSellers have been more than eager to share their tips and advice about shipping your products.

›› Continue to buy things on eBay

"Continue to buy things on eBay," recommends a PowerSeller specializing in hobbies and crafts. "That way, you'll never forget what it feels like to open a package you've been waiting for. You'll always remember the difference between opening a well-packed package and a poorly packed one." This advice goes back to the old Golden Rule. Still, when you're busy and looking for fast turnaround of your products and inexpensive sources of packing materials, it's easy to lose sight of the final goal. You never want your customers to be disappointed by the packages they receive. In this way, eBay shopping is very different from shopping offline. When you go into a store, you physically remove the product yourself, and the bag doesn't make much difference to you. But, eBay shopping has an element of surprise akin to receiving a present. That's part of the fun. Make sure you don't forget that when you send things on to your customers.

Packaging Your Items

How you package your items for shipping will depend, of course, on what you sell. Some sellers are lucky, such as PowerSeller Steve of 1busyman, who specializes in video games. His packaging challenge is simple because the items are all the same size and shape. He determines the right packaging and how much each item will cost to ship just once, and then he can move on from there. Most sellers, however, are not that lucky.

What you sell will determine which shipping method you choose and what types of materials you'll need to prepare your packages. But one thing will not change: it is your responsibility to protect your items and make every effort to get them to their destinations whole and undamaged. You can say whatever you want in your listing about your buyers needing to purchase insurance, and your not being responsible for damaged goods, but in the end, you are responsible. You enter a contract with your customers to deliver the products they purchased. If you deliver a broken product, your customer has every right to a refund. Not only will you lose any dispute with eBay or PayPal over this, but you'll also lose the customer. So get it right from the very beginning.

» There's no such thing as too much packing material

"When I pack my items, I pretend someone is purposely going to try to damage the package." "I pack my items so they could

There's no such thing as too much packing material

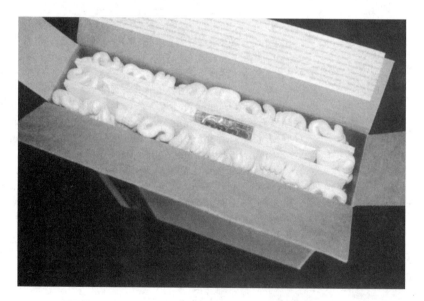

FIGURE 8-1 (a) PowerSeller Davidk57 starts packing his comic book by wrapping it carefully to prevent the case from being scratched or damaged. (b) When packaging is complete, this comic book is so well protected that only a catastrophic event could damage it.

potentially survive if a truck drove over them." "I double-box everything I ship." These are the voices of PowerSellers who told us how important it is to package everything carefully. We spoke with PowerSeller DavidK57, who was kind enough to share his packing techniques with us. When we asked about why he packages everything so carefully, he responded simply, "It's how I want to be perceived by others." Figures 8-1a and 8-1b show DavidK57's product before and after he's finished packing it. First he places the comic in a protective envelope and wraps it tightly. Next he wraps that package in a sleeve of bubble wrap. He then places the bundle between two pieces of foam board and tapes it all down securely. Finally, he places the whole thing in a Priority Mail box and fills the surrounding space with packing peanuts. A computer-printed label finishes the package neatly for an exceptional example of an eBay shipment.

On the other hand, you'll also see items sent out in packages like the one in Figure 8-2. Inside this discarded Blockbuster video box, we found a handful of packing peanuts and a bent and damaged vintage advertising card. Obviously, this seller was more interested in moving his merchandise and collecting his money than he was in making sure his customer was satisfied. That's not to say a seller shouldn't creatively use recycled materials. (At least we hope this video case was discarded and recycled!) We're all for that as you'll soon see. But if you use them, make them presentable. When we received this, we felt as though someone had mailed us his trash! Obviously, we will not be return customers.

» Spend less (or nothing) for packing materials

Getting the materials you'll need for packing your items is an opportunity for you to use your creativity. PowerSellers have discovered all types of sources for packing materials, including some that cost money and some that are free. Some of the best advice we heard follows:

- **Use the USPS Priority Mail** If you ship via Priority Mail, the box, tape, and labels are all available to you for free. Yes, the shipping rate is higher, but often if you factor in the cost of the materials and the faster

Spend less (or nothing) for packing materials

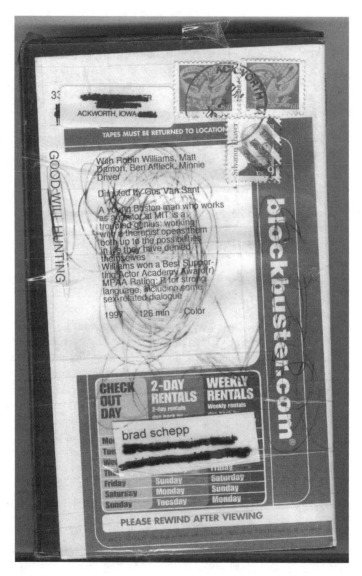

FIGURE 8-2 We blanked out the names and addresses on these labels to protect the seller's privacy, but all the rest of the scribbling was his own handiwork. The result is an extreme example of a poorly done package that came through the USPS.

Spend less (or nothing) for packing materials

shipment of your Priority Mail items, the additional cost is worth it. A wide variety of materials are available including boxes with the eBay logo.

A number of flat-rate Priority Mail boxes are available, so you pay the same price regardless of the final package's weight. The boxes are available in several sizes including one that's shoe-boxed size. You can order them at no charge from eBay's shipping center (http://pages.ebay.com/services/buyandsell/shipping .html), as long as you have an eBay account. Click on the link and your carrier will bring them by the next time he delivers your mail. What service! Currently, each box ships at a rate of $8.70, no matter what the package weighs or what the destination is. This makes Priority Mail even more cost-effective.

■ **Buy boxes in bulk**   Once you determine the most useful size box for shipping your items, buy your boxes in bulk. "I buy my boxes from a local cardboard manufacturer," says one clothing manufacturer who is also a PowerSeller. "I buy boxes printed with my own logo," says a PowerSeller from the Southeast. "I just consider it one of my many business expenses, but it is also good advertising." If you shop in bulk, you'll be able to buy your boxes at a reduced rate. Explore your local resources to see if there is a good source of cardboard products nearby.

■ **Reuse the boxes you receive**   eBay sellers are forever receiving packages in the mail, both from eBay purchases and from product sources such as wholesalers and manufacturers. Save all the clean boxes and all the packing materials you receive. A good sturdy box can be reused several times. When you do this, you get to use a product that someone else has already paid for! You may need to apply some extra packing tape to further reinforce it, but still it's free.

■ **Offer yourself as a recycler**   Think of the local businesses that may be receiving boxes routinely, and approach them with the offer of taking the used boxes off their hands. You'll want to get only clean boxes, so stay away from food stores and restaurants. Also, you don't want boxes that have been cut open with a razor.

Spend less (or nothing) for packing materials

Approach local gift shops, for example. Unless they sell on eBay, they have no use for their discarded boxes. They'll be happy to have you stop by routinely and pick them up. This will save them the time an employee must spend breaking boxes down for recycling or the trash. You may also suggest they sign on as a consignment customer for eBay selling if you'd like!

- **Get free bubble wrap**   That gift shop is also a good place to pick up free bubble wrap, but the best source for free bubble wrap and plastic is your local furniture store. Furniture stores get huge quantities of bubble wrap, and they don't have a need to reuse it. It's more a nuisance to them than anything else, but to you it's clean, perfectly reusable packing material. Again, make a schedule to routinely pick up all the discards you need.

- **Use clean shredded paper**   With your office shredder you can create this excellent packing material. It's free, and you can produce as much of it as you need. What a great way to put that junk mail to work!

- **Think environmentally friendly**   All of these recycling ideas have the added benefit of a smaller footprint on the environment. You are entering a business that requires you to use resources. You can't deliver your products safely without them. So, be mindful of what you use and choose materials with the environment in mind. More and more of your customers will appreciate it, and you can even incorporate your environmental concern into your advertising materials.

- **Save those newspaper bags**   Clean plastic bags from your daily newspaper can easily be transformed into air-pocket cushions for packing your items. Just blow them up and tie the end. Now you have a cushion much like the ones other people are buying from the office supply store.

Labeling Your Packages

If packing your items carefully is the way to ensure they arrive at their destinations in good shape, labeling them carefully is the way to ensure that they arrive there at all. You can print labels using your auction management software, or you can print them online when you buy your postage (more about that in a minute). Either way, printing your labels on a printer makes them neater and more legible. If you must do it by hand, print them—don't write. "I always ask my customers to e-mail me their addresses, because I don't trust myself to type the address correctly," admits one PowerSeller from the Midwest. When he receives the e-mail, he simply cuts and pastes the address, and he doesn't need to worry about making a mistake. You may decide you don't want to take on this extra e-mail step, but just be certain you are careful when you make up the label, and then double-check it one more time. Once you have your label affixed to the box, cover it completely with a piece of clear packing tape. That way, nothing can smear if the box gets damp, and the label is much less likely to be damaged or lost.

» Include a packing slip with every package

Including a packing slip in every package leaves your customers with a sense that they are dealing with a professional seller. Every customer deserves a receipt, and your packing slip will provide that. In addition, you can use it to add a little note of thanks for the purchase, a greeting about your business, or a reminder that you plan to leave positive feedback for the buyer and hope for the same. Be friendly, and you'll close your transaction on a happy, positive note. As a practical consideration, including a packing slip protects you in the event that the package gets lost or damaged. Since it will include both the buyer's name and address and your business's name and address, the carrier can open the box to investigate who owns the contents and where those contents belong should something happen to the label or to the box.

Should You Use Delivery Confirmation?

PowerSellers are not of one mind on this question. Whether or not you should include delivery confirmation for your packages depends largely on what you sell. You don't need to bother with it if you sell items that are so inexpensive that you won't mind occasionally bearing the cost of replacing a shipment. For sellers of inexpensive items, for example, $5 to $10, it may not pay to spend the extra $0.50 or $0.60 (through the USPS) that delivery confirmation costs. For the random problem with

Pad the item, not the shipping charges

delivery, it may be more cost-effective to just take the loss and replace the item. For most sellers, however, delivery confirmation is worth the cost.

Another benefit of delivery confirmation is that it helps make you less vulnerable to scam buyers. If a customer claims never to have received an item you shipped, you'll have proof that the package was delivered. Usually it takes nothing more to get one of these dishonest buyers out of your life than just sending an e-mail with the tracking numbers in it. The dishonest buyer who now knows you're savvy is likely to just move on to the next victim. Through the USPS you will have automatic delivery confirmation by purchasing the following services:

- Signature confirmation service
- Certified mail service
- Registered mail service
- International registered mail service

It's also available for a small extra fee for Priority Mail (free if you paid for your postage online), parcels sent as First-Class Mail, Parcel Post, Bound Printed Matter, or Media Mail.

Note that if you ship through PayPal with USPS, delivery confirmation is free for Priority Mail postage printed online, and available at a nominal charge for other postage classes. Your buyer can track the shipment by clicking on a link from his PayPal My Account page.

Pricing Your Shipping and Handling

PowerSellers may not agree about delivery confirmation, but they do agree that you should not be using shipping and handling charges to generate profit and income for your eBay business. Your chance to make a profit is on the sale of the item; once it's sold, you are only being dishonest if you overcharge for the cost of shipping and handling.

» Pad the item, not the shipping charges

You don't want your customers to feel resentful about being overcharged for shipping fees. You also don't want to discourage potential customers by shipping charges that will easily send them on to your competitors' auction listings. Now that shipping charges are included in search results, if yours aren't competitive your buyers may not even bother looking at your listing. "Don't pad your shipping costs. It makes your customers resent you, and you want them to come back to shop some more," advises a PowerSeller who deals in collectibles. At the same time, he advised, free shipping doesn't work either. "I tried free shipping, but I was just losing too much money that way."

How Much Is Too Much?

So how do you determine a fair rate of pay that covers your expenses but doesn't fleece your buyers? First keep in mind the term shipping and handling. Although this term can sometimes seem distasteful to a buyer (What's handling, anyway?), considering all its meanings helps you set pricing policy. Shipping and handling includes a good deal more than just postage.

In addition to paying for postage, your customer should expect to contribute toward your costs for preparing and sending the package. These are some of the costs:

- The materials you must purchase to prepare the package
- The time you spend getting the package ready
- The time you spend driving to drop off the package, and the gas it takes to do that
- The time you spend waiting in line to mail the package
- The cost of the salary you pay someone to prepare your shipping

Time is money, and you deserve to be paid for the time it takes you to carefully send an item along to the customer. It's a service you provide, and you deserve to be paid for it. On the other hand, you may want to reconsider some of these charges in the light of your business practices. For example, if you claim your boxes as a business expense, is it fair to also charge your customers for them? If you have a daily pick-up arrangement with your postal carrier, is it fair to charge your customer as though you spent time and money going to the post office? Be fair, but also be realistic about what you are actually spending and which parts of those expenditures you can honestly pass on to your customers.

≫ Don't disclose your postage costs

"I use Stamps.com and hide my postage costs," says one PowerSeller from New Jersey. "Shipping is more than just postage, and if my customer can't see the postage charge of $1.05, he can't get angry and ask me why I charged $2.50 for shipping." Stamps.com is not the only online postage service that will allow you to keep your postage charges private, but it's a good piece of advice to use one that will.

Flat-Rate Shipping Versus Variable-Rate Shipping

When you create your auction listing, you'll be asked to include shipping costs. You can handle this part of your listing in two different ways. You can calculate a flat rate for your shipping expenses and list that figure, which will apply to all your bidders. Or, you can include a rate calculator in the auction listing that will allow prospective bidders to calculate their specific shipping costs on the basis of their ZIP codes. You specify the weight and size of the package and the shipping services you wish to make available. The bidders then input their ZIP code and a price for shipping appears, calculated to that specific location, and shipping option. This price will include the handling charge you specify and insurance, if you're offering that, too. You don't have to specifically itemize each of these fees, as the total price is all that the bidder will see. You can easily include a shipping calculator in your auctions. When you're creating your auction, you'll see it listed as an option from the Create Your Listing page.

Some sellers find it simpler to just create the flat-rate price and then state it in the auction listing, leaving nothing further for the bidder to have to calculate. This is especially good when postal rates are in a state of flux, because online calculators may not be up-to-the-minute with these changes. Sellers may also use their shipping rates as sales incentives, keeping them as low as possible to attract buyers who watch their pennies in shipping charges. Sellers using this method prefer the simplicity, even if they occasionally charge slightly less than they should. Other sellers prefer the more precise estimates they get with the shipping calculators and expect their bidders to be willing to take that extra step in determining what their final costs will be. PowerSeller Arthur Clem has found that his customers appreciate that he offers variable-rate pricing, rather than just stipulating a flat rate. They feel it keeps their costs reasonable. Try your shipping fees each way to determine which is right for your business.

» State your shipping charges clearly

Just be sure that when you list your item, you are very clear in stating your shipping charges and policies. Everyone who shops on eBay expects to pay shipping charges. When your item appears in search results, if you haven't included shipping charges, "Not Specified" will appear in the shipping column. Rather than take the added step of contacting you or closely examining your listing for clues, many buyers will move on. If you clearly state what your charges are, your customer will have all the facts needed to make a decision.

Customers who feel a seller's shipping charges are too high are free to move along and shop with someone else. But if you clearly state your charges and a buyer wins your auction, it's the buyer's responsibility to live up to the shipping charges you published in your listings. If the buyer then gets back to you to ask you to adjust the shipping charges, you are within your rights to decline. The buyer should have made that decision before bidding, and you are under no obligation to comply with such a request.

At the same time, calculate your shipping fees carefully and then be prepared to live with them even if they turn out to be wrong. You'll get better at estimating your shipping fees with experience, but you must abide by your estimates from the very beginning. Every seller has sent out packages and taken a hit on the shipping fees. You can't go back to the buyer after the auction ends and explain that you made a mistake, and you'll need more money for shipping. That's just wrong. So be prepared to take one for the team. You'll be more accurate in your estimate the next time around.

Overall, PowerSellers clearly state their shipping and handling charges whether they choose to ship using variable rates or flat rates. Clearly stating all associated fees for each listing enables your customers to calculate exactly what they

State your shipping charges clearly

will have to spend to purchase and receive the items you've listed. From a psychological viewpoint, this will encourage them to take that final step and make the bid. If you leave it open-ended, requesting that buyers contact you for shipping and handling charges, you leave open a great unknown that will make your shoppers much more likely to move on to the next seller. They'll move on not only because they don't want to bother with that extra step, but also because, psychologically, it suggests that perhaps you have some reason not to be up front about the charge right in your listing.

On another note, you can use your shipping and handling charges as a marketing tool and an incentive to get your customers to bid on your items. "We found shipping charges were a powerful place to incent multiple-item purchases," says PowerSeller David of Blueberryboutique. No extra charge for additional items shipped together and totally free shipping for sales of three items or more worked very well for him. Buyers appreciate low shipping charges, and eBay statistics prove that keeping your costs as low as possible makes it more likely for you to get increased bids on your auctions. Since you've already learned how to get free or very inexpensive shipping supplies, consider cutting your shipping and handling charges to the bone to entice customers to bid on your items. In this way, your shipping and handling charges will not only cover the expense of sending your items on their way, they will also become part of your overall marketing strategy. As a rising PowerSeller, you will work hard to distinguish yourself from the pack on every score, and shipping and handling is one more area where you can do that.

Shipping Oversized Items

If you're planning to deal in furniture, appliances, computers, or other large items, you'll have special shipping concerns that go beyond the scope of the average eBay seller. You'll need to do some research locally to determine your best shipping options. Very often you'll get the best price quotes from local shipping companies. Canadian-based PowerSeller Joe of Carrocel-antiques specializes in antique and restored furniture. Almost all of his shipping is via truck freight, and nearly 90 percent of his items get shipped to the continental United States. He does ship furniture to Europe, however, and when he does, he uses a combination of truck freight and ocean freight. His shipping fees are quite expensive, but that doesn't deter his customers from purchasing his beautiful furniture. Since he operates his own woodworking shop, he creates his own wooden customized crates for every piece he ships.

If your oversized items are less specialized than this, you'll want to explore a company such as freightquote.com. This company provides online business-to-business freight and logistics services for sellers who need to ship heavy items. Visit their Web site at www.freightquote.com. Another company that eBay sellers use is Craters & Freighters at http://www.cratersandfreighters.com.

Insuring Your Shipments

In almost all cases, the items you ship will arrive at their destinations without trouble. But in those very few cases when this is not true, insurance saves you and your buyer a huge headache. What type of insurance you choose will depend on what you sell, how you ship it, and how much risk you are willing to take. One collectibles PowerSeller told us he purchased a special collector's insurance policy for his inventory. This insurance covers his collection when it's stored at his site, when he travels to sell it at shows, and when he ships items to his customers. He has no worries about insuring anything, and the yearly premiums he pays for his insurance are less than he would pay if he insured every shipment. This might be a solution for you if you plan to deal in collectibles.

You certainly want to offer insurance to your bidders as an option with their shipping costs. Shipping via the USPS, you can purchase up to $50 worth of insurance for $1.30. Bumping that up to $100 of coverage will cost just $2.30. When you ship with UPS, you automatically receive up to $100 of insurance included in your shipping charges. If you want additional insurance it's $0.55 per $100 of coverage with a minimum charge of $1.60. An alternative to offering insurance to your bidders is to fold insurance charges into your total shipping costs and list your shipping fees as including insurance. This way, you are assured that the package will be covered from the

State your shipping charges clearly

time it leaves your hands until it arrives at your customer's location.

When you purchase insurance, you buy peace of mind, but you also buy simplicity in resolving problems if they arise. When you ship an item insured through the USPS, for example, you simply hold on to the insurance receipt. If your package doesn't arrive at its destination, you send the receipt on to your buyer, and he will then pursue it with the USPS on his end. Because you purchased insurance, the problem will now be resolved with no more input from you.

Scheduling Your Shipments

Once again, how frequently you send shipments out depends entirely on you. Some sellers ship every day. Others create a schedule of two or three shipping days a week. Neither approach is right or wrong, as long as you're up front with your customers about your policy. Obviously, from your buyer's viewpoint you should ship products every business day. "Buyers expect to receive their shipments in seven days or less, so the faster the shipping the better," says PowerSeller Cynthia Lizana of texcyngoods. She recommends that you ship within one business day if possible. If you sell items that are more time-sensitive, for example, gift items near the holidays, you may agree. Keep in mind, your business may work more efficiently if you can process a maximum number of orders at each shipping session. That will require you to set aside a couple of days each week for shipping. Make it clear in your auctions which days those are and include them again in your end of auction e-mails.

Your Carrier Options

We've all sent packages, so there's really not much mystery about the process of getting something sent to a distant destination. Which carrier you choose depends largely on what you ship and where you live. For some sellers, geography makes one carrier more convenient than another. For others, one carrier offers better rates for the oversized packages they ship. You'll have to make your choice for yourself, but we'll offer you a look at some of the most common options.

❯❯ Consider eBay's own shipping center

eBay makes it easy for you to pay for postage and print labels for both the USPS and UPS. You can buy postage through your PayPal account and print the labels directly from eBay's site. Then with the postage paid and the labels in place, you can take your packages to the post office or drop-off center and simply drop them off all ready to go. As an added benefit, when you use eBay's shipping center, your customer's address is automatically printed on the label from your eBay records. Then both you and your customer receive an automatically generated e-mail that includes the tracking information for the package. You can even purchase insurance through PayPal and eBay. Go to http:// pages.ebay.com/services/buyandsell/shipping center9.html for more information.

The USPS

The USPS is a steady and reliable means of shipping your items. It also offers you a wide variety of options and prices for mailing your packages. If you sell books, magazines, CDs, or movies, you can use Media Mail, which is the least expensive way to send a package. Remember though, it also takes the longest to arrive, so be clear that this is the shipping method you will use when you list the item. Other choices range from Parcel Post all the way to Express Mail, which will give you overnight delivery. You can get a complete listing of fees and services by going to www.usps.com.

If you use Express Mail or Priority Mail, you can arrange to have your regular mail carrier stop by your house every day to pick up all your packages. If you choose not to ship every day, you can still arrange for free next-day carrier pickup by the USPS for Express Mail and Priority Mail. Simply go online to http:// ebay.com/usps/usps_tools.html to arrange for your carrier to stop by on the next delivery day to pick up your packages

If you find yourself caught in a bind that requires you to ship an item even before your next delivery day, you can arrange for an on-demand pickup of an unlimited number of packages for $13.25. To use the on-demand pickup, you'll have to be shipping your packages via Express Mail, Priority Mail, Global Express Mail, or Parcel Post. Of course, you'll have to have already affixed the proper postage in order to use these services. You can do that through online postage services, Stamps.com among others.

» Use Stamps.com

"We have found it is faster to use Stamps.com, than PayPal Shipping," says texcyngood's Cynthia. With Stamps.com you can purchase all your postage online using your credit card. You can print postage in any amount, including individual stamps and shipping labels, too. A rate calculator helps you ensure that your postage is correct, and you can purchase extras such as Delivery Confirmation. With the postage and labels already in place, all you need do is take your packages to the post office and drop them off. "I have an arrangement with my post office so that I can actually drive around back and just drop them off. No waiting in line at all," a PowerSeller from the Midwest told us. The software is easy to use. It has very modest hardware requirements, and it supports address books from many popular software applications including QuickBooks and Microsoft Outlook. For more information, go to www.stamps.com.

» Consider Endícía.com

Another source of online postage is Endícía.com. Endícía Internet Postage is a service from Envelope Manager Software, a leading provider of desktop mail software for more than 15 years. Through Endícía.com's attractive and easy-to-use Web site at www.endicia.com (no accent marks in the URL), you can sign up to purchase postage for all classes of mailings from Media Mail and Library Mail to Express Mail. Endícía.com offers three different pricing plans for users; each comes with a discount if you purchase a one-year subscription in advance. For the basic service known as the Windows Standard Plan, you'll pay $9.95 per month or $99.95 per year. You'll have access to all of the postage services plus an address book, free Internet address corrections, and interfaces to the Outlook and Act! e-mail programs. The Windows Premium Plan costs $15.95 per month or $174.95 per year. It gives you all the features of the Standard Plan, but it also allows you to hide your shipping and handling charges on your postage labels. It further allows you to search for packages from any Web browser, not just where you created the shipping labels. You can search by name of recipient, address, company, ZIP code, reference ID, tracking number, and/or approximate shipping date. This feature could be very handy when you're trying to track down a missing package. Finally, Endícia.com offers a plan for Macintosh computer users. The MAC Premium Plan offers many of the same features as the Windows Premium Plan and costs $15.95 per month or $174.95 per year. With all of these plans your usage is free for the first 30 days.

UPS

For the most part, UPS is somewhat more expensive than the USPS. Billing for UPS is based on zones, so calculating your shipping is a little more complicated and the final postage fees will vary depending on where your winning bidder lives. Still, you can do all the calculations online, and UPS has done its best to try to simplify the process. You can get complete rate information at www.ups.com. When you sign up on the Web site, UPS will deliver a package to you with a tremendous amount of information to get you started. In that package you will receive some free UPS Express envelopes, shipping labels, and a map of the zones based on your own ZIP code.

Some advantages to using UPS are that the company has a higher weight limit than the USPS. UPS will ship packages up to 150 pounds, while the USPS won't go above 70 pounds. Also, when you ship UPS you receive automatic online delivery confirmation and insurance of up to $100 per package at no extra charge. However, if you want to arrange for an on-demand pickup, you'll pay a fee for each package you send. You can offset that by arranging for a routine daily pick-up schedule. You will then be charged a weekly rate based on the total value of what you ship each week. You can get free shipping supplies, including boxes, tape, and envelope mailers.

FedEx

"We go with FedEx because for our oversized packages they are actually cheaper," says a PowerSeller who ships golf equipment. That may be so for his specialized shipping needs, but for the most part FedEx will be more expensive than either UPS or the USPS. However, as with UPS and USPS you can get your shipping supplies for free, as long as you have an account (no charge to open one). Keep FedEx in the back of your mind for special shipping needs, but for the most part, the PowerSellers we spoke with chose either the USPS or UPS for the bulk of their shipping needs.

When choosing your carrier, remember that prices may not be set and may, in fact, be negotiable. It depends on the amount of business you can offer. PowerSeller Art Clem scheduled both UPS and Fedex to arrive at the same time on the same day. Once both drivers knew they were competing for his business,, better pricing was the result.

International Shipping

International shipping can seem intimidating, but more than anything it just involves extra paperwork. As you saw in Chapter 7, some PowerSellers believe the opportunities for selling to international markets far outweigh the challenges of arranging overseas shipping. Considering that eBay's international revenues are consistently growing more rapidly than the domestic ones, you may find it difficult to maintain solid growth without international sales. If you do decide to sell internationally, be sure to clearly state that bidders from outside the United States must contact you for shipping costs—that the standard shipping offered for U.S. customers will not apply to those who live outside of the United States. Shipping internationally is far more expensive, and you don't want to be stuck with the difference coming directly from the profit you made on the sale.

To ship internationally, you should stick with the well-known shipping providers. Both UPS and the USPS handle international shipping. Sticking with the big names makes sense, because everything you ship internationally must clear customs. The big name shipping providers are most experienced in getting packages through customs without a hitch.

When you ship internationally, you must complete customs forms for each package you send. These forms require you to declare both the contents and the value of the package. Most countries charge taxes and duty fees based on the value of the item you are shipping. It's very important for you to value the items carefully to avoid increasing these fees unnecessarily. The value of your item is the final price it brought on eBay. When you want to send a package that requires custom forms, you must take them directly to the post office or the UPS shipping center. These packages cannot be dropped off at a box or picked up by a carrier. To get more information about shipping internationally, stop by eBay's International Trading Discussion Board. You'll find a lot of experienced sellers there willing to help you get started in the global market.

Bob Buchanan and Greg Scheuer— avforsale

Just over seven years ago, Bob and Greg worked together for a large audio-visual rental and production company based in Atlanta, Georgia. When the company decided to move to California, both friends were laid off. They gave up their jobs rather than to uproot and move across the country. One of their last responsibilities was to sell the inventory that remained in the

Atlanta warehouse. The equipment was high-end, production quality, audio-visual equipment, and therefore not the kind of thing that individuals, or even most large companies, would need to own. The two faced an interesting business challenge, and turned to eBay to solve it.

In retrospect, they were in the right place at the right time! Having worked for the largest audio-visual rental business in the country, they had a ready supply of product to sell. Because they'd worked in the industry for more than 20 years, they also brought a technical expertise to the task that is priceless to their customers. Not only can they sell you what you need, they can also help you figure out the best products to satisfy your needs. "We had a business problem that we solved with eBay," Bob told us. "That in turn led to an eBay business."

Today Bob and Greg have more than 200 different suppliers of audio-visual equipment. "We really have two sets of customers," they explained. "We have our selling customers and our buying customers, and we have to keep them both happy." Because of their expertise, they can serve as consultants to both groups. "The resale pricing curve is a pretty straight line down," they explained. "An item only holds its value until the latest version from the manufacturer. Then it goes down. Six months makes a big difference." Because they so completely know their industry and marketplace, they can advise their suppliers of upcoming changes in time to get the best price possible for the used equipment. "We sell a lot on consignment," they said. "Working on straight commission, it's in our best interest to sell our products at the highest price possible." The two set a goal of moving a tractor trailer full of product out of their operation every week. They have 15 employees to help them achieve this goal.

Although these two friends operate in a pretty specialized niche, they have some advice that can be applied universally to eBay sales. For example, they recommend that, as an eBay seller, you should remember that eBay is not a retail sales venue. Set your sales expectations accordingly, and start your pricing low. "Trust eBay to do what it does well, which is sell things," Bob said. At one time their sell-through rates were running between 60 and 70 percent. They decided to cut their listing price in half, and within a month their sell-through rate moved up to 85 percent. "If you list a $100-item for $100, you won't sell it for that," he noted. "If you list it for $9.99, it may go for $100. If it doesn't sell for $100, then it wasn't really worth $100."

Bob and Greg also advise specializing in an item and growing to know it so well that you can advise your customers. Of course, you must start out as an honest businessperson and provide great customer service too. Shipping items is a place where you can really distinguish yourself, according to Bob and Greg. "We take full responsibility for everything we ship," they said. To ensure that shipping goes well, the two have invested $11,000 in a foam packing system. They also have a global insurance policy through UPS that covers everything that comes in and goes out. "It's an all-harm, worldwide insurance policy," they told us. The two noted that they learned about the policy through UPS, a great business partner, according to the friends.

They also focus on learning from their customers. The two make it a point to watch the questions that come in regarding their policies and their descriptions. If they see patterns to those questions, they review their own work to see if they can clarify things for their customers. That way, they can avoid customer service issues before they become problems.

So the old question remains, was getting laid off good news or bad news? At the time, it must have seemed like bad news, but seven years and a lucrative business of their own later, it may just have been the lucky break of a lifetime!

You Sold It, Now Ship It Checklist

✓ I shop on eBay so I can see how my competitors handle packaging and shipping.

✓ I am generous, very generous, with my packing materials.

✓ I'm thinking about sources for free packing materials that are in good condition.

✓ Shipping is not one of my profit centers, but I try not to lose money on shipping either.

- ✓ If I need to ship oversized items, I'll get at least two quotes from companies such as freightquote.com and Craters & Freighters.
- ✓ I know when I need to insure an item for my own peace of mind, and I've reviewed my insurance options.
- ✓ I know my customers expect fast shipping, so I keep them informed about my shipping schedule.
- ✓ I am exploring my options for carriers, and I plan to make them compete for my business.
- ✓ I've researched services such as Stamps.com and Endícía.com.
- ✓ I am learning about shipping internationally.

Chapter 9

Your Customer Is Always Right (Even When He's Wrong)

O f all the subjects we discussed with PowerSellers, no other found the unanimous agreement that we saw on the subject of customer service. It didn't matter if the product they sold was an $8 DVD or a painting that went for $20,000; all of them agreed that outstanding customer service is the hallmark of a PowerSeller's business. Providing great customer service may seem a daunting task when you're processing hundreds or even thousands of orders a month, and the volume of e-mail from customers can feel overwhelming. But what can seem so complicated is really, at its core, fairly simple.

"It's funny how the most important thing we know about business is what we learned as children," noted a PowerSeller who specializes in collectibles. He was talking, of course, about the Golden Rule. Treat others as you would like to be treated yourself. Even as your business grows this should remain your motto. "We're a family business and we try and give the customers what they want," says PowerSeller Chris Chapman. "We treat them like we'd want our family to be treated."

It's so simple. It's so pure. It's so easy to lose track of when you're busy, hurried, and feeling hassled. You've already begun to live this rule, however, because you've gone into your eBay business with the intent to provide good-quality products. Since you are selling products you truly believe in, standing behind every sale will be easier. Starting from this position of strength will give you the solid foundation you need to handle whatever customer service challenges you may face.

The first thing to remember is not to be afraid of your customers. We've spoken before about the fact that ultimately every transaction on eBay comes down to a moment of trust. Your customers trust that you will send the products that they expect to get, and you trust that your buyers have come to transact business with you in good faith. In the vast majority of cases, customer service will be no more difficult than fulfilling this commitment and leaving positive feedback. "PowerSellers meet all kinds of people: sincere, unreasonable, some you could never make happy in a million years. Out of 100 percent of my customers, 95 percent are people I want to deal with," says PowerSeller James of Jeralinc, who sells jewelry.

In this regard, great customer service on eBay isn't different from great customer service in a brick-and-mortar environment. If you dealt face-to-face with your customers, you'd have the opportunity to come to know them by face, personality, and preference. Most would come and go without much note, but there would be some who stuck in your memory for either pleasant reasons or unpleasant ones. While you'll find your eBay experience to be much the same, you do have some special challenges when you deal with your customers online. It's easy to lose track of the person on the other side of the computer. Don't allow yourself to forget that most problems with customers are more a matter of miscommunication and misunderstanding rather than misdemeanor and misanthropy.

But, don't be intimidated. You've already gone a long way toward providing your customers with the service and support they deserve. When you write accurate descriptions of your products, that's customer service. When you state your policies clearly, that's customer service. When you provide your customers with a variety of payment options, you're providing great customer service. When you package your items carefully and arrange for them to be shipped properly, that's great customer service too. Even your About Me page is a step toward providing your customers the service they deserve. Look at all you've accomplished already! PowerSellers all agree that customer service is what distinguishes a great seller from a good one. They've shared their tips with us, and with those tips you'll find your own level of comfort. After all, you are the boss.

E-Mail: The Way Customer Service Is Done

Almost all of your customer service efforts will happen via e-mail. It is the medium through which you'll know your customers, but e-mail is a flawed method of communication. It is easy to misinterpret the intent and tone of a person's e-mail communication. Remember that when you receive e-mail from your customers, but never forget it when you send your own e-mails. "The most important, and time-consuming, part of this job is answering e-mail," said a New England PowerSeller. You will have to respond to questions your customers pose about your items before the auction ends, and then you'll have a series of e-mails to swap as the auction ends and the transaction closes. Some of these can be automated, but don't ever let them seem automated. Don't forget that, although you may send out a dozen e-mail notifications of products shipped today, each of your customers is probably only receiving one. Don't let your e-mail feel processed to the point of removing the human touch.

"I feel the personal touch is what makes it different," says PowerSeller Frank of tessies-toys. The idea is to let them see you as a person.

❯❯ Your e-mail should be letter perfect

The first thing you want your customers to know is that the person on the other side of the e-mail is a professional, committed to the business he or she operates. Your e-mails are the face you show your customers, and you want that face to represent you well. You don't have to be a great writer, but you do have to be sure your e-mails are grammatically correct and filled only with proper English; no slang here. You should also use your spell checker to ensure that you don't send e-mails off with misspellings or typos. That's really not excusable, because it's just too easy to prevent. Answer your e-mails promptly.

Your goal is to respond to e-mail the same day you receive it, and when it comes to queries about your item before the auction closes, you must respond even more quickly. Chris of snowsportdeals confided that early on he didn't realize this. "I got some early negative feedbacks, because I didn't know to respond to e-mail over the weekend. It seemed early enough to me to respond on Monday, but it's very important to respond incredibly quickly. Even if you just acknowledge that you received the e-mail and will respond on Monday." If you keep your customer waiting, that customer may find just the right item in some other seller's listings.

E-Mails Throughout the Transaction

Most of your transactions will happen with just a minimum of e-mails passed between you and the buyer. PowerSellers couldn't possibly process the volume of orders they do if each transaction required multiple e-mails. As your volume increases it's likely you'll automate some of these e-mail communications, and that's a great time-saver, as long as you don't allow the e-mails to seem "processed." You will surely send an e-mail when the auction ends, and you must send one when the item ships, but some PowerSellers go even further. "We send five e-mails for every transaction," reported PowerSeller Shelly of Shoetime. "We send three end-of-auction e-mails, one payment-received e-mail, and one item-shipped e-mail." Certainly with more than 80,000 feedbacks, this

Answer the query and add a little bit more

PowerSeller has found a reliable method for automating these e-mails, but her customers still feel they are being tended through each step of the process.

You may find that you are able to combine some of these e-mails to cut down on your e-mail effort, but you still want to be certain that your customers feel you are taking good care of them through every step of the sale. We'll look at e-mails for each part of the transaction, so that you can see how PowerSellers keep their customers informed and interested. Remember that with each e-mail you send, your customer learns a little bit more about you. It doesn't take more time to be friendly and helpful, and your efforts are sure to pay off when your customer feels that shopping with you has been a pleasure. The first e-mail you receive is likely to come before your item is sold.

» Answer the query and add a little bit more

When a customer requests more information about your item, be friendly in your responses, but keep it professional. Answer the question directly, and then go on to add a bit about the product and how the person might use it, if appropriate. Use this e-mail as bait to make the person want the product just a little bit more than before asking the question. You want the customer to actually see himself or herself using your product and enjoying it. That's really not a difficult thing to do, especially since you're selling items you are familiar with and can stand behind. Here's an example:

The question has been answered, you've personalized the item, and you've given the customer a reason to see that she will enjoy owning this pattern book. You've also proved to her that her transaction is important to you, because you've given her a response that proves you value her interest in your item and you've thanked her. You may secretly be annoyed because your description clearly stated the patterns in the book included both crocheted and knitted projects, but your customer must never detect that annoyance. No matter how carefully you craft your auction listings, some customers just need to ask before they buy. They may actually view this as a way to "test" a seller before they bid. That can be frustrating, but think of it as the online equivalent of the smile you'd share with a customer who walked into your brick-and-mortar store.

Answer the query and add a little bit more

Yes, I'm happy to say that the pattern book you're asking about does include instructions for both knitted and crocheted sweaters for children. You'll also find instructions for matching hats and mittens. I especially like this book, because there are instructions for using multiple colors for each project. The patterns can be adapted for either the beginner or the more experienced crafter. You'll be proud to give these finished projects as gifts or to enjoy seeing your own children dressed in your creations! Thank you for shopping with me.

End the Auction on a High Note

When the auction ends and you have a winning bidder, eBay will send an end-of-auction (EOA) e-mail on your behalf. That e-mail may include your standard policy information about payment and shipping, and it should set the stage for a smooth ending to your sale. But, of course you can follow up with your own, more personal e-mail. First, send this e-mail out immediately after the auction closes. Chances are your customer is well aware of the auction's closing time, and sending out this e-mail quickly proves that you are right on top of your business details. Keep the tone friendly and upbeat. Remember this is a celebration. They don't call this person the "winning" bidder for nothing! Congratulate your winner and assure the person that you're committed to providing complete satisfaction with the item. PowerSellers recommend that you include certain details in this e-mail to help ensure a smooth transfer of your item to its new owner:

- The item number should be both in the body of the e-mail and in the subject heading. This helps the buyer identify which auction item is yours if the buyer has purchased more than one thing at a time. It also helps you quickly identify the e-mails you've sent and the responses you receive.

- Include your payment options. Yes, you stated them before, but that doesn't mean this buyer was actually paying attention when payment was a theoretical thing. Now that it's a reality, clearly state what your payment options are.

- Tell the customer when payment is due and provide your address.

- Detail your shipping options and how they will be affected by payment choices. If you hold personal checks for 10 days or more, state that here. If you only ship twice a week, no matter what method of payment is used, be sure your customer knows that. Clearly state which days you ship. If you have not already calculated shipping charges and listed them in your auction, do it now before you send this e-mail. Make sure your customer knows everything necessary about completing the transaction before you hit Send.

■ Ask the buyer to e-mail you in return stating his or her shipping preference, intended method of payment, and correct shipping address.

■ Sign off with a hearty "thank you" and good wishes for the buyer with the new purchase.

This is not the time to ask for feedback. It's also not the time to be harsh and strict in detailing what the buyer must do and what will befall the buyer if he or she doesn't do it. Remember, the tone is celebratory, cooperative, and upbeat. Here's a sample you can use as a template for your EOA e-mail:

Congratulations! You're the winning bidder for item #123456789! You've just purchased a great set of screwdrivers, and I'm sure you'll get many years of good service from them. I am committed to your 100 percent satisfaction with your item, and here are some details that will help us complete your transaction:

You may pay for your purchase through PayPal or by money order, certified check, or personal check. If you send a personal check, I will hold it for 10 business days before I ship your item.

Please send payment within three business days to me at:

>1234 My Street
>Hometown, NY 23456

I will gladly ship your item to you via USPS or UPS. The cost for first-class mail will be $5.50. Priority Mail will cost $7.75. UPS will cost $9.95. Your shipping costs include delivery confirmation, and I can add insurance for $1.30. I ship my products every Monday, Wednesday, and Friday.

Please send me a return e-mail to let me know your preferred payment method and your shipping preference. Also, please include your correct shipping address. Thank you for shopping with me. I look forward to completing this transaction with you.

If you have any questions or concerns, please be in touch.

Sincerely,

Send the package and the e-mail too

Now you've made yourself clear. You've shown your buyer that you are partners in the transaction, and you've given him clear instructions for completing the sale. You've taken a big step toward completing your transaction with customer satisfaction and without any misunderstandings.

» Send the package and the e-mail too

Some PowerSellers choose to send an e-mail when they receive payment from the buyer. If your customer pays through the mail, it's good to let the customer know when payment has arrived, but you can easily combine that communication with the shipping notice you send when you ship the item. Again, be sure to include the item number in the body and the subject heading of this e-mail.

Also send along any tracking numbers the customer can use to keep an eye on the delivery. Finally, thank your customer once again, and feel free to politely mention the subject of feedback. We'll talk about feedback in much greater detail soon, but when you broach the subject with your customer, be delicate. It's one thing to note feedback, it's another thing to solicit it outright. The latter is common, but also commonly considered tacky. Here are some examples of shipping e-mails you may use as templates if you like:

> Hello! I am happy to tell you that I received your personal check today as payment for item #1234567. Thank you for sending this along so quickly. I plan to ship your item on the 23rd of this month, after the required time my bank needs to clear your check. I will be sending it via USPS Priority Mail, and I will send along all the tracking information once I've posted the item. Thank you again for your business.
>
> Sincerely,

> Hello! I received your PayPal payment today for item #1234567. I have already packaged your purchase and will send it out to you on my next shipping day, which will be Wednesday of this week. I will e-mail you then with all of the tracking information so that you can watch the progress of your item as it comes your way. Thank you again for your business.
>
> Sincerely,

Hello! I sent your package for item #1234567 today via UPS. Your tracking number is 987654, and you can check on your package at http://www.ups.com. I am sure you will enjoy your new sunglasses. It has been a pleasure doing business with you, and I hope you share my enthusiasm for this transaction. I plan to leave positive feedback for you, and if you agree our transaction was successful, I would be pleased if you'd do the same. If you have any questions, concerns, or comments about my products and services, please e-mail me directly. I welcome the opportunity to address any issues you may have had and ensure your 100 percent satisfaction. Thank you, once again, for shopping with me.

Sincerely,

Hello! I sent item #1234567 to you today through the USPS with delivery confirmation and insurance. Your tracking number is 9876543. You can track your package at http://www.usps .com.

Please let me know that you've received your item and are completely satisfied either by sending an e-mail or leaving positive feedback. I plan to leave positive feedback for you, too.

Thank you again for shopping with me.

Sincerely,

In the preceding e-mails, when you have reason to believe this will be your last interaction with your customer for this transaction, you have politely brought up the subject of feedback and informed your buyer that you'll be adding a positive feedback comment. But, you've been polite and positive and given your buyer every reason to think well of you. That will go a long way toward getting the positive feedback you would like.

Doing What's Right When Things Go Wrong

Despite all your best intentions and efforts, you will have customer service problems to deal with. In a way, that's not entirely a bad thing. It actually means you've attracted enough customers and sales to have some of them present you with problems. Sellers who are not selling never have trouble with customers. By sheer percentages alone, you have to expect that some of your transactions will go sour. It's more important to

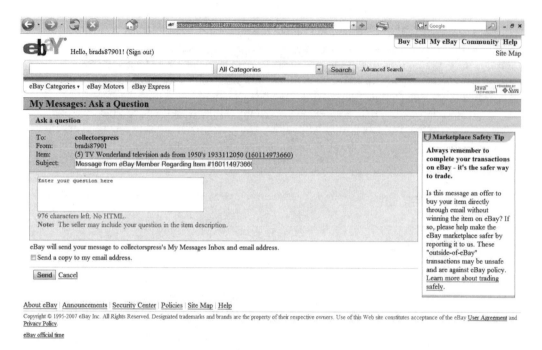

FIGURE 9-1 Use the My Messages part of your My eBay page to send verifiable e-mail to buyers.

know what to do when that happens than it is to worry about whether it will happen or not. It will.

Should you need to contact your trading partner about any kind of problem, be sure to go through the My Messages part of your My eBay page, shown in Figure 9-1. It's ok to set up your auction automation program to handle routine e-mails announcing an auction's been won or an item's been sent (although eBay would prefer you go through My Messages for all correspondence). If you send the e-mail through My Messages, the recipient will know with certainty that the message is valid, because it will be automatically copied to his My Messages area, as well as yours. Also, this will provide added insurance against an e-mail getting "lost."

» Think like the store manager, not the store clerk

This advice comes from a PowerSeller who started his eBay business with nearly 15 years of experience in the offline retail world. He recommends that you keep in mind what happens when you have a problem in a brick-and-mortar store. If the clerk is not able to fix your problem, because of store rules or policies, you are likely to ask that clerk to get the manager. You know when you're dealing with the manager that this person has the authority to address your concerns. The store manager also has the perspective to know that sometimes you must bend to your customer's needs if you're going to run a successful business. You are the store manager of your eBay business. You want to be as resourceful as you can in solving your customers' problems before they escalate into contentious issues that require mediation.

» Remember, it's business, not personal

You may get rude and insulting e-mails, and they will seem personal. Keep in mind that they can't be personal attacks, since your customer doesn't know you personally. They speak much more clearly about the sender of those e-mails than they do about you and your business practices. Bite your tongue, cross your fingers to prevent them from typing, step back from the situation, and keep your emotions out of the encounter. Acknowledge the customer's frustration, and calmly offer to do what you can to make the situation right, but don't allow this person to drag you into a nasty e-mail exchange. You cannot control what the other person says or does, but what you say and do is within your control. Always act in such a way that you can look back and note you did your best to satisfy the problem professionally and without rancor. Not only will it help keep the lid on your blood pressure, but these e-mail exchanges will also prove invaluable if you do ultimately go to mediation with a customer.

» Give your customer the benefit of the doubt

If you get an e-mail that seems insulting, give your customer the benefit of finding out what the problem is before you decide you're angry. This could be a person who doesn't have very good e-mail skills and may not have meant to come across negatively. Or, you could be dealing with a newcomer who is overly fearful of eBay trading. The customer may just need some reassurance, and fear may make the person seem overly defensive. Again, that's about the customer, not you, so don't allow yourself to be insulted. The first thing to do is respond in a professional and reassuring manner. Tell the person straight out that you are committed to your customer's complete satisfaction, and you will go out of your way to make sure the eBay shopping experience is pleasant. You may decide to ask the customer what you can do to make the sale seem right. Not only will you likely diffuse a potential problem, you'll go a long way as an ambassador to the world of online commerce. That's bound to benefit you and all the other eBay sellers too.

» If the mistake is yours, own up to it

Everyone makes mistakes, and as a busy eBay seller, you won't be immune to the occasional blunder. If you've made a mistake, admit it right away and offer to fix the resulting problem. "Any time I receive an e-mail from an upset or disappointed customer I begin my reply with 'I am sorry. . . . ,' " says Texcyngoods' Cynthia. Don't spend time or energy trying to put a better face on a bad situation.

Your buyer is human too, and you will be surprised to see how many eBay buyers will show understanding for your missteps. You'll gain more from being honest than you ever could by trying to pull one over on a buyer who may very

---

Hello Sir!

I am dreadfully sorry about this! I will also give it my full attention to make you "whole" in this purchase. We can do two things:

1. You ship the book back to me . . . I can resubmit it and return it to you, and I will pay all shipping costs, or
2. I can refund you in full the cost of the grading, and the extra shipping fees = $13.00 (my grading cost) plus $2.00 (extra shipping fee for graded book) = $15.00 by check or PayPal.

Please let me know which one you prefer. I am REALLY sorry about this . . . it has never happened before.

With true apologies,

---

well know that you goofed it up anyway. No customer can ask more from you than that you'll stand behind your actions and work to make them right. PowerSeller David from CarrerasComics shared the wonderful e-mail (shown on the preceding page) with us. He sent it out when a customer received his collectible comic with a cracked protective case that voided the grading guarantee.

Now, no one could stay angry with a seller who responded to a problem with an e-mail like that. The e-mail response was nearly immediate. This PowerSeller fixed the problem, and he even offered the buyer his choice of methods to correct the mistake. He also turned a disgruntled customer into a trading partner who respects his business ethics and plans to shop with him again. Yes, the seller had to pay $15, and that wasn't his first choice. But the buyer had expectations in this transaction that weren't met too. The seller proved himself to be just the kind of trading partner buyers can depend on, and that was certainly worth the money he had to spend to make his accident right. Not only did the customer understand completely how the incident could happen and appreciate the seller's response, but he also appreciated the honesty the seller showed in standing behind his service. This type of customer service can often lead to the best feedback a seller has. A buyer who has been treated with this kind of consideration and respect is likely to speak more specifically about the virtues of this seller's customer service and honesty and less generically about fast shipping and good products. Because you can now receive ratings of from one to five stars on a number of criteria, the more specific your buyer is about your service, the more impact his feedback can have. Imagine how this transaction could have ended if this seller instead suggested that maybe the customer himself had cracked the case!

» When a problem comes up, know who you're dealing with

We don't want to suggest to you that PowerSellers should be spineless wimps who fold at the sign of trouble and always take the loss. We're just recommending that you enter into every potential encounter with a positive attitude toward your trading partners and a philosophy that says you'll go out of your way to make a customer satisfied with your service. Armed with that

When a problem comes up, know who you're dealing with

philosophy, you can take some steps to ensure your own interests are protected. As soon as you get a problematic e-mail from a customer, take some time to research who this person is. Check the customer's feedback rating, limiting it to feedback from sellers. You'll soon see if other sellers have had problems too. But also go one step further and check the feedback this person left for other trading partners. Simply click the "Feedback left for others" tab from this person's feedback page, shown in Figure 9-2. Now you'll see how this customer conducts business with other sellers, and you'll learn a lot about the personality this customer brings to your transaction.

If you see that you've gotten involved with a problem bidder, offer to void the sale. Do what you must to cut your losses, and move on. Don't fuel the fire. Don't send incendiary

FIGURE 9-2 Here you can see all of the feedback this eBayer left for other trading partners.

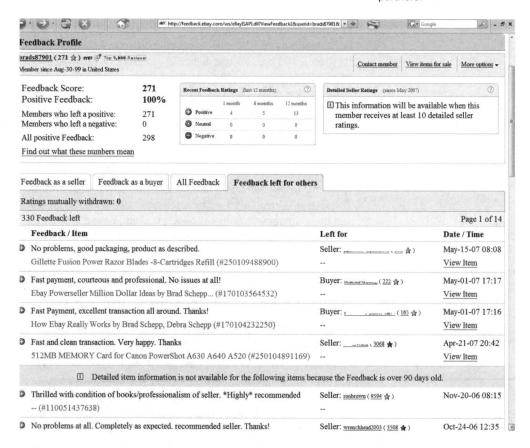

e-mails or threaten this person with anything. This person is a problem already and can probably think of more things to do to damage you and your reputation than you can think of to do in return. Once you've gotten away from the problem customer, block that person from all your future auctions, and essentially, you've made your problem go away. You may remember this from Chapter 7, but if not, go back and see just how it's done.

If, on the other hand, you see the person in question has a clean feedback history and has not spent his or her time on eBay sending horrible feedback to other sellers, you know you're most likely dealing with someone who has a legitimate customer service problem. Now you can move ahead with confidence. You know that you have a reasonable trading partner who will appreciate your efforts to correct the problem and close the deal.

» Use the Negative/Neutral Feedback tool

If you're searching through feedback comments from someone with many transactions, you must wade through page after page to find the negatives and neutrals. eBay doesn't provide you with a simple way to call out only the ones you need. Fortunately, there's a clever little tool you can use for this job. It's called the Negative/Neutral Feedback tool and you can find it at http://www.toolhaus.org/. You can see from Figure 9-3a just how simple it is. Once you're at the site, enter the user ID of the eBayer you are researching and click either "Received by" or "Left by." The results will list every negative or neutral comment made about the user. We searched for our own records under the Received by link. As you can see in Figure 9-3b, you'll find the user's total feedback score, the positive feedback percentage, and the individual comments left by other users. Each comment comes with the complete statement by the party leaving the feedback, the reply left by the user who received it, the time and date of the comment, and the item number under discussion.

Using this tool will allow you to quickly see the person's history and evaluate whether the comments are consistent, indicative of a pattern, or reflective of a new user who may have needed some time to learn the ways of eBay. As you can see from our example, you could have found all three of our neutral feedbacks, but you would have had to scroll back through years of eBay feedback records to get a complete look at all of them.

Use the Negative/Neutral Feedback tool

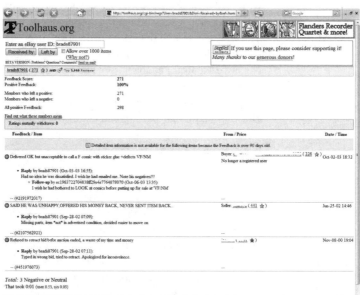

FIGURE 9-3 (a) The Negative/Neutral Feedback finder makes it simple to spot problematic eBayers. (b) Here you can see the results of the search for this user's negative and neutral feedback.

Use the Negative/Neutral Feedback tool

Once you've built up your feedback number, you can use this tool to test yourself. Enter your own user ID to see if the negative and neutral feedback comments you've received suggest a flaw in your operation that you can improve.

If you decide to use this little tool, please keep in mind that it's dangerous to view a seller's negative and neutral feedback all together and out of context. If a seller has 30,000 feedbacks, that seller is bound to have more than a few negatives. Taken in context of page after page of positives, you can view these feedbacks in the proper perspective. It's unlikely that any seller is going to please all buyers 100 percent of the time. Instead of paging through the list of negatives and neutrals with a growing sense of foreboding, evaluate them for what they are. See how the seller may have responded to the comments. It could be the seller was a victim of a perpetually unhappy buyer. Also consider if the negatives all came within a certain period of time. That could mean the poor seller was caught in an emergency, whether medical, family, or economic. You can't know what was happening in this person's life that may have made their eBay performance slide, but they certainly deserve the benefit of the doubt if all their negatives occurred together. So, by all means, check out their negatives, but keep them in perspective too. This tool, like so many other ways of evaluating an eBayer, is part of the whole picture, not the whole picture itself.

This tool, which was created by Win Bent, is free for you to use. If you use it, and like it, please support Win's great work by donating to his site through PayPal. And, be sure to bookmark this site so that you can get to it quickly.

What If Your Customer Is One of Those Scammers?

As you remember from Chapter 7, there are people who use eBay to scam legitimate sellers. They are a small minority of eBayers, but they can wreak havoc on the unsuspecting seller. Of course, you're no longer quite so unsuspecting, because PowerSellers have helped you to see what scams can happen. You're in a much better position to spot them than sellers who haven't taken advantage of the PowerSellers' secrets. Still, you may fall victim to a scam or a scheme, and if you do, be prepared to act quickly.

If e-mail fails, pick up the phone

If you determine before the auction is ended that the person you are dealing with is out to cheat you, do everything you can to void the sale. That may mean you void the bid from this buyer. Or, you may have to actually end the entire auction. That will cost your listing fees, but if this is truly a scam in progress, you'll be better off losing those fees than losing the cost of the entire sale or the item itself. But what if the buyer cheats you after the auction's ended and you've mailed out the item? Unfortunately, sometimes you have to send a replacement or eat part of the item's cost if PayPal's Seller Protection Program, for example, isn't applicable.

Archive every e-mail you send and receive. This will be your paper trail and will be valuable evidence if you end up in mediation. It will prove both what you did to resolve the issue and what the other person did to scam you. If you suspect this person is perpetrating a fraud or crime, report it to eBay customer service as soon as you realize it. You may also try to mediate the problem through PayPal dispute resolution, knowing you can escalate the dispute to a claim if needed.

In the end, you may just have to face the harsh realities of being a victim of a thief. "Sometimes you just have to take one for the team" is a philosophy a PowerSeller and trading assistant from the Southwest shared with us. Accept that life isn't always fair and sometimes the bad guys really do win. But at the same time, keep in mind that any single encounter, no matter what the outcome, isn't going to make or break your business as an eBay seller. Keep your perspective, take your hit, and move on with the business of earning an income from the millions of honest eBay buyers who are still out there waiting.

» If e-mail fails, pick up the phone

eBay will provide you complete contact information for another member, including their phone number, only if you are currently involved in a transaction with that member. You can't indiscriminately request contact information for eBayers who are not currently participating in a trade with you. That's only reasonable to protect the privacy of the community in general. Also, you may find it more difficult to get the contact information for someone from outside the United States, but it is possible to obtain this information for some international traders.

If e-mail fails, pick up the phone

To get to the form you'll complete to get contact information, click on the Advanced Search hyperlink at the top of most eBay pages, then click on the Find Contact Information link. The screen shown in Figure 9-4 will appear. Once you request the contact information, eBay will send an e-mail to that user notifying the person that you've requested contact information.

"If I can't get through with e-mail, I always pull the contact information and make that phone call," says PowerSeller TraderNick. "Sometimes just that next level of person-to-person contact helps." Other PowerSellers agree with Nick. It's much more difficult to be ugly to a person on the phone, especially after this person willingly called to try and straighten out the problem between you. It shows your real commitment to making the situation right, and it personalizes you to your buyer in a way that e-mail can't.

That's especially true if you approach this as a chance to help instead of a chance to tell off someone who has angered you. If you send e-mails through the My Messages link on your

FIGURE 9-4 The Find Contact Information screen gives you access to the phone number of a trading partner with whom you're currently involved in a transaction.

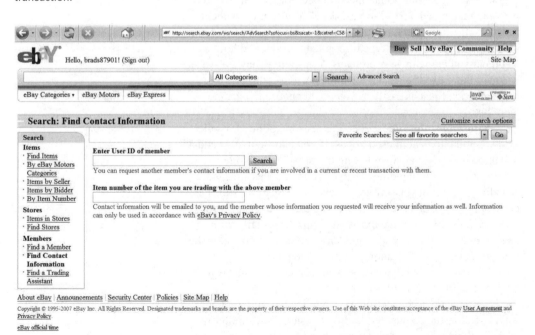

If e-mail fails, pick up the phone

My eBay page and the buyer never responds, it's possible that the person is ignoring you, but it's also possible that the person has an e-mail program with an overzealous spam filter. Not all users are disciplined about checking their My Messages area, and they may not even realize that they are missing e-mail. In that case, the customer may wonder why you're not reaching out. Check your own filter periodically to ensure that it's not catching legitimate e-mails, and of course check your own My Messages area through your My eBay page. If you do find that you're missing some e-mails, adjust your e-mail software's settings to allow more e-mails to get through.

What's the Word on Your Guarantee?

"In the beginning eBay was a typical Internet site. 'It is what it is. You get what you get, don't bother me. Too bad? So sad!'" remembers PowerSeller Jeffrey of Hessfine. "Now it's almost like Macy's with returns for everything." Most PowerSellers offer their customers some form of guarantee on their purchases. It's important for them to do that to stay competitive with other sellers and safeguard their feedback ratings. These guarantees range from "Guaranteed to be as described" to "100 percent, guaranteed, no questions asked." You'll have to decide for yourself where you fit on this sliding scale of options. Much of that will depend on the type of product you sell and how confident you are with your products. Your policy may evolve as you gain more experience, and that means you could choose to become stricter just as easily as you could choose to become more lax.

Guaranteed to be as described is a sensible policy for sellers who are going to deal in used goods. If you choose it, also add a line to your policy statement telling the prospective bidders to ask questions before bidding. That, of course, doesn't mean they actually will. But in your effort to make your auction listings as clear as possible, this is a small step you can take toward your own protection. Unfortunately, as you know, especially with new eBay users, it's easy for a bidder to get caught up and make a bid, not clearly understanding that it's a legally binding contract. Still, you will have done what you could to make your policies clear before a bid occurs.

If you handle used electronics or appliances, you might want to follow the advice of a trading assistant PowerSeller we spoke with who handles similar merchandise. He guarantees his buyers that the item will not arrive "Dead on Arrival (DOA)." Beyond that he offers them a three-day review period to ensure that the product works to their satisfaction. Within those three days, they are free to return the item for a full refund, once he verifies that the item is returned in the same condition he sent it. Beyond the three-day period he is no longer obligated to accept the item for return. He makes this policy clear in his EOA e-mail and with his shipping statement too. This reasonable policy assures customers that they won't be getting a box of broken junk without a return option. It also supports the PowerSeller, who knows that beyond the three-day review, he won't hear back from the buyer if the used item stops working.

PowerSeller Shane of Balkowitsch takes yet another approach. He offers his customers a 100 percent, no questions asked, satisfaction guaranteed return policy as long as the item is returned within 10 days, with all of its original packaging. He even agrees to pay shipping for both sending the item to the customer and returning it to him. He uses his generous return policy within his auction listing to build bidder confidence in both his products and his services. This liberal return policy is a good way to go when it comes to returns. Your bidders are likely to pay a bit more if they know they can return an item, and they may be more likely to shop with you than with one of your competitors if they know you will honor their returns.

» Don't hesitate to offer a refund

"I hate giving money back, but I do it anyway," says a PowerSeller from Rhode Island. "Once they have a refund, or an offer of a refund, I have nothing more to prove about my willingness to support my products." Offering your bidder a refund is hard to do, especially when you're first starting out. But you need to be prepared to do it, and you need to be gracious about it when you do. It's the best way to turn a disappointed and potentially angry customer into a satisfied one. Once a buyer finds that you'll be refunding the money, everyone can be ready to move on. Your buyer will recognize that you are a professional and not out to cheat anyone. Of course, sometimes the buyer won't bother returning the item for a refund. But your offer goes a long way to diffusing misunderstandings.

"The first thing I do is refund their money. Then I work at getting my product back," says PowerSeller Joe of Carrocel

Restorations. This Canadian-based PowerSeller deals in restored and antique furniture. He ships his products throughout the United States and Europe. Even so, when a customer is dissatisfied, he returns the money first and claims his product second. He told us he's never had a serious loss using this approach to customer service.

Tools That Support You While You Support Your Customers

PowerSellers have discovered some tools they've found useful in helping them provide great support for their customers. You might find some of these recommended tools immediately useful. Others you'll want to keep in mind and bring into your business once you've grown big enough and busy enough to make them reasonable for you.

» Consider giving a telephone number and customer service hours

"You should offer a phone number for your customers to call," recommends a PowerSeller with more than 13,000 feedbacks and a 100 percent positive feedback rating. "I list a phone number in all my auctions and make it clear my customer service hours are from 8 A.M. until 10 P.M. Mountain Time, Monday through Friday. In all the years I've been on eBay [and that's since 1999], no one has ever called outside of those hours. I've gotten international phone calls at 8:01! But, never before or after my official hours." Other PowerSellers agree, and it isn't at all unusual to find customer service telephone numbers listed in their auctions. This is a customer service feature that you can actually offer at little or no additional cost to you. If you decide to use your own phone number, you are adding a customer support feature to something you already pay for. Your customer will pay the long-distance charges to reach you. If you decide not to use your own number, you'll have the connection costs of a new phone line and the line's monthly charge.

Whether you choose to make your hours as flexible and convenient as our Rocky Mountain–based PowerSeller or decide instead to provide more limited access, it's definitely worth a try, since it seems such an effective tool for PowerSellers. Ultimately, you may be able to afford an 800 number, and then your customers will be even more likely to get in touch before they bid.

» Get ready for Skype

When eBay bought Skype for $2.6 billion in 2005 it hoped "Skype" as in Skype Me would become a verb, just as Google has. What's Skype you ask? Skype is a service that allows people to talk to each other over the Internet for free. Skype users don a headset or microphone, call each other's Skype numbers using their computers, and talk away as much as they want. The only requirement is that both users have the Skype software and those headsets or microphones.

While there are more than 196 million registered Skype users worldwide, Skype hasn't impacted business on eBay very much yet. eBay hoped its members would Skype each other if they had questions, rather than just rely on e-mail. To facilitate this, sellers can now add a Skype button to their listings once they've signed up. But those buttons aren't appearing in many listings yet. When we searched in April 2007, we found about 25,000 eBay listings mentioned the word Skype. Considering that millions of new listings appear on the site every day, that's a very small number.

That will change. We already know PowerSellers who are Skype fans. eBay is hugely committed to the company and technology. While relatively few members use it now, those that do seem to be using it in the way eBay envisioned they would. eBay surmised that being able to speak with someone by entering a few keystrokes on your computer would be less imposing than picking up the telephone. Our research found that a high proportion of current Skype users sell high-end items such as automobiles and jewelry. Those are sellers who have the most at stake and therefore the greatest need to communicate with buyers.

You can learn more about using Skype with eBay at http://pages.ebay.com/help/account/managing-skype.html. We suggest that you stay on top of Skype developments by checking eBay's Skype discussion board. When the time is right you should sign up for Skype and let buyers know you have an account. And then be sure to list the times when you'll be available to receive Skype calls!

» Try a Message Tag (MSGTAG)

You may have a tool to use if you come across the customer who claims "I never got your e-mail!" Message Tag is a little software tool you can add to your desktop. You'll find the company at www.messagetag.com. As you can see in Figure 9-5, you add a little capsule to your desktop that allows you to "tag" an e-mail. Once you do, you will receive an e-mail notifying you of the time that e-mail reached its destination and another message noting the time the recipient opened it. Now when you hear the old excuse, you can double-check for yourself and see if the problem might be a Spam filter, or if the problem is a bidder trying to dodge your e-mail. You surely won't want to tag every e-mail you send, but if you suspect that

FIGURE 9-5 With a click on this capsule, you can add a tag to your e-mail messages that will notify you when they have been opened by the recipient.

a customer interaction might get sticky, you'll be ready to get to the truth.

You can sign up for the basic Message Tag option for free. This will allow you to tag your e-mail, but the e-mail you tag will include a line at the end identifying it as being tagged by Message Tag. That's not necessarily a bad thing, but it does eliminate your element of surprise, if that's important to you. For $19.95 you can have Message Tag Plus. This gives you all the same features of the free version, but it also lets you personalize or hide the footer tag, and you get unlimited e-mail technical support too. Finally, you can pay $59.95 for the Message Tag Status version, which includes all of the features of the other products but also gives you a "dashboard" monitor board from which you can see all the e-mails you send and the status of each one.

You can also create groups of e-mail contacts, with different tagging rules for each one. If you have some concern about keeping in touch with your customers through e-mail, the free product offered by Message Tag seems like a good idea. At this point, the Cadillac service you'll get from Message Tag Status is very likely much more information than you need to concern yourself with. Stop by at www.messagetag.com to learn more about this tool.

Feedback: A Human (and Therefore Imperfect) System

We all have eBay feedback ratings, and you probably know all about how feedback works. We saw in Chapter 1 what PowerSellers think about their feedback ratings and how they work to maintain as spotless a feedback rating as possible. As you progress from seller to PowerSeller, you'll develop a whole new perspective on the subject of feedback. This perspective will grow almost as quickly as your feedback rating itself as you sell more, buy more, and gain more experience in doing business on eBay.

Feedback is one of the main subjects of discussion among PowerSellers. They debate when sellers should leave feedback. Is it when they receive payment from the buyer or when they learn the buyer is satisfied with the item received? They discuss who should leave feedback first. Is it the buyer or the seller? They talk about whether you should leave feedback for someone who hasn't left feedback for you. And they even debate whether or not you should leave feedback at all. You probably have your own opinions about the feedback system already. These will grow and shift as you face some of the special challenges feedback presents to PowerSellers.

The feedback system is at once the heart of eBay ethics and a source of great injustice on eBay. For example, did you know that a nonpaying bidder (NPB) may leave negative feedback for a seller? That's something PowerSellers struggle with. Some eBayers even use feedback for extortion. Here's how it works. The buyer you've just completed a transaction with may leave you a negative feedback. Then the buyer will contact you and offer to enter a mutual feedback withdrawal, if you refund a percentage of the purchase price. This is a complete violation of eBay's rules of trade, but while you do what's necessary to clear up the mess, you still have a negative feedback on the first page of your feedback comments. Also, you'll lose valuable time you could be spending listing and selling your products. Fortunately, PowerSellers share lots of wisdom about navigating the feedback system with all of its flaws, and most of the time, your transactions will result in positive feedback or no feedback at all. We'll help you gain a good perspective on the whole subject, and we'll offer you some guidance about keeping your feedback rating solid.

» This is going on your permanent record

Oh no, that dreaded permanent record. It has kept many a middle-school student on the right track. Now that you've decided to join the upper echelon of the eBay world, your permanent record—your feedback rating—is more important than ever. When it's your turn to leave feedback, remember that what you say cannot be taken back. There are only a few instances when eBay will remove feedback, and then only the feedback score gets altered. In most cases the comments must remain. When you receive neutral or negative feedback, you have the opportunity to leave a comment in response to the one left by your trading partner. That comment also becomes part of your permanent feedback record, so watch yourself to make sure that your statement is worthy of being viewed in perpetuity. You're just like Charles Dickens' Jacob Marley in this case; you'll forever wear the chains you forge in life. Be conscious of how your actions might drag you down if you're not careful.

» Try for eBay's Mutual Feedback Withdrawal program

If you find yourself in a situation in which you've left negative feedback and so has your trading partner, you can mutually agree to withdraw each others' ratings through eBay's Mutual Feedback Withdrawal (MFW) program. Now keep in mind that if you keep on reading and follow our advice, you will be much less likely to be in this situation, but just in case, it's good to know what to do if you need to undo the damage.

Let's suppose you've had a very contentious and difficult interaction with a buyer who flamed you with a negative feedback. You were so caught up in the event that you responded in kind. Now you both have a spot on your feedback rating. Let's further suppose that within a short while, you both calm down. You try one more time to make things better, and the buyer agrees. Now you can both go to the Mutual Feedback Withdrawal page http://pages.ebay.com/help/feedback/ questions/mutual-withdrawal.html and begin to resolve the confrontation.

At the bottom of that page is a hyperlink to the screen that appears in Figure 9-6. This is where your journey begins. Once you enter the item number of the contentious auction, you will be stepped through the form and finally the whole issue will be submitted to eBay for resolution.

Once both parties have agreed and worked together to remove the feedback, eBay will simultaneously remove both of the negative numbers from both of the parties' feedback scores at just the same moment. That way, neither party gets an advantage. The comments left cannot be removed, but they will be amended with the statement "Rating Mutually Withdrawn: Buyer and seller mutually agreed to withdraw feedback for this item." Now you see, firsthand, why you must be so careful about what you say in your feedback comments.

Sometimes, But Only Rarely, eBay Will Step In

eBay purposely leaves feedback up to the trading partners. You can't expect eBay to step in and fix an unfair feedback someone has left for you. eBay does, however, remove feedback for some very specific reasons. For example, if you accidentally leave

Try for eBay's Mutual Feedback Withdrawal program

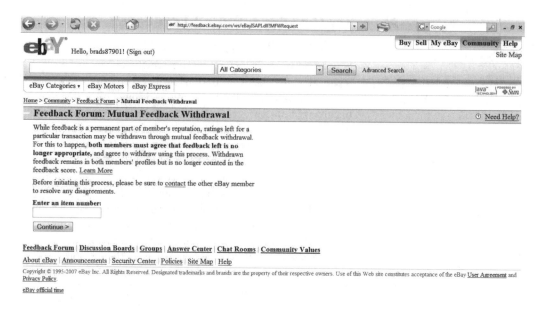

feedback for the wrong customer, you can work to make that right.

The first thing you must do is leave exactly the same comment for the correct person. It must match word for word. Once you've done that, you can inform eBay of the mistake and provide the usernames for both parties. Now, eBay will remove the negative from the score of the innocent buyer, but again the comment must remain with an amendment explaining that it was left by mistake.

Here are other reasons that eBay will step in:

- eBay receives a valid court order finding that the feedback in question is slanderous, libelous, defamatory, or otherwise illegal.

- The comment contains profane, vulgar, obscene, or racist language, or adult material. (On the other hand, although eBay discourages name-calling such as "fraud," "cheat," "liar," and "scam artist," these comments will not be removed.)

- Personal identifying information about another member is included in the comment, such as real name, address, telephone number, or e-mail address.

FIGURE 9-6 Mutual Feedback Withdrawal is one option you have for resolving a bad interaction.

- The feedback includes references to a PayPal, eBay, or law enforcement organization investigation.

- The person who left the feedback was ineligible to participate in an eBay transaction at the time of the transaction or when the feedback was left.

- The person who left the feedback gave eBay false contact information and couldn't be reached. For the most part, the transaction period is considered to be 90 days from the end of the listing or 30 days from the date the feedback was left.

- Someone has bid on your item or purchases strictly to have the chance to leave negative feedback with no intention of completing the transaction.

This last person is not automatically the same as an NPB, because NPBs can claim that they did intend to complete the transaction at the time they made the bid or won the auction. It is difficult to prove intent. If you suspect that one of your feedbacks qualifies for removal for one of these reasons, you can contact eBay to get the process started. Remember, these are the only instances under which eBay will remove a negative feedback.

» If all else fails, consider SquareTrade

As you learned in Chapter 6, SquareTrade can provide a feedback review and withdrawal service through a mediation process. At the cost of $29.95 per review, you will work with a SquareTrade mediator to review the entire transaction and decide on the course of action. Even with this review, the negative comment can not be removed from your feedback, but you can have the negative point taken from your score. Consider how much you are willing to spend for the removal. Is it worth it to you to put out the money to remove the point?

Feedback Is Strictly Voluntary

Although the feedback system is the ethical backbone of eBay, participating in it is strictly voluntary. No one can force you to leave feedback, and there's nothing you can do to force someone else to leave it for you. Among the more experienced eBayers, actively soliciting feedback is considered quite tacky.

Feedback is the last step in a transaction

So what can you do to encourage your partners to give you the positive feedback you deserve? First let's look at what you shouldn't do.

Don't send messages that say, "I'll leave good feedback for you after you leave good feedback for me." This reads a lot like a seventh-grader's diary. Also don't ask outright for positive feedback. It looks greedy and coercive.

Instead, frame your mention of feedback in the form of a thank-you note. You can include a phrase in your invoice, or you can attach a statement to your business card or giveaway that you slip into each of your packages. Below is a recommended statement that couldn't possibly offend anyone.

> It's been a pleasure to trade with you. I hope you're completely satisfied with your purchase. I plan to leave positive feedback for you. If you agree, I'd be pleased if you'd also leave it for me. If you have any questions or concerns with your purchase, please be in touch directly with me. I'll do my best to see you're satisfied.

Now all you can do is let it go. If the person doesn't leave a positive feedback for you, don't focus on it. You're right—that person who was completely satisfied should have left you a positive feedback. You earned it and you deserve it. But, we don't always get what we deserve in the world, and it isn't worth your time or energy to focus on each individual feedback.

» Feedback is the last step in a transaction

It's easy to know when you should leave feedback if you're the buyer. When you receive your package and inspect your item, if you're satisfied, go right to your computer and leave a feedback for the seller. If you're not satisfied, contact the seller and hold off on leaving the feedback. Give the person a chance to make the sale right. Remember that Golden Rule? You'd want one of your buyers to do the same for you. Either way, there's really no dispute. You can clearly see the point where feedback is called for.

As the seller, it's not so simple. Some sellers feel that the buyer's main responsibility is to pay for the item. They leave positive feedback for the buyer when they receive payment. If

Feedback is the last step in a transaction

the payment is prompt and complies with the seller's policies, then these sellers believe the buyer completed his or her part of the transaction and has earned a positive. Other sellers disagree. They feel that the transaction isn't complete until the buyer has received the package and is satisfied with the purchase. Until you hear from that buyer, either via e-mail or through feedback, you can't be sure the transaction is complete.

Feedback is the final step in any eBay transaction. Any problems you may have with a transaction should be resolved long before you get to the feedback part. Leaving feedback before the transaction is complete and closed leaves you vulnerable. If you've already left feedback when the buyer paid, then you will have lost your chance to comment on the buyer's total behavior. You can't know how reliable a trading partner a buyer is just by judging how quickly that buyer paid. After all, paying for an item you bid on is just complying with the legal contract you entered when you placed the bid. On the other hand, how this person handles a potential disappointment or problem speaks volumes about what that person's like as a trading partner. So, wait until the transaction has actually ended with the buyer having received the product before you leave feedback.

Should You Ever Leave Negative Feedback?

"I have almost 6,000 feedbacks, and I can count on one hand the times I've left a negative feedback," says a PowerSeller who specializes in coins. This seller feels it just isn't worth the risk of retaliation and the aggravation negative feedback creates. You will find many PowerSellers agree. "It's just more important to me that I relist the item and get on with my business," says an Arizona PowerSeller. Indeed, you will find that the greatest percentage of negative feedbacks come from inexperienced eBay users. You can check on this yourself using the Negative/Neutral Feedback finder we described earlier. The next time you come across a seller with a feedback rating ranging between 98 and 99 percent, enter that person's user ID into the finder and check your results. You are bound to find that most of the negatives come from people with fewer than 50 feedbacks of their own.

Other PowerSellers feel differently about leaving negative feedback. "Feedback is the way this community polices itself," says a PowerSeller from Georgia. "If I'm not willing to take a risk and make a statement against a bad eBayer, I'm only hurting other sellers who come along after me. That damages the whole community." This seller views it as her civic responsibility to accurately relate her experience so that others can learn from her misfortune. She doesn't view it as a burden to add to the feedback record of a bad eBayer, and she's willing to take the risk of retaliation. Chris of snowsportdeals may have the best strategy of all: "Give a negative when someone pours a bucket of cold water on your head, not when it starts to rain."

» If your customer goes ballistic, don't go with him

Getting a negative feedback or dealing with a difficult customer will absolutely make you furious. In many of these instances, your anger is justified, and we're completely on your side. But, as we've said, never respond to a customer when you're caught in a fury. It's the same thing that keeps you from fighting it out on the highway with an aggressive driver. In the end, you're entering into a confrontation with a stranger. You are also dealing with someone who will be in your life for only a very brief period of time. Be angry, but also be smart. Never leave feedback when you're furious. We can guarantee you'll regret it, even if you will always believe the other party deserved it.

Any time you find yourself in a confrontation, the one who keeps cool has an automatic advantage. It's easy to get caught up in an escalating screaming match, and much more difficult to stay calm, but calm is what you need. When you're calm, the other person starts to look ridiculous, and he also starts to make mistakes. Emotions take over and control the brain. If you keep calm, you're much more likely to be thinking clearly, and you'll be more likely to see the solution to the confrontation. In the end, what you want is resolution, not vindication. You can be vindicated when you block this person from your auctions, making it impossible for you to ever be bothered again by this hothead.

❯❯ When it comes to a negative, stick to the facts

Just as you should never leave feedback when you're angry, you should never leave feedback that strays from the basic facts of the issue. You won't gain anything by name-calling, or by insulting or threatening an errant buyer. Also, don't use that Caps Lock. If you leave feedback in all caps, it makes you look like a hothead. Instead, make clear statements and include dates. For example, "EOA sent 10/24; no payment r'cvd; filed NPB 11/15; FVF r'cvd 11/30."

Now, everyone viewing this person's feedback will see that your customer received a negative feedback because he or she didn't pay for your item, but you've conducted yourself in a businesslike manner. You've also not invested the situation with more emotion than it deserves, and you've safeguarded your blood pressure too!

Beyond these reasons for controlling yourself, you should never forget that the negative comments you leave for other people speak more about you than they do about the eBayer who receives the comment. If you flame this person or leave rude and insulting comments, your future buyers will see that when they check the feedback you've left for others. Savvy buyers will do that before they buy a relatively expensive item from you. You don't really want other customers to think of you as a loose cannon, just waiting to blow up at someone. You may know you're completely justified in calling this guy for what he is, but no one else is ever going to know the details of that deal that went wrong. They'll only be able to see how you conducted yourself, and you want that conduct to represent you well. Finally, remember that if you actually libel someone, you can be sued. Then, the single transaction that went bad will seem like a fond memory compared to the aggravation of a lawsuit.

❯❯ When the negative comes, let it go

Given everything you've learned, you'll probably go a long way without a negative feedback. When you're careful in your eBay business, you'll find it's much more likely that you'll be getting positives. Just keep your goals realistic. Getting your first negative feedback is much like getting that first scratch on your

When the negative comes, let it go

new car. It hurts, but at the same time, there's a bit of relief in the pain. Now that it's happened, the pressure to prevent it is off. A 100 percent positive feedback rating is a wonderful thing to have, but it certainly isn't essential to a successful eBay business, and it isn't a requirement to guarantee your life as a PowerSeller. In fact, if you have a 100 percent positive feedback rating, but you have thousands of feedbacks, you may be spending too much time focusing on the minority of problematic customers. That makes it more likely that you're distracted from providing the best possible service to your problem-free customers.

You are bound to displease someone eventually, and that person may very well resort to a negative feedback without giving you the proper chance to make it right. Once you have the negative, you can amend it with a comment. If you add something like "buyer never told me she was unhappy. Would have refunded her money," the comment gains a bit of perspective. Now, you keep your perspective, too. It's not the end of the world.

During the first month or so, that negative comment will be right there on your first feedback page for all the world to see. As long as you stay busy and please more customers, that comment will get pushed further and further down on your list of feedback comments. It won't be too long before it's off the first page completely. Anyone who bothers to scroll through your feedback comments is likely to understand that every seller can get a stray negative comment here and there. It won't dramatically alter your rating, and in time it will be subsumed in the sheer volume of your positive feedbacks. No reasonable buyer will wade through page after page of positive feedbacks to find the occasional neutral or negative, and even those buyers who use the Negative/Neutral Feedback finder will keep the comment in context. So, pick yourself up, brush off your pride, and get back to the work of PowerSelling.

For this chapter, we decided to profile a professional mediator instead of a PowerSeller. Because this mediator's job requires complete anonymity, we're not going to reveal any details that could identify him or her. Instead we will call this person "Mediator" and switch pronouns between the feminine and masculine, so that no one will ever guess Mediator's true identity. From talking with Mediator, who currently works with SquareTrade, we gained an interesting perspective that isn't tainted by this individual's personal experiences as either a buyer or a seller.

It's gratifying to learn that most of the mediations that come before Mediator have nothing at all to do with "outright fraud or malice." Most often, parties come to resolve disputes that began with miscommunication and escalated to rancor, creating a situation where neither party was able to step back far enough to see a resolution. A good many problems begin when the buyer simply doesn't read the auction listing. If he doesn't bother to read it, he may miss the fact that the item is used. He might not follow the seller's procedures for payment, and he may not get the shipping he thought he was going to get. Then he gets angry, because his expectations haven't been met. The seller is angry, because this buyer didn't have realistic expectations to begin with.

Another source of conflict is shipping. If an item gets damaged in shipping, the buyer is going to be disappointed. The seller must respond to this situation without blaming the buyer, but that doesn't always happen. If the seller responds to the buyer's complaint with suspicion or an accusation that the buyer may have caused the damage, the problem is likely to go to mediation.

Mediator recommends that before either party resorts to mediation, they try to resolve the issue between themselves through direct, calm, and reasoned communication. If that's not possible, the matter can be turned over to SquareTrade, and Mediator or one of his associates will be assigned to intervene. eBay actually subsidizes the mediation, and one party, usually the seller, pays the fee of $29.95 to have the matter mediated. The first step is for Mediator to review all of the interactions between the buyer and seller, both through eBay and through e-mail outside of eBay, too. (Didn't we tell you to watch your e-mail tone and content?) Then she tries to see where the problem came about and attempts to suggest a reasonable resolution to the issue.

Mediator says that very often the issue is just getting everyone to stop blaming and shouting. He tries to get the aggrieved party to see that the other person meant no harm. Sometimes just an apology is enough to make the parties see each other more clearly and find a resolution. She reminds both parties that they want to be buyers and sellers on eBay for years to come, and that they are losing track of the big picture. She reports that she has seen a greater than 50 percent success rate with this approach.

When the negative comes, let it go

Mediator makes some clear recommendations for preventing problems between buyers and sellers. These should all sound familiar to you by now:

1. Take clear photos that show the flaws, if there are any.
2. Be very careful in your descriptions.
3. Be rigorous in shipping your items.
4. Follow up with your customers to make sure they're happy.
5. Behave professionally.

Additionally, he recommends that you take certain things into consideration. Don't deal in products that are easily marked for fraud or misrepresentation. Mediator notes that Louis Vuitton bags are commonly mediated items. People sell them as genuine when they're not. They also sell them used and in excellent condition, only to find that the buyer detects a smell or marks on the bag that the seller didn't mention. Steer yourself away from things that could leave you vulnerable.

She also reminds you to be aware of your trading partner's feedback history. "With less than a 97 or 98 percent rating, get suspicious. Look at the individual comments, not just the numbers for these sellers, so you can see what the issues are. Remember that on eBay, a 91 percent does not mean this person is a good student."

Mediator further reminds us that participating in eBay is something of a game of chance. You take risks, and you reap rewards. When things go sour, do your best to fix it yourself, but if all else fails, turn to mediation. "It's a great alternative to lawyering up."

Your Customer Is Always Right (Even When He's Wrong) Checklist

✓ I turn questions from my customers into opportunities to make my item shine.

✓ I'm adding a little flare to those sterile eBay end-of-auction e-mails.

✓ I coddle my customers! I know that I'm the store manager, not a clerk.

✓ I work to always take the high road in disputes with customers. I know it dissipates dissatisfaction.

When the negative comes, let it go

✓ Before I respond to a disgruntled customer's correspondence, I check out his feedback for insights on how to best deal with him.

✓ I use the Negative/Neutral Feedback tool to quickly analyze less than positive feedback.

✓ The phone is a powerful tool for personally handling customer concerns, so I know when to use it.

✓ Refunds are repellant, but a necessary part of doing business, so I offer them.

✓ I'm curious about Skype, and I'll keep on top of its developments, because I know I'll want to use it.

✓ I'm thinking about using Message Tags so I'll know if and when my e-mails are read.

✓ I guard my feedback carefully, but I don't allow myself to be held hostage by it.

✓ I know I'll use eBay's Mutual Feedback Withdrawal option to keep my feedback record as blemish free as possible.

✓ I understand when eBay will intervene in a dispute and when it will not.

✓ I think carefully about the kind of feedback I leave.

✓ I will leave negative feedback if it's warranted, but I will be strictly businesslike when I do.

✓ I know that negative feedbacks may be unavoidable if I do enough business, so when I get one, I'll be able to move on with my life.

Chapter 10

Keeping Records—or Let's Have a Look at Those Books, Buddy

We hope that by now you've begun to think of yourself as a real businessperson. You've certainly been submerged in subjects that only businesspeople must consider. You've built yourself a PowerShop with all the tools necessary to operate an eBay business. You've considered the best approaches to customer service. You've created your own policies for receiving payments from customers and shipping your products to their final destinations. Now it's time to take a look at that other part of being a businessperson. Keeping your books and managing your records is a vital part of managing your own business. It's also the part where many new and small business owners begin to stumble.

To us it seems that record keeping is a lot like housework. Who among us really loves it? Yet, we all have to do it. Like housework, it's best done routinely and consistently, and we've all managed to find our own systems that work and our own schedules for getting the tasks done. Start managing your records and keeping your books from the very beginning. Do it right, right from the start. You'll reap the rewards of your efforts in the form of taxes that you can prepare without anguish, reports that will help you analyze your business growth, and nights of restful sleep knowing you've got everything in order.

Don't be hard on yourself if you're dreading this part of your business life. Many PowerSellers told us it's the part they dislike the most too. We'll help you to get started, and we'll make some recommendations that should lessen your load, but please remember we are not accountants or tax attorneys. We'll give you some guidelines, but you'll want to make sure you're complying with all of your state and local tax and business laws. We can't help you much with that. Not knowing what your local laws are will not excuse you if the regulating agencies in your area come calling. So, make sure you consult the proper professionals in your area to ensure that you are in compliance with zoning and licensing laws, and you are meeting the requirements of all local and state taxes.

Getting Off to a Good Start

That's not to say that keeping your business records and accounts is all challenge and no benefit. Yes, you have more work to do because you have these records to keep. But on the other hand, you now have business deductions that you were not eligible to take as an average taxpayer. Plus, it's never been easier to get help with having your own business than it is now, thanks to the Internet. Millions of others run successful businesses, and you can too. Now, let's get off to the right start.

» Visit SCORE

Since 1964 SCORE has been providing valuable support to people who want to start and build their own businesses. SCORE is a national nonprofit organization that works in partnership with the Small Business Administration. Its mission is to "provide professional guidance and information, accessible to all, to maximize the success of Americans' existing and emerging small businesses." You can visit SCORE online at www.SCORE.org, or you can arrange to meet in person with one of the 10,500 volunteers who work through 389 SCORE chapters across the country. These volunteers are local working or retired businesspeople who have already operated successful businesses and want to help newcomers to the business world get started.

You will find that these businesspeople include accountants who are more than happy to answer your questions about how to get your business started. "The first thing I did was to schedule an appointment with an accountant through SCORE," said a PowerSeller specializing in gift items. "He sat with me and showed me all the records I'd need to keep, and how I might store and organize them." This PowerSeller isn't alone. In the last 43 years, SCORE has helped more than seven million people who wanted to start businesses. Today you'll find that SCORE not only offers person-to-person meetings, but also low-priced ($25 to $75) local workshops, e-mail advice, and a toll-free number (800-634-0245) to help you find your local SCORE chapter.

The SCORE home page, shown in Figure 10-1, is a good place to start gathering information from professionals who are only there because they want to help you. You'll find a Reading Room with dozens of articles about every type of business concern from hiring employees to managing your office. You can also use SCORE's 60-Second Guides, quick tips on subjects as varied as cash flow, obtaining a loan, and writing a business plan. There is also an archive of business articles written by experts in fields as varied as information technology and human resources. Plus, you'll find specialized information

Visit SCORE

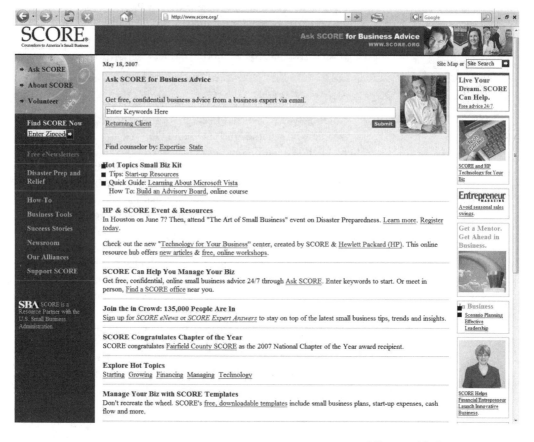

FIGURE 10-1 The SCORE home page lets you easily see the resources available to you through this all-volunteer program.

for aspiring minority, women, veteran, and young entrepreneurs. Finally, sign up for SCORE's free e-mail newsletters. SCORE eNews is a monthly newsletter that discusses the latest trends and resources to help small business owners. SCORE Expert Answers discusses marketplace trends and provides advice from both small business experts and industry leaders.

You'll be able to find the SCORE volunteers closest to you by searching the site via ZIP code. Once you've selected a volunteer from those listed, you fill out a form in which you describe your business needs. Your SCORE volunteer will respond within 48 hours. While SCORE is a pioneer in providing online assistance, we recommend you arrange for a one-on-one meeting.

When you meet with your SCORE volunteer, prepare some questions in advance. Here are a few to get you started:

- What information should I be recording for each of my transactions?

- What records should I be keeping to document my expenses?

- What are the local regulations for zoning, taxes, and licensing in our area?

- Can you advise me about incorporating or registering my business?

- Should I use cash-basis accounting or accrual-basis accounting? (Cash-basis accounting means you report income when you actually receive it and cost your expenses when you actually accrue them. Accrual-basis accounting is inventory-based. When you sell an item from inventory, you report the earning even if you haven't yet been paid.)

- How can I best depreciate my computer and office equipment?

- Can you recommend an accountant and/or bookkeeper?

» Educate yourself

Your meeting will be more productive, and so will your business, if you educate yourself a bit about accounting. Even if you ultimately hire a bookkeeper and an accountant (more about that in a minute), you'll be better able to explain your needs and assess their work if you at least understand the vocabulary they use. You can, of course, get some great basic accounting books at the local library or invest in one for your own library.

Here's a tip an editor friend once gave us for researching complex new topics: Start with books aimed at a young audience, say high school or even middle school students. They'll be easier to grasp. You can always move on from there.

Aside from books, you can find some help online. BusinessTown.com, shown in Figure 10-2, is a valuable site you'll find at www.businesstown.com. The site offers a wealth of information about all types of business concerns, but it has a whole separate section for accounting information. Here you'll find easy-to-digest bits of information about accounting and

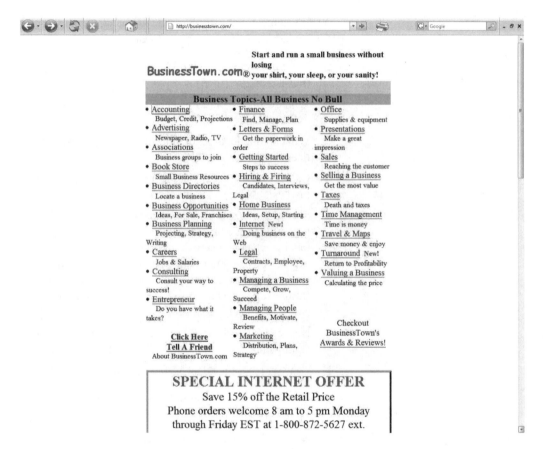

FIGURE 10-2 BusinessTown.com makes it easy for you to quickly learn about all types of business issues.

very clear descriptions of accounting vocabulary terms. You will also learn how to read an income statement or a balance sheet, how to manage a general ledger, and the details of both amortization and depreciation. It's a great place to start your accounting education.

» Start with all new accounts

If you're going to run a legitimate and successful business, you must separate your personal banking from your business banking. This makes it so much easier to actually see how well your business is earning, how much you're spending, and where your money is going. You'll need a business checking account for paying bills, a business savings account for storing your profits with interest, and a business credit card. Once you open your business accounts, make sure all of your expenses are drawn directly from them and all of your earnings go directly into them. Your business credit card should be the one you use to register with PayPal and eBay. Now all of your monthly fees will come on a credit card statement that does not include the new sneakers your son needed last month and your spouse's charge for the dentist. When you're gathering your records for your tax returns, everything on the statements for this account will be for your business. That will make life easier for both you and your accountant.

Think Like a Business Now

In your regular life, it probably works for you to stick your receipts in your pocket or purse. You may have to uncrumple them and try to decipher what they once said. That's not going to work for you anymore. You'll need to come up with a system for keeping every receipt, bank statement, and canceled check. Your system should be both thorough and simple. If you make it too complicated, you're likely to sidestep it, and then you'll be missing valuable documents when it comes time to do your taxes or assess your actual business costs versus profits.

We've found the easiest way to keep paper records straight is to use an expandable accordionlike file folder. Ours comes with a little clasp that catches the fold-over top to keep things secure. Each tab inside the folder has an alphabetical label, but you can alter the label to suit your own needs. Every time you get a receipt or a statement from your accounts, slip the paper into this folder according to your own filing system. Resist the temptation to let them build up on your dresser or in your purse. Keep your records straight as they come in and you'll avoid those horrible hours of trying to re-create documentation that you received months earlier. When the time comes for you to use the information, just pull it out of its folder and you're ready to go.

» If it's deductible, don't forget to deduct it

To offset the aggravation keeping your books can bring when you operate your own business, you acquire lots of deductible business expenses you may never have had before. Now that

If it's deductible, don't forget to deduct it

you're thinking like a business owner, don't forget to account for these. Using part of your home exclusively and regularly for operating your own business allows you to deduct a portion of your homeowner's expenses as business expenses. You'll want to figure the estimated square footage of your home that is used exclusively for your business. That percentage then becomes the percent of your home's expenses that you can attribute to your business. If, for example, your home office constitutes 10 percent of your total living space, then 10 percent of the cost of maintaining, heating, and insuring your home can go toward your business expense. Just remember, that means this part of your house is used just for business. If the kids have been using your computer for homework, you'll have to get them one of their own.

All of the supplies and incidentals that you need to run your business count as expenses so long as you use them exclusively for that purpose. That includes all of your office supplies such as paper for your printer, labels and boxes for shipping your items, and postage too. But it also includes other things you may not have thought of. Your high-speed Internet connection is a business expense. So is all of your long-distance calling for tracking down sources and working with your customers. The software you purchase is an expense, and so is the book you buy to teach yourself how to use the software. If you take a course to learn more, that's also deductible. If you subscribe to a newsletter that will help you educate yourself about your business, you can deduct the subscription fee. The same is true of the dues you pay to join an association or gain an accreditation in your particular field of expertise. You can even count the fees you pay your accountant for doing the taxes for your business.

Your travel expenses are deductible when you travel for business too. That includes the trip to the post office and the office supply store, or the trip you make to a trade show or to purchase inventory. Keep a small pad in the car and record the mileage for every trip you make for your business. It's not just your mileage that's deductible either. All of the tolls you pay, the meals you eat, and the lodging expenses you pay are deductions, as long as you made your trip on behalf of your business.

Now, you can't just claim you incurred these expenses. You have to prove it. You have to have paper documentation in the

If it's deductible, don't forget to deduct it

form of receipts, canceled checks, bill stubs, or credit card statements. For each expense you have to provide the date you incurred the expense, the person or company providing the service or product, and the business purpose of the expense. That's simple if you're buying a piece of software, but not quite so clear-cut if you're staying the weekend at a collector's show to build your inventory. Be sure to document the purpose of the expense when you incur it. That's so much easier than trying to figure it out months down the road. When you get home, file them all away into that simple, but thorough, filing system you devised.

For a much more complete list of business expenses, talk to your accountant. He'll know exactly what you can claim and how you can document everything you spend. Our suggestions are meant to get you started.

Uncle Sam May No Longer Want You, But He Does Want a Piece of Your Income

When you work for someone else, it's pretty clear what your tax liabilities will be. You complete a W-4 form when you sign on telling your employer what to withhold for your tax bill. Every year your employer gives you a W-2 form that states what you earned and how much federal income tax was withheld on your behalf. Those easy days are gone once you become your own boss. It will be up to you to estimate your tax bill for each year and pay estimated taxes quarterly toward your annual tax bill. Quarterly tax payments are due January 15, April 15, June 15, and September 15. If you fail to pay at least 90 percent of the tax you owe or an amount equivalent to your tax liability of the previous year, you could be facing penalties and interest charges. Work with your accountant to determine what your quarterly tax payment should be, and don't forget to make those payments on time.

When you complete your income tax return for your business, you will now have to use a Schedule C form along with your Form 1040. The Schedule C is the Profit or Loss from Business form. You'll use this form to itemize all of your business expenses for the year. Then you'll factor the cost of your operation against the profit you earned to determine your earnings and your tax liability.

He's Here to Help

Our only wish for you is that you'll have to pay a big tax bill next year. That's the best kind of problem to have, since only people who earn good money have to worry about big tax bills. While you make your transition from individual filer to business filer, you'll find the Internal Revenue Service hasn't left you all alone. Go to http://www.irs.gov/businesses/small/index.html for the online resource center established by the IRS for the small business owner or the self-employed individual. You'll see the home page for this site in Figure 10-3. Here you'll find online workshops for helping you manage your taxes. You'll also find downloadable forms. In addition, you can order a free Small Business Resource Guide on CD containing critical information

FIGURE 10-3 This online resource center from the Internal Revenue Service helps you learn about managing your records and preparing your taxes.

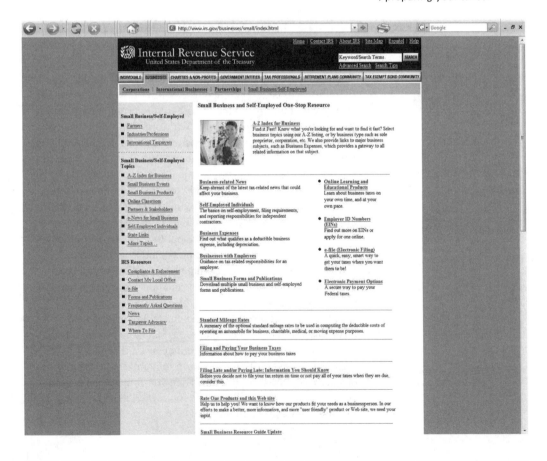

from a variety of government agencies, educational organizations and nonprofits, including forms, instructions, and publications. This is great information designed to help you successfully operate your small business.

Tax laws are very complicated, and only those who are well educated on the subject can claim to be completely up-to-date with huge and ever-changing codes. Educate yourself, of course, because you need to be an educated consumer, but never take the word of any book published about your individual taxes. The subject is too complicated. Each case is individual, and books about taxes, by virtue of their medium, can become inaccurate between the time their authors write them and the time you read them.

Social Security

Just in case you're already having too much fun with the subject of your income taxes, we'll spread a little more joy your way. You also have to pay for your own Social Security taxes while you're at it. When you were an employee, you paid part of the tax, which your employer deducted from your regular pay, and your employer paid part. Now the entire bill is up to you. Plus, if you hire employees, you'll have to pay their Social Security taxes and withhold income tax from them too.

That's one reason why some people hire only independent contractors. If you want the fellow down the street to come into your home office twice a week to do some packing and shipping for you, you'll need to decide if he's your employee or if he's an independent contractor. If he's your employee, you'll be responsible for his Social Security and tax withholding. If he's a contractor, it will be his responsibility, but you'll need an invoice from him for all of the hours he works for you each week. Then he'll have to pay the taxes on his return.

Sales Tax

Of course, by now, you've taken our advice from Chapter 2 and gotten yourself a tax ID number. That's good, because as soon as you start selling things, you'll have to start collecting state sales tax too. As of this writing, you only have to collect sales tax for items shipped to customers who live in your own state. That may change very soon, but it's been difficult for the states to agree on how to collect the taxes for items purchased and shipped across state lines. You are exempt from this only if you live in one of the five states that currently, as of this writing, doesn't have a state sales tax. Those lucky individuals already know who they are, but for the rest of us, those states are Alaska, Delaware, New Hampshire, Montana, and Oregon. All the rest of us have got to collect sales tax. There are no exceptions. Once you're clear on the taxes you must collect you can set up eBay Checkout to automatically calculate the tax due, based on the buyer's address. That amount gets added to the total amount the buyer must pay.

» Hire an accountant

This piece of advice probably doesn't come as a surprise to you, after you've read what we've had to say about setting up your accounts and dealing with your taxes. We'd tell you this even if it weren't the advice of countless PowerSellers. But, it is. PowerSeller after PowerSeller told us the same thing. Accountants earn their livelihoods by knowing all of the details of tax codes and money managing. Unless you are a trained accountant yourself, you couldn't possibly match the knowledge and expertise of a professional. Besides, we suspect that you'd rather spend your energies staying current with the changes in your own market rather than staying current with the ever-changing tax codes. Find yourself a good Certified Public Accountant, and make friends. Begin your search by asking your friends or other small business owners for recommendations. You'll be glad you did, and so will your business.

The Tools You'll Use

Now, just because you're going to hire an accountant, that doesn't mean you're going to get away with not using any tools of your own. You don't want to pay an accountant's hourly rate to manage the day-to-day earnings and expenses of your business. You'll be going to your accountant for help with the big picture and to have someone do your taxes for you, but you'll be responsible for keeping track of the incidentals from one tax year to the next. Fortunately, when you built your

PowerShop after reading Chapters 3 and 4, you included some important tools that will help.

Use Your Auction Management Software

As you saw in Chapter 4, your auction management software will track a great deal of information for you about what you spend, sell, and ship. You can use it as a vital part of your record-keeping toolbox. Most auction management software packages offer similar features and functions, whether the program you choose is Web-based or a desktop application. We'll discuss the features of eBay's own auction management software to serve as an example for you. As you will remember, Blackthorne Pro is desktop-based, and Selling Manager Pro is Web-based.

Both products allow you to track your inventory. They both offer you automatic incrementing and decrementing of inventory items, so you don't have to manually add or subtract each item individually. They both offer you automatic restocking alerts to let you know when you're running low. And, they both allow you to create listings linked to a specific product.

Using either program, you can preview, edit, reschedule, or cancel scheduled listings online. You can also monitor active listings in real time. This allows you to quickly see what's happening with all of your auctions and make adjustments to your listings easily. You can review your previously sold items, including such details as sale date, item number, sale price, total price, the buyer's e-mail address, and feedback status.

In addition, Selling Manager Pro, because it's Web-based allows you to track your buyers' communications and note whether the items you've sold have been paid for and/or shipped. You can gather this information for both individual sales and those made in bulk. The communications features of Selling Manager Pro also allow you to record your buyer communication to help you with resolving issues with Nonpaying Bidders. You can also note and send automatic payment-received notification e-mails and automatic item-shipped notification e-mails. These help you keep track of the items that have actually sold and/or moved out of your inventory.

Finally, Selling Manager Pro offers you the option of creating printer-friendly reports. But on the other hand, Selling

Hire accountant

Manager Pro will store your records for only a maximum of 120 days, while Blackthorne Pro will allow you to keep them indefinitely, because they are all stored on your own computer.

PayPal Will Help

PayPal will store for you and allow you to view all the details for any PayPal transaction. This information is available through your History Log. To view this:

- Log into your PayPal account.
- Click the History tab.
- In the Show drop-down menu select All Activity-Advanced View.
- By default you'll see details for transactions that occurred within the past 30 days. To view specific time periods click the Within drop-down menu.
- Click Search to see the transactions.
- Click the Details hyperlink for further information regarding a particular transaction.

QuickBooks

"I used to recommend QuickBooks to my enemies," says CPA and QuickBooks Advisor Terry Lanier of LMGW Certified Public Accountants, based in California. That was before Intuit greatly improved their software. Now he says it's the easiest and most intuitive way to keep track of your business. An estimated 75 percent of LMGW's clients use the program to record their invoices and cash receipts, write checks, create financial statements, and prepare tax records for their accountants at the end of the year. Terry explains that the beauty of QuickBooks, its ease of use, is also its greatest disadvantage. Because nearly anyone can use the program, people often don't use it properly. The software, according to Terry, "was designed for people who don't know much about accounting, but who can follow rules." Problems occur when people don't follow the rules and either fill out the forms incorrectly or stray from the forms completely.

Terry has identified seven common mistakes that new QuickBooks users typically make:

1. **Initial set-up**   People often choose the wrong starting date. They don't properly enter bank account balances and outstanding checks or deposits. They don't properly enter amounts owed to the company by customers or amounts owed by their company to vendors. They select an inappropriate or incomplete chart of accounts.

2. **Use of the forms**   People often bypass the form for invoicing, check writing, and other functions and instead use journal entries for these activities.

3. **Receiving payments from customers**   Users often don't properly reduce their inventories when they receive payments. They also bypass the cash receipts form when processing their cash sales.

4. **Making payments to vendors**   Users often make mistakes when using the check writing function after entering a bill.

5. **Using credit cards**   Users commonly enter only the amount to be paid on a credit card bill, not the entire balance owed.

6. **Paying sales or payroll taxes**   People often neglect to use the "pay payroll taxes" or "pay sales taxes" functions.

7. **Setting up items and classes**   Users often improperly set up items to categorize sales and identify gross margins. They also improperly set up items for sales tax reporting, and they fail to use classes to separate profit or cost centers.

As long as you will be shopping around for an accountant anyway, why not look for one who is also a QuickBooks advisor? Your accountant can then help you establish your bookkeeping procedures, and you'll have someone to turn to when you have specific questions. You may also want to consider taking a QuickBooks course. Many local community colleges offer them.

Excel

We mentioned in Chapter 3 that you should also be using Excel, the spreadsheet program from Microsoft. If you're comfortable with Excel, you can download your PayPal account history directly into the spreadsheet software. Download My History is one of your options from your PayPal History tab. You can specify a date range (up to one year) Or, select Last Download to Present to pull up payments that have occurred since your last download. Of course, for working with your data within Excel, or any spreadsheet for that matter, you need to download that data as a comma-delimited file (you do this through the Files Types for Download drop-down menu). You can also produce Excel-compatible reports with Selling Manager Pro, Blackthorne Pro, and many other auction management software programs.

» Hire a bookkeeper

"I used to do all my own books," says a PowerSeller from the Midwest. "Now I've hired a professional bookkeeping service, and I turn it all over to them." Many PowerSellers agree that their time is better spent in other parts of their businesses, and the money they spend for a professional bookkeeper is money well spent. You can easily hire a bookkeeper as an independent contractor and avoid having to pay all the payroll taxes and Social Security taxes you'd pay an employee.

Hiring a professional bookkeeper doesn't mean you can avoid learning about the bookkeeping aspects of your business, because you'll need to be educated in order to work with your bookkeeper. But you don't have to carry the entire burden of keeping your own records once you've gotten yourself organized and under way.

Meet a PowerSeller

Steve Grossberg—1Busyman

Steve started his eBay business as a hobby. But, it was a hobby he started to pursue after he'd spent 22 years as a sales manager for a leading corporation. Steve came to eBay with a clear understanding of what it takes to sell. Yet, when he began, his goal wasn't necessarily to become a successful PowerSeller. He was trying to help his wife stay occupied and busy during her pregnancy. It was all just in sport. Today, nine years later, he is among eBay's top sellers with a feedback score greater than 120,000!

Steve sells video games. "I started by selling video games, just to break even, or make a small profit," he told us. "Back then, I reinvested everything into the business." Today, distributors of video games actually seek him out when they have inventory to sell. They

know he can buy enough inventory at one time to make him a profitable business partner. It may be surprising to learn that Steve doesn't compete on price alone. He knows what margins he has to make, and he distinguishes himself from the competition through his broad selection of items and his extraordinary feedback. He knows that lowering prices in his category will only lead to reduced margins, so he keeps plenty of listings current and sticks to his pricing. When we wrote this, he had more than 3,800 listings on eBay, and that didn't include his store inventory.

Research isn't at the top of Steve's task list. "I read AuctionBytes, but I don't do too much analysis. I know from my time in sales that the main thing I should do is buy more and list more items. Nothing happens till you make a sale, and there's only limited time in the day," he noted. He uses his sales acumen to understand the process of stocking his eBay business and moving inventory. For example, when video games go out of distribution, he tries to buy up as many as he can. Then he "slow sells" them waiting for his competition to run out of their inventory, leaving him as the exclusive seller of the game. He has noted that too often, his competitors are happy making smaller margins in exchange for the cash flow, but he'd rather bide his time and go for the higher profit margins.

Steve also knows how to control the inventory on its way out the door. He has organized his inventory with his own SKUs and grouped by gaming systems. When he prints his shipping labels, they're printed, according to the SKUs, in the same order in which they are stored in the warehouse. When his shipping person pulls the items for shipping, he can easily go straight up and down rows of the warehouse pulling everything he needs, in the order the games appear on the shelves. With this technique, one person can easily complete all of his orders, on a slow day, numbering 300 to 350 packages!

His advice to sellers trying to achieve success on eBay is to stay focused on one thing. For Steve that means buying inventory, listing it, selling it, and shipping it. He does write eBay guides to help drive traffic to his listings and increase sales. He notes that his guides get a lot of views, because he writes effective guides that don't have a lot of competition. "I try to write meaningful guides," Steve notes.

"For example, 'which games work on the X-Box 360?' This information isn't easy for people to find." Steve cautions newer sellers to not get too distracted. He attributes his success to the fact that he spends his time largely selling. He further recommends that sellers stay focused on eBay exclusively until they've grown large enough to venture out on their own. "Don't get overwhelmed in the beginning by multichannel selling too soon," he advised. "How will you drive traffic to your site?" he asked. "My sales in my Web store are all coming from my past customers."

Hire a bookkeeper

Keeping Records—or Let's Have a Look at Those Books, Buddy Checklist

✓ Because SCORE is such a great (and free) service from the federal government, I've visited their Web site and I am planning a counseling session with one of their volunteers.

✓ I'm learning enough business accounting so that I can be familiar with the basics.

✓ My personal and business accounts are now separate. I have a credit card just for my business.

✓ With apologies to Gershwin, when it comes to taxes if it's deductible it's delicious. So I track my deductions!

✓ The IRS's Web site isn't as much fun as Youtube .com, but I do check it out.

✓ Since I'm going to have to collect state sales tax, I make it easier by using eBay Checkout to automatically calculate any tax that is due.

✓ I know I prefer crunching potato chips to crunching numbers, so I'll hire an accountant.

✓ I've learned how to let my auction management software help with my record keeping.

✓ I'm looking into QuickBooks to automate my bookkeeping. I expect there to be a learning curve, and I know that's ok!

✓ I know that just as hiring an accountant makes sense, so may hiring a bookkeeper.

Chapter 11

From eBay Seller
to e-Merchant

Now that you've got your eBay business off to a great start, you may be thinking about your next step. Maybe it's time for you to join the more than 500,000 eBay sellers who now operate their own eBay stores. It's a relatively simple process to open an eBay store (although running a profitable one month after month is challenging). With an eBay store you're still within the safe confines of eBay, and can take advantage of its tremendous marketing apparatus and huge customer base.

After you've been running your eBay store for a while, the time may come when you're ready to become a bit more independent, and set up your own place on the Web. Much as a child who is living apart from Mom and Dad for the first time, when you do this you may want to stay connected to eBay. The way to do this is with ProStores. And finally, just as your child will become completely independent too, and may even move to another state, you may want to cut the cord entirely. That means having your own Web site, as well as selling through other sites such as Amazon. These are the exciting options we'll explore in this chapter.

Almost all of the successful sellers we know have their own eBay stores, or did so at one time. When you open your store, you'll stock it yourself, and it will reflect your own personality and interests. If you're still thinking of eBay as a giant mall (the real Mall of America), your eBay store makes it easy for you to rent space in that mall, present your own store to the world, stock it with your items, and manage and promote it yourself. Topping it off, you'll create your eBay store using the same type of simple eBay templates you've used to create the listings you've already been running.

There are many reasons why you should have a store. Establishing yourself as an online retailer is cheaper through eBay than it would be if you set out to do it on your own. Plus, through an eBay store, you have ready access to eBay's 200-million-plus customer base.

Listing items is cheaper in your store than it is through regular eBay auctions outside of the special store environment. You determine how long your item remains for sale in your store, and as we'll explain, cross-merchandising (upselling) between your regular auctions and your store is simple. Having your own store gives you added credibility as an eBay seller.

If you're still not convinced, eBay reports that sellers see a 25 percent boost in their revenues, on average, during the first three months after they've opened a store. Of course, that could just reflect the fact that overall, they have more items for sale once their stores open. Take a look at Figure 11-1 for an example of a great eBay store.

Even though you have an eBay store, you will still want to create regular auctions. Your auction listings will drive buyers to your store, because each of your auctions will include a direct link to your store. Once you've created your store, your regular eBay auctions will automatically appear in your store too. In addition to your auction inventory, you'll also use the Store Inventory Format to list items for less than you would through auctions outside of the store environment. Note that because of the reduced rates, Store Inventory Items only show up in regular eBay searches when there are 30 or fewer results in auction or fixed-price format

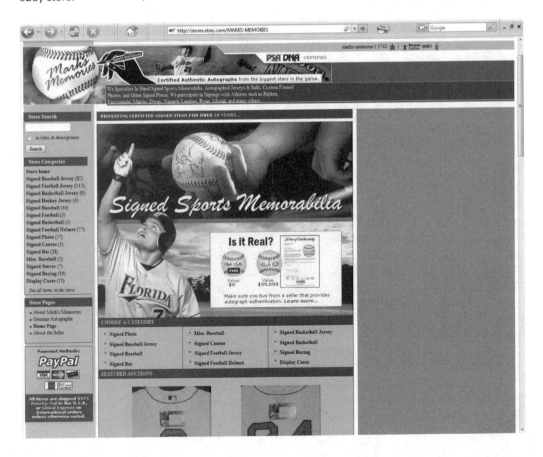

FIGURE 11-1 Here's an example of a popular eBay store.

listings. These Store Inventory listings matching a search will appear after the "regular" search results list.

Many storeowners use their stores to sell add-ons, such as memory cards for digital cameras or other items that are normally purchased concurrently with an item if they are being purchased in a brick-and-mortar store.

Although a part of eBay, eBay Stores have their own set of guidelines dictating how they are "stocked," managed, and promoted. There's no reason at all to feel intimidated, because setting up an eBay store is simple. The rules about who can set up a store are quite broad—anyone with an eBay seller's account can do so if they also have a feedback rating of at least 20 or have a PayPal account in good standing or are ID verified.

A Word about Fees

If you consider just listing fees, the question of whether to open an eBay store requires little thought. You're giving away money if you don't because eBay stores are not expensive. If you have a month's worth of success, and are grossing over $500 per month, it's worth getting the basic eBay store already, according to a New Jersey Platinum PowerSeller.

For store items you can pay a listing fee of just $0.05 for every 30 days per item with a starting or reserve price of less than $25; $0.10 for items that cost more than that. As mentioned, these are for Store Inventory Items; they are not regular auctions. Listings can contain any quantity of items you want (e.g., a listing for 1,000 individual widgets, each separately for sale, still costs only $0.05). Also, listings can be set up as Good 'Til Cancelled (often referred to as GTC), meaning the listing runs until the seller ends the sale or the item sells (or sells out, in the case of multiple items in a listing). You will be charged relisting fees every 30 days. You just won't have the bother of relisting your unsold items. In calculating your costs, you also have to figure in Final Value Fees and the normal fees for listing upgrades.

In your eBay store, you'll be able to use some listing upgrades at greatly reduced prices for store inventory items. You can add the Gallery feature, for example, for only $0.01 for each item. This feature will run for as long as you've listed your store item at the same low price. You can also add a Subtitle for your store inventory items. This feature will cost only $0.02. As you can see, not only can you save money on your listings by placing your items in your store inventory, but you can make use of some upgrades that you might not generally try in your regular auction listings.

When deciding about opening a store, you should factor in the subscription fees (the equivalent of rent) you must pay. These vary depending on the complexity of your store and where eBay promotes it for you. The three categories are Basic ($15.95 per month), Featured ($49.95 per month), and Anchor ($499.95 per month).

Opening a Basic store is a great way to get started with your eBay store. With it you will receive five customizable store pages. When you're ready to upgrade, you can move up to the Featured store. This will give you 10 customizable pages for your store. You will also get a free subscription to Selling Manager Pro, which will definitely help offset the extra expense of the store if you've chosen this as your auction management program. You will also gain additional traffic-reporting tools that will help you analyze your store's performance and advanced sales data to help you determine your sales effectiveness. Your store will appear on eBay's Stores Pages. Finally, the Anchor stores will provide you with all of these features, but you will also gain 15 customizable pages and 24-hour dedicated live customer support services.

» Stick with a Basic store until you've built up your inventory and profits

PowerSellers have consistently advised us that new store owners start small. The Basic store's five customizable pages will give you room for merchandise and space for building your brand and promotional work. The danger for relatively new sellers can be in overreaching and opening a larger more expensive store too quickly, before their businesses can support the extra overhead. "I don't think the Anchored stores do too much," observes Ben of skulls615 who not only operates five eBay stores, but works as a consultant to other sellers. It's interesting that Ben has observed that sellers with feedbacks ranging from 100 to 500, open an Anchored store as their first eBay store, taking on the monthly charge of $499.95 and assuming that the additional promotion eBay gives its Anchored stores will justify the expense. In Ben's experience, this just isn't true.

Stick with a Basic store until you've built up your inventory and profits

Getting Started

As with everything else on eBay, you should first look to eBay's online help pages for assistance in opening your store. From the site map follow the center column. Down near the end of the page you'll find the heading, Web Stores, which includes a link to information about eBay stores. Start by going to the Stores Overview page, http://pages.ebay.com/storefronts/seller-landing .html, shown in Figure 11-2. From there you can find just about any information you need to explore the idea of opening a store, as well as managing and promoting one.

FIGURE 11-2 The Stores Overview page is the place to start gathering information about opening your own eBay store.

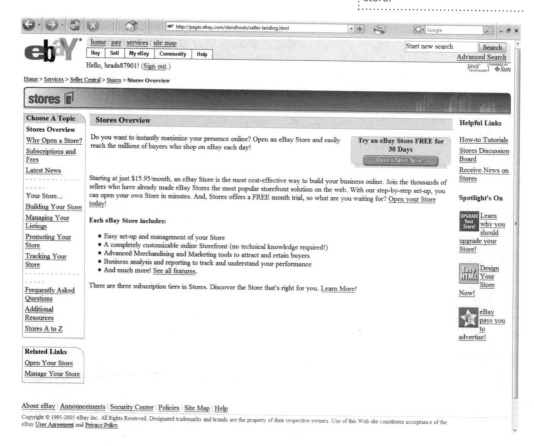

Stick with a Basic store until you've built up your inventory and profits

The eBay Stores Discussion Board

We think the eBay Stores Discussion Board is one of eBay's best boards. As a prospective and even current shop owner, you'll find many helpful discussions there. If your question hasn't yet been answered, the many experts who frequent that board will be glad to help you.

Driving Customer Traffic to Your Store

The help files and other information sources we have mentioned include all the information you need to manage your store. But a topic that's even more important is how you get customers in the "door." Your regular eBay auctions are the best tool you have for driving people to your store. That's because each one will contain a direct link to your storefront in the form of a red door that appears next to your feedback number. As we've mentioned before, you can also add an HTML link to your listings that will take your shopper directly to your store for a great cross-marketing tool. "It's very important to put in all your auction listings, 'Click here to buy it now through my store,'" advises Ben. This will grab the shopper who not only loves what you're offering, but doesn't want to risk losing it in an auction. Once you open your store, be sure to continue to have plenty of auctions going at all times to promote your store as well as sell your products.

Another good way to direct customers to your store via regular auction listings is to use the Cross Merchandising tool that's part of the store seller package. It allows you to show additional items similar to the ones a buyer is viewing within your regular auctions. When buyers click the icons for these items, they'll be taken directly to the relevant page in your store. This tool can work on a "mega" level as well. You can also use it to promote related categories, not just items.

Finally, be sure your customers know about your eBay store! Include a link to it in all your electronic correspondence, and discretely mention it in all the paper invoices and freebies you send along with purchases. Since your eBay store will have its own unique URL, this is your opportunity to create a memorable Web address that helps you brand your business.

Of course, just because people have entered your store doesn't mean they will buy anything. Getting browsers to buy once they're in your store is another challenge. Strategies

Stick with a Basic store until you've built up your inventory and profits

include making use of your store's customizable header to highlight certain items (e.g., NEW THIS WEEK). This header shows up on the storefront page and every other store page. You can also use eBay's Markdown Manager feature to create sales that coincide with holidays, are seasonal, or reflect the discount you specify.

As with auctions, research tools can help here. You can put counters on your storefront, just as you can in your regular auctions. There is also a powerful traffic-reporting tool, which uses technology similar to the technology eBay uses to understand its own traffic. It's available to all store subscribers; you'll find the details at http://pages.ebay.com/storefronts/traffic-reports.html. Through these "Traffic Reports" you'll receive real-time data on the number of times your eBay auctions or areas within your store are viewed, as well as the keywords buyers used to get to your listings. This tool is extremely powerful, and any PowerSeller could make excellent use of it!

Move Your Store Off eBay

It may be hard for you to believe at this moment, but if all your efforts toward building your eBay business are successful, the day will come when you need to move most of your business off eBay and onto the Web at large. Most of the biggest and most successful sellers we've worked with have their own Web stores and work at selling through other channels beyond eBay. It comes down to the old idea of not putting all of your eggs in one basket called eBay. But they also caution about taking this step too quickly. "You have to establish a base first," says PowerSeller Steve of 1busyman. "I waited till I was pretty big before I started my Web store."

"If you're just in one marketplace, you're missing 75 percent of the market," warns Scott Wingo of ChannelAdvisor. Both ChannelAdvisor and MarketWorks offer help in moving into multichannel sales. If, by the time you decide to make this move, you're already using the services from one of these companies, you'll want the seamless integration of your inventory to your Web store that they make possible. If you haven't yet signed on with one of these companies, you will have a broader decision to make about what to do next.

Stick with a Basic store until you've built up your inventory and profits

---

ProStores: eBay's Own Web Store Solution

ProStores is an eBay company that provides tools and services you'll need to operate your own Web store. eBay describes ProStores as "a complete, affordable, e-commerce solution for established eBay sellers." Unlike an eBay store, a ProStore Web store is accessed through its own unique URL. There is no eBay branding. There are more than 180 templates available through ProStores, which eliminates the need for you to understand HTML code when you build your store.

Because ProStores is still an eBay company, you can create your own Web store and easily display your eBay auctions within that store. You can also manage your eBay listings from your ProStores Web store. As with an eBay store, ProStores offers you multiple levels of store size. A good place to start is with the ProStores Business Tier store, for $29.95 per month and a successful transaction fee of 0.5 percent. If you decide to use ProStores and you're already an eBay store subscriber, you'll receive a discount of 30 percent off your monthly ProStores subscription.

Keep in mind that ProStores, as an eBay company, will not support your efforts to branch out into competitive market venues such as Amazon. If multichannel marketing is your goal, ProStores may not be your best choice.

Build Your Own Store

One of your critical goals is to have your own Web store completely independent of eBay. You can do that with the help of many of the auction management companies we discussed in Chapter 4, but those are not your only alternatives. In our book *eBay PowerSeller Million Dollar Ideas* we introduce readers to inexpensive sites that will let you create a Web store cheaply and easily with simple software, which steps you through the process. ShopPal (http://www.shoppal.com/), shown in Figure 11-3, is one of those sites. For a nominal fee you can use their software to create a store than can handle all the basic e-commerce functions (display your merchandise, provide shopping carts, brand your store with your own logo and colors that suit you, accept orders, etc.). You can set the store up to accept PayPal and credit cards and even offer coupons.

To get started, you pay a reasonable setup fee (as little as $49.99); after that you pay a monthly fee ($14.99 to $49.99) to keep the virtual doors open and the lights on. That fee will vary with the number of items you carry in your store. ShopPal's software can even work with eBay's site so you can easily direct

Stick with a Basic store until you've built up your inventory and profits

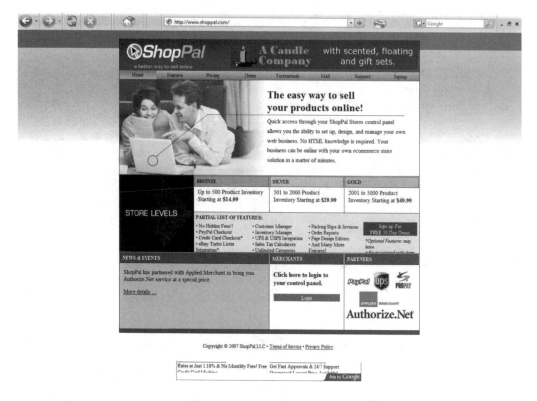

FIGURE 11-3 Sites such as ShopPal can take a lot of the sting out of opening your own e-commerce site.

your eBay customers to your Web store. ShopPal claims you can have your own store up within minutes, but our discussions with storeowners suggest you should take a bit more time than that to get it right.

Float Your Boat on Amazon

Moving to Amazon.com seems a natural next step for people who are already selling on eBay. We asked Amazon for some guidance to help eBay sellers branch out into this new market.

1. About how many third-party businesses sell on Amazon? Any idea how many of these could be classified as small businesses?

Stick with a Basic store until you've built up your inventory and profits

Amazon.com currently has more than 1.1 million active seller accounts worldwide. This number includes, for example, a person selling books out of the basement to major retailers like Target.

2. Do you think it's important to have prior e-commerce experience to be successful selling on Amazon?

No. Everyone is welcome to list items for sale at Amazon.com. We offer several ways to sell your items to our millions of customers, each with its own advantages. For example, Amazon Marketplace is the best place to sell new, used, refurbished, and collectible items—you list your item right alongside the same item carried by Amazon.com. Amazon.com collects no fees unless you sell. Selling on Amazon.com is extremely easy for those new to e-commerce as they have the opportunity to leverage Amazon's already popular shopping features, such as recommendations and listmania. Amazon provides the e-commerce skills for them.

3. Do you have any advice for eBay sellers who are looking to branch out, and who are considering selling on Amazon?

eBay sellers will find many similarities and some differences, and the best advice is to be prepared for the differences. On Amazon.com, the focus is discoverability for the buying customer, so product classification is more robust. Since the sales are retail, inventory and fulfillment management expectations are high, and at the same time the need for interaction with the buyer is reduced. Merchants need to take the time to learn how to best classify products, have products available in inventory, price them competitively, and ship them in a timely manner. In addition, providing the highest-quality customer service will result in positive feedback thus ensuring merchant success on Amazon.com.

4. What tools (e.g., software and reports) does Amazon have in place to support its sellers?

Considering Amazon.com is a technology company, we have outstanding tools in place to support our sellers. Merchants can choose the appropriate tools, ranging from a simple user interface for a small catalog to desktop and feed tools for larger catalogs, all tailored to position their products for maximum discoverability with near real-time access to order and fulfillment management.

5. Can you give examples of some successful sellers? What makes them so successful? Any pointers you could share with others who'd like to follow in their footsteps?

Kevin Harmon who owns Inflatable Madness, a bookdealer and consumer electronics merchant, has this to say:

What makes you so successful on Amazon?   Amazon is simply a good fit for what we do. We sell media products on a media-driven site. Amazon's Web services and tools give us everything we need to intelligently list and sell product.

Any pointers you could share with others who'd like to follow a similar path? Start small! Get some items listed and follow everything through the listing, sales, and shipping processes. When you've got your system down pat, then expand your offerings. This is from personal experience—we made a mistake early on of diving in with all guns blazing without being ready to handle it—it was a big mistake.

What are some advantages of selling on Amazon as opposed to eBay?   We are finding that there are many advantages including these: (a) The A-to-Z guarantee program ensures a smooth transaction for both the buyer and the seller. As a seller, I know that Amazon protects me from fraudulent buyers. A buyer shopping on Amazon is also protected from a fraudulent seller. The net result of this is a worry-free transaction for both. Amazon also holds sellers to a higher standard than eBay does. If a seller does not meet certain criteria on an ongoing basis, that seller is removed from Amazon. (b) Payments are easier. Amazon handles the payment process for you. A sale is actually a sale! (c) Tools and programs are available. Amazon provides a complete suite of software that really makes it simple to manage your listings, and their developer tools allow you to either use third-party tools or develop your own application fairly quickly. (d) Amazon is a partnership. There are no listing fees. That means that Amazon does not get paid unless you sell your item. We win—they win. This is the most important difference for me.

» Float your boat with Amazon, but watch out for shallow waters

Within the space of a very short time, Amazon (see box) has seemingly become the new eBay—the hot e-commerce site where small sellers can make a bundle just by setting up shop there. During 2006 and 2007, eBay sellers corralled Amazon reps at various conferences, eager to jump aboard their ship. We've sold quite a few books on Amazon ourselves and must admit the process is quite easy. On any Amazon item description page you'll see a button labeled, "Sell yours here." Simply click that button to reach the screen shown in Figure 11-4. Complete that form, and you have a live listing. Considering the many, many PowerSellers who are so enthusiastic about selling there, we wouldn't be doing our jobs if we didn't include an Amazon tip in this new edition of *eBay PowerSeller Secrets*.

However, for budding e-merchants, Amazon is not the promised e-land. As PowerSeller and tech editor extraordinaire David Yaskulka explains it, it's important for online merchants looking to create their own Web stores one day to build their own client lists and brands. You can accomplish both of these tasks more readily on eBay than on Amazon. On eBay, you can create an About Me page that can include links to your own Web site. You can build mailing lists and sign up subscribers to your newsletter through your eBay store. And, of course, you can

FIGURE 11-4 This is the screen that appears when you click on the "Sell yours here" button, which appears on most Amazon pages.

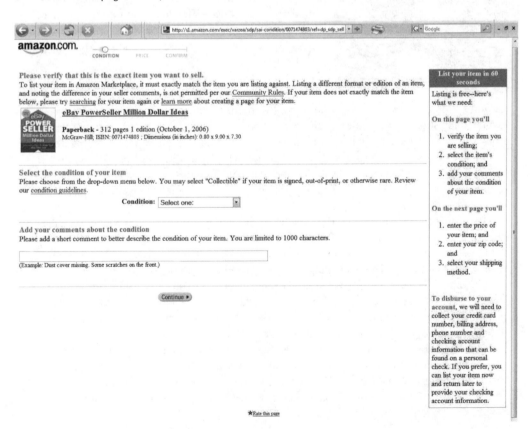

Float your boat with Amazon, but watch out for shallow waters

include your own branding on store pages as well as on About Me and My World pages. As of this writing, your brand gets lost on Amazon, and there's no easy way to compile customer mailing lists.

Meet a PowerSeller

Ben Thompkins—Skulls615

Ben Thompkins started his first eBay store with a couple of his friends when they were all still in college. Back then, they'd decided to sell electric scooters. When they discovered that the scooters they'd sourced were falling apart, they abandoned their original plan and set out to become the "Wal-Mart of eBay." Their plan was to offer a huge selection of merchandise at low prices. They soon expanded to include selling on Amazon and started working on their own Web store, too. They discovered that some of their prices were so low they had customers who were interested in buying quantities of hundreds of products. This led them to implement a system that could give their prospective customers price quotes based on quantity discounts. And that was the beginning.

Today, Ben works as the operations manager for five eBay stores, and his client base is growing monthly. "My job should actually be titled, 'Marketing Manager,'" says Ben. "I'm responsible for generating sales, seeing what trends are happening on eBay, handling keywords, and overseeing the general operations for the stores. New stores are managed on a microlevel and then progress to a macrolevel where I just monitor the product to make sure customer service and sales are perfect." So, Ben has turned his early interest in online sales into a successful consulting business, helping others create successful online stores.

Ben believes you can take two approaches to selling on eBay and online retail in general. "Either you sell a small number of items that have high margins, or you sell tons of items with low margins." Ben reports that many people get so caught up in selling that they fail to track what doesn't sell. That's the only way to determine which of your products are working and which are not. It's not simply of matter of what you can earn for a particular item. You have to also track how much you're spending to make that sale, including fees and handling. Sometimes, however, you can use those products that are not selling as advertising to drive customers to your more profitable wares.

Because online marketing is still so new, Ben believes it's important to experiment as much as possible to find out what your customers want and how they perceive you. He finds e-mail campaigns to be a great way to get your business name out there and offer deals to your customers. He also believes that repeat customer discounts can be very useful.

Float your boat with Amazon, but watch out for shallow waters

From eBay Seller to e-Merchant Checklist

✓ Many of eBay's most successful sellers operate stores. Is it time for me to join them?

✓ I will plan a Basic Store until my business can support a more expensive one.

✓ I am looking at my product line to identify which products would be successful store inventory items.

✓ I understand how I can use my eBay listings to drive customers to my eBay store.

✓ I will explore eBay's ProStores as a route to my own e-commerce Web site.

✓ I am considering other options available to me for building my own Web store.

✓ I am looking into other non-eBay venues to sell my products.

✓ I have listed my first item for sale on Amazon.

Index

About the Authors

Brad and Debra Schepp met as Rutgers College students and have been collaborators ever since. Cheerfully blending their interests in technology and popular culture, they write about cutting-edge technologies and how those technologies are changing our lives. Together they've written 14 books, from *The Complete Passive Solar Home Book* to *The Telecommuter's Handbook* to *Kidnet: The Kid's Guide to Surfing Through Cyberspace.* Their most recent book is *eBayPowerSeller Million Dollar Ideas.*

Their work has been featured in publications such as *Newsweek, The Chicago Tribune*, and *Life Magazine.* They have both worked as writers and editors for McGraw-Hill. Brad was also editorial director for America Online's book division.

Brad and Deb have been buying and selling on eBay since 1999 and have maintained a 100% positive feedback record. They are associate members of the Internet Merchants Association and the E-Commerce Trade Association. They are also regular contributors to AuctionBytes. If you have any comments or suggestions regarding this book or eBay in general, feel free to contact them through their Web site at http://www.bradanddeb.com.